THE THERAPEUTIC PROCESS

THE THERAPEUTIC PROCESS

A Clinical Introduction to Psychodynamic Psychotherapy

J. MARK THOMPSON
AND CANDACE COTLOVE

JASON ARONSON
Lanham • Boulder • New York • Toronto • Oxford

Published in the United States of America
by Jason Aronson
An imprint of Rowman & Littlefield Publishers, Inc.

A wholly owned subsidary of
The Rowman & Littlefield Publishing Group, Inc.
4501 Forbes Boulevard, Suite 200, Lanham, Maryland 20706
www.rowmanlittlefield.com

PO Box 317
Oxford
OX2 9RU, UK

British Library Cataloguing in Publication Information Available

Library of Congress Cataloging-in-Publication Data

Thompson, J. Mark.
  The therapeutic process : a clinical introduction to psychodynamic
psychotherapy / J. Mark Thompson and Candace Cotlove.
      p. cm.
  Includes bibliographical references.
  ISBN 0-7657-0329-7 (cloth : alk. paper)
  1. Psychodynamic psychotherapy.   I. Cotlove, Candace. II. Title.
RC489.P72T485 2005
  616.89'14—dc22

                                                    2004022720

Printed in the United States of America

∞™ The paper used in this publication meets the minimum requirements of
American National Standard for Information Sciences—Permanence of Paper for
Printed Library Materials, ANSI/NISO Z39.48-1992.

CONTENTS

INTRODUCTION

The Therapeutic Process presents an informative, well-defined, and clinically rich guide to the process of psychodynamic psychotherapy. It is specifically designed to have broad appeal and value for both beginning and more experienced clinicians, as well as those who also teach psychoanalytic psychotherapy. For the beginning clinician, many illustrative examples are included and important terms defined. For the long-practicing clinician, the book clearly states what many of us have thought about all along.

This book arose from a series of lectures that were part of a course for the psychiatric residents at UCLA Neuropsychiatric Institute and Hospital, as well as from the instruction of many therapists from other mental health disciplines. The challenge in the initial instruction of psychoanalytic psychotherapy is to introduce fundamental concepts and convey the importance of a solid theoretical background, while concurrently addressing the clinician's pressing need to understand the clinical process. To meet that challenge, clinical vignettes illustrate and describe novel heuristic models that quickly integrate clinical and theoretical terms with the practice and process of psychotherapy.

The organization of the book is designed to conform to the progression of a psychoanalytic psychotherapy. Since anticipating a realistic outcome of a psychodynamic therapy is a valuable starting point for patient and therapist alike, the first two chapters review initial patient assessment and the goals of psychodynamic therapy and describe difficulties to anticipate with patients. Five conceptual dream models offer both a method for understanding dreams and a template for listening to the clinical hour. Psychodynamic principles and theories in conjunction with clinical examples present an outline for the conceptualization of the dynamic formulation, which is a preface to the analysis of character structures. Clinical examples illustrate individual defenses and coping mechanisms. The authors define a variety of therapeutic interventions, including advice, educational comments, supportive comments, clarifications, resistance-oriented comments, transference-related interpretations, reconstructions, and self-revelations. Important discussions focus on the timing of interpretations, the use of tact, and the role of interpretation. Transference in everyday life and as part of the therapeutic process is explored, and different types of transference patterns are defined, including the classical and more contemporary relational theories of transference. Empathy and countertransference and their role in the clinical process are also explored. The role of working through in the clinical process is detailed, and more significantly, the microelements of working through as seen on a day-to-day basis in a treatment are elaborated. The last chapters speak to the end of a psychotherapy with a discussion of termination and a review of the phases of a psychotherapy process.

1

THE GOALS OF PSYCHODYNAMIC PSYCHOTHERAPY

A ll forms of psychotherapy attempt to be "therapeutic," that is, to "treat, heal, or be curative." Psychodynamic psychotherapy is used by the therapist as a "treating, healing, or curative" medium, because the process offers the possibility of receiving or procuring something of importance and value for the effort extended.

We begin our study then by attempting to understand what are potentially achievable goals of psychoanalytic psychotherapy, and what are not?

"Normalcy" is not the goal of psychotherapy, and a psychologically ideal human is impossible to define. Yet certain conditions seem important for human happiness. Freud (1996) suggested that psychic health relates to the capacity for work and love. If we broaden his definition to include the capacity to relax and have fun, this becomes a succinct and effective description of psychic health. However, the ability to work, love, relax, and have fun is an overly broad and vague goal.

What does one really obtain from psychotherapy? The magnificent and thorough results depicted in fictional accounts or even in some professional articles are rarely achieved. Inevitably, what is gotten from psychotherapy is bittersweet. More specifically, people rarely find what they are unconsciously seeking, hoping to avoid the experience of loss and pain. At the same time, however, people often also get something of very real value. What one gains from psychotherapy parallels existential life struggles. Many people live life searching for something impossible, pursuing dreams derived from and intended to erase or reverse disappointments and frustrations of childhood. This kind of pursuit can result in the failure to perceive real possibilities that might currently be available. Psychotherapy attempts to enhance awareness of those currently available possibilities.

1

While it can be difficult, particularly for the patient, to define clearly the specific individual benefits derived from psychotherapy, most patients gain an appreciation of its value. Because the effects of psychotherapy are diffuse and affect many strata of the patient's personality, even clinicians struggle to precisely define the elements of change. The following are criteria that many psychotherapists would agree are positive indicators of change.

SYMPTOM ALLEVIATION

Specific symptom alleviation is the most obvious and straightforward goal of psychodynamic psychotherapy. Symptoms can be specific, as with claustrophobia, depression, and difficulties encountered in intimate relationships; symptoms may be more diffuse, such as existential confusion about the meaning of life and feelings of boredom, apathy, and lack of vitality. Some of these symptoms are best addressed with psychotherapy; some of these symptoms are best addressed with psychopharmacology. Some symptoms fall in the gray zone between psychology and biology. Often the patient will identify one symptom and the therapist will identify another. For example, a male patient may only be aware of some sexual difficulty in dealing with women. The therapist may quickly realize that the patient has more global, unresolved feelings about women. Understandably, symptom resolution, rather than the other psychological changes delineated below, is often the most important goal to the patient. However, separating symptom resolution from the achievement of broader psychological understanding and change may not be possible. The alteration of one symptom may require the achievement of more complex, intrapsychic change.

Conversely, some symptoms can be more rapidly addressed with non-insight-oriented therapies or by medication. Symptoms that are transient and less interwoven with chronic characterologic patterns may respond more therapeutically to specific behavioral or cognitive treatment. Biologically driven symptoms, such as those arising from bipolar illness or schizophrenia, require medication treatment. Psychodynamic psychotherapy offers a unique form of treatment for those symptoms that are woven into the person's enduring psychological fabric or character structure. Psychodynamic psychotherapy and psychoanalysis are the only therapies that attempt to understand and to modify "character" (character describes the complex, enduring, psychological and behavioral patterns that make each person unique, and allow that person in a stable and somewhat predictable way to interact with the self, others, and the world). As some symptoms inevitably reflect this substructure, character must be addressed and understood.

UNLOCKING DEVELOPMENTAL IMPASSES OR FIXATIONS

The late Robert Stoller used to say that if we, as therapists, could allow ourselves to step back and observe, we would see elements in most people that are reminiscent of a particular age or developmental stage (personal communication). That is, qualities or styles that we observe are reminiscent of phases of the life cycle, adolescence and latency and even prelatency (reflected in casual observations such as, that person is so "infantile," "childish," "adolescent," etc.). The more we observe, the more accurately we will discern the residuals of earlier developmental periods. When developing formulations to guide us in psychotherapy, we think of certain questions. The first question is "What present-day developmental challenge confronts the patient?" The second question is "How or in what way does this current developmental challenge relate to previous developmental difficulties?"

To explain further, in the first place we consider the place in which a person might be currently stuck or derailed in the adult life cycle (e.g., leaving home, beginning a career, marriage, parenthood, menopause, etc.). In the second place, we try to understand the way in which the impasse recapitulates an earlier and incompletely traversed developmental phase.

Struggles in the present often reflect an incomplete resolution at a previous developmental crossroad, at which time mastery of key psychological capacities was disrupted. These capacities are fundamental to the attainment of a fully functional range of ego strengths. We speak here of the following:

1. the capacity to develop attachments to others (object relations).
2. the capacity to separate and the capacity to have an appreciation of one's own unique identity and abilities (separation–individuation).
3. the capacity to maintain positive feelings toward significant people in one's life, even in the face of disappointments in and frustrations with those people (object constancy).
4. the capacity to maintain a stable sense of worth and to function autonomously, without the constant companionship of another person (self-constancy and the capacity to be alone).
5. the capacity to achieve a reliable "gender identity" (sense of being masculine or feminine) is an essential developmental achievement.

Developmental discontinuities may arise at different developmental phases, such as the phallic–narcissistic or phallic–oedipal phases. A character type that owes its origin to this level might be reflected in preservation around issues of competition, assertion, or exhibitionism; conflicts with authority figures or difficulties with sexual fulfillment may be evinced.

An example of a developmental impasse and its resolution during the course of therapy follows:

> Ms. X was a competent woman in her late twenties who lived with a man whom she loved and thought was an appropriate marriage partner; however, she was unable to take the next step and commit herself to marrying this man. She sought psychotherapy in an effort to help her resolve her inability to commit to this relationship. Ms. X was an attractive and poised young woman, but curiously, she always wore men's shoes. This was a stylistic choice that aroused her therapist's curiosity. Was this particular accessory choice simply the style of the day and nothing more ("sometimes a cigar is just a cigar") or was this preference a manifestation of a masculine identification (or female "disidentification"), the analysis of which would help to understand her presenting complaint?
>
> Early in her therapy, Ms. X talked about her very dysfunctional mother; she saw the mother as depressed, emotionally paralyzed, unhappily stuck at home. These perceptions were condensed into a recurring memory: Ms. X's mother would come to retrieve her from school, poorly groomed and still wearing a bathrobe from the morning. This painful memory and others like it, reminded Ms. X of the extent of her mother's dysfunction and unhappiness. The memory also exposed the mother's distaste for the maternal role and her disregard for her own daughter.
>
> With time, it became clear that the patient feared getting married because, to her, marriage meant becoming like her mother. In fact, she strove to be as different from her mother as was possible. Particularly in her choice of a career, she chose a *male*-dominated profession that was closely related to her *father's* line of work. Marriage also had the meaning of bidding good-bye to a family she had defensively idealized in order to protect herself from the anger, disappointment, and sadness that might emerge were she to face her true feelings. For Ms. X, to get married and fully move into her own life symbolically meant giving up on the possibility of ever having a mother who would be pleased with and excited to have a daughter like her.

As therapy progressed, Ms. X was slowly able to relinquish her idealized vision of her mother and acknowledge the anger and then disappointment she felt about her mother's failure to provide her with an inviting feminine role model. She was also able to recognize the guilt she felt about her true feelings. As Ms. X focused on her mother and then on other family members, she mourned the loss entailed in not having a family without very significant psychological and vocational limitations.

Ms. X did eventually marry, having understood and worked through the issues stimulated by the developmental milestone of facing marriage.

For Ms. X, the decision to marry revived an earlier developmental conflict regarding identification with a feminine role model (because the role model presented by Ms. X's mother was not positive). The idea of marriage also evoked feelings of deprivation and sadness; to get married meant emotionally moving on, and acknowledging and accepting her less-than-ideal family.

Another theme that seemed to apply to Ms. X had to do with competition with her mother and siblings. This was a conflict that had old roots; Ms. X had always tried to please her father, consequent in part to her perception of her father's disappointment with her mother.

With the treatment, Ms. X was able to readdress earlier ideas and problems, allowing her to move on to another phase of her life. Ms. X still wore shoes that were clearly masculine at the end of her treatment, and this was never addressed. Perhaps the shoes reflected some degree of continued struggle around feminine identity, or perhaps the shoes were just a distinct stylistic preference.

INCREASING SELF-ESTEEM

Difficulty with self-esteem is a common if not universal symptom and/or complaint among individuals who seek psychotherapy. Self-esteem may improve rapidly, particularly in the context of a therapeutic relationship (see transference and transference "cures"); more typically, improvement gradually solidifies as therapy progresses. Improvement in self-esteem often parallels other "structural changes" that occur during psychotherapy; by this we mean, for example, expansion of ego capacities (ego strengths), the development of a more realistic superego and attainable ego ideal, and changes in internal object images (imagos) that then allow for the improved ability to relate to and form relationships with other people.

Kohut (1984) has suggested that we require significant other people in order to maintain our sense of self and self-esteem throughout our lives. However, we also hope to make self-esteem less dependent upon the approval of authority figures who may function as "transference objects," and to liberate the patient from repetitive and perhaps futile attempts to find love or other gratification from those unable and/or unwilling to provide it. In other words, we hope to free our patients from persistently seeking approbation from people who are unlikely to fulfill the patient's wishes (idealized authority figures, charismatic leaders, stars); instead, we hope that our patients will begin to look for reasonable feedback and/or support from those who would be likely to care enough (about the patient) to respond meaningfully (close friends, loved ones, teachers, mentors). At the same time, we hope that our patients will develop sufficient independence from other people so that self-esteem is relatively stable and/or can be recovered autonomously when outside sources are not available.

MODIFYING THE SUPEREGO AND EGO IDEAL

The stability and flexibility of the superego and the reasonability of the ego ideal are critical components of self-esteem regulation. These factors are also important diagnostic variables to consider when establishing "treatment goals" (see chapter 10, "Termination"). Although a more extensive review of the theoretical and technical aspects that pertain to superego and ego functions in psychotherapy will be covered later, a brief review here may be illustrative. The superego dictates what one "should do" or "should not do"; the ego ideal determines one's aspirations and goals. If what one "should do" or "should not do" is too restrictive or too loose, or significantly out of touch with current reality, the result is an unworkable system of ethics and morals. For example, if ideals and goals are unrealistic, a hopeless cycle of never being able to live up to inner requirements ensues; this results in lowered self-esteem, consequent to the inability to feel the experience of mastery and competence. With psychotherapy, we hope to help our patients develop an attainable ego ideal so that more realistic goals and opportunities can be preferentially pursued. The following example is that of a patient who came to understand that his internal expectations were extremely unrealistic.

Mr. B was a middle-aged man who came to psychotherapy as a last resort; he was so distraught that he was considering the possibility of suicide. Mr. B had been very successful in his academic career as a scientist. He had written numerous papers and books, and routinely obtained grants. At the time that Mr. B came to treatment, he had for the first time been turned down for a grant. This caused him to reflect upon his career and to come to the conclusion that he would never win the Nobel Prize. The realization that he would never meet this goal was devastating to Mr. B's sense of himself. To win the Nobel Prize had been the sole reason for Mr. B's existence, his raison d'être. Mr. B saw no reason to continue with life if this did not occur.

Psychotherapy enabled Mr. B to contain his acute self–destructive urges so that he could begin to explore the harsh and rigid nature of his expectations, reflective of a harsh and unrealistic ego ideal ("treatment goal"; see chapter 10, "Termination"). Slowly, and with much disbelief at first, Mr. B began to see that a goal of winning the Nobel Prize was an extreme but also limited and simplistic way to evaluate his success or failure in life.

Over time, as Mr. B's curiosity about himself grew, he began to think about early experiences with his mother, in particular her anxiety about a minor birth defect that he had had, and that was surgically corrected when he was a young boy. He recalled the ways in which his mother had communicated her view of him as disappointing and defective. Mr. B's sense of defectiveness was worsened by the fact that his father abandoned the family shortly after he was born and his mother never recovered from the anger she felt at being "scorned." From the patient's perspective, she developed a hatred of all males, including himself.

In the context of therapy, Mr. B was able to recall feeling impotent and like a failure from as far back as he could remember. He recalled that when he discovered his scientific capacity in his latency years, he swore to himself that he would use his talent to show the world (especially his mother) his "incredible" ability and desirability. This drive (that is, the need to restitute his sense of himself as powerful and potent) provided a significant motivation that, along with his very real abilities, led him to many successes. However, Mr. B was never able to really enjoy his successes; the underlying experience of himself as inadequate and a failure was always lingering in the background.

Psychotherapy allowed Mr. B the opportunity to reexamine his ideas about himself. More specifically, Mr. B was able to piece together the connections among his expectation of himself, and the relationship to his mother's conscious and unconscious perception of him, the loss of his father in his childhood, and his hidden shame about his birth defect.

Mr. B's superego pathology exists at one pole of superego development. At the other pole are individuals with uneven or inadequate superego functioning, resulting in lapses of moral judgment with the expected consequences for behavior. Inadequate superego functioning results in a more serious and difficult problem to address than the problem that results from an overly restrictive and punitive conscience. This will be addressed more fully in the evaluation and formulation section of this book.

IDENTITY CHANGES AND CONSOLIDATION

Psychotherapy often results in the development and consolidation of a positive, more integrated identity. A "positive identity" means to have a reasonable sense of who one is and to like that person, a consequence of sufficient experiences that lead to a sense of mastery and value. Periods of confusion and painful disintegration can occur before identity stabilizes, as the patient deals with various unintegrated aspects of the self. This can take the form of an "identity crisis," manifested by questions like "Who am I?" or statements like "I am not who I thought I was."

During the process of psychotherapy, lost parts of or from the patient's affective experiences, fantasies, memories, and so on that had been projected, denied, or repressed are reintegrated into the patient's schema of him-/herself. This gradual process of integration leads to a more consistently experienced "real" self, or to quote Winnicott (1965), the "true self" (which takes the place of the "false self"). The "true self" experiences, feels, and intuits in order to guide the person's emotional life and make decisions. The "true self" feels *alive*! (For further discussion, see chapter 9, "Working Through.")

Psychotherapy also addresses incongruent and negative identities. Erik Erikson (1950) used the term "negative" identity to refer to those individuals whose identity is not recognized and valued by society. These individuals, who have no way of anticipating a valued role in the world, are also unable to value themselves, resulting in feelings of pain and alienation. The goal in psychotherapy is not to push the patient into a more "socially acceptable" identity; psychotherapy attempts to understand why the patient has been unable to define a workable identity that feels "true" to the self.

The following example describes a patient who *adopted* an identity that caused difficulty for his family and for himself.

Z, a young man in his late teens, was brought to therapy by his parents. Although Z appeared to be bright and articulate, he was considered by both the family and himself to be the "family idiot." Z's parents were intelligent, successful academicians. His father was uniquely "brilliant"; this brilliance seemed not to protect Z's father, however, from the necessity to constantly reassure himself of his brilliance by achieving new heights and then soliciting approbation for his accomplishments from his family.

Therapy revealed that Z had formed an identity as a "pseudo-imbecile." Analysis of this identity revealed a number of components. Z was unable to reconcile his angry and competitive inclinations toward his father with his experience of his father as fragile and therefore breakable. Because Z found his father threatening, he was unable to identify positively with those traits of his father that might have been useful to assume as part of his own identity (intelligence, belief in education). Z unconsciously rebelled against his father and his father's ideals, but paid an enormous price in his resultant negative self-concept. The rebellion, which expressed Z's hostility toward his family, took the form of an attack upon the values of intellect and brilliance. The patient felt excluded as a consequence of this particular familial preoccupation, which he perceived to limit any potential for him to attain love and affection from his parents.

Gradually Z became aware of the anger, disappointment, and sadness that he had harbored toward and about his father and family. In the context of a therapeutic relationship, as Z was able to understand the conflicts that had created his identity (as described above), he became free to appreciate his intelligence and excel in his own right.

IMPROVE COPING ABILITY AND THE QUALITY OF THE DEFENSES

A goal of psychotherapy is to enhance the likelihood that people will have the *intrapsychic ability* to recognize options and that coping skills will involve *sufficient flexibility* to allow the person to cope when necessary, that is, to ensure that defenses are not rigid. Psychotherapy works by setting the stage to allow for sufficient internal (intrapsychic) freedom as well as by decreasing the need to defend against certain experiences and feelings; psychotherapy does not eradicate defenses. Psychotherapy hopes to increase the capacity to make use of more mature, defenses (defenses will be discussed in greater detail in chapter 5, "Resistance and Defense"). Changes in the capacity to

cope and to make use of mature defenses are always relative. In the primitive borderline patient, the goal is to develop middle-level, "neurotic"
defenses such as reaction formation and intellectualization. In the neurotic individual the goal is to develop higher-level defensive operations
such as suppression and altruism (for delineation of specific defenses, see
chapter 5).

The following example illustrates the evolution of defenses in the course
of psychotherapy:

> Mr. P came to feel unloved by everyone—his fellow workers, his
> wife, his children, and his family of origin—whenever he felt over-
> whelmed by work. During these periods of feeling unloved and
> overwhelmed, Mr. P would regress to a position of withdrawal, in
> which he felt anger toward other people. He then (unconsciously)
> projected his anger onto these other people, thus creating a situa-
> tion in which he experienced them as hostile toward him.
>
> Psychotherapy sought to explore with Mr. P the origin of his
> anger. As he explored its significance, gradually, Mr. P developed
> a greater capacity to tolerate his anger and acknowledge that it
> might belong to him. With this understanding, Mr. P was able to
> *limit the projection* of his anger onto other people, and instead,
> appropriately express his concerns when necessary. With these
> newly acquired capacities, Mr. P became better able to accept
> support and closeness from his wife, and address frustrations in his
> work situation tactfully and as needed.

INCREASE CONTINUITY WITH THE PAST

Accepting the past, and mourning for what one did not get in life, is not an
easy task. Therefore, understanding that damage may have been done, and
living with the realization that some opportunities are irretrievable, presents
a substantial and at times impossible challenge to many.

Memories serve as cognitive links with the past; this means that memory allows for the continual reworking and reweaving of the past and of our
personal understanding of from whence we have come (Kris 1956). One has
to be able to remember and appreciate the impact of past experiences in order to accept and integrate them. Some people remember little or nothing
of the past and have little appreciation of how they have been affected by
familial and life experience. The novelist Thomas Wolfe (1929), once said,
"Each of us is all the sums he has not counted."

Psychotherapy hopes to improve appreciation for the "sums . . . not counted," to remember and consider the past (not have to disavow the past), resulting in an ability to comfortably live with an awareness of past experience. *The capacity to recall the past with fluidity*, not to be preoccupied with or overwhelmed by affectively laden memories, *demonstrates the achievement of continuity with the past*. During the process of psychotherapy, surprising recollections sometimes occur as the past gradually becomes better integrated into current experience. The following is an example:

> J. C., a young woman with a somewhat resolved eating disorder and mild chronic depression, was being seen in psychotherapy. Late in the first year of treatment, an erotic and frightening theme began to emerge in her associations. Several weeks passed, during which J. C. spoke of sexual feelings toward two male coworkers; J. C. than began to comment about her therapist's neckties, which she referred to as "attractive." During this period of time, J. C. became increasingly anxious, and she had not been anxious in the treatment in recent times. J. C.'s therapist (a man) offered a tentative clarification in the form of a question; perhaps J. C. was having sexual feelings toward her therapist and this was disturbing to her?
>
> The next session arrived and J. C. reported that an unsettling but interesting thing had occurred. J. C.'s husband had approached her about having sex the night before. He had approached her from behind, placing his hand on her thigh and putting his hand between her legs. J. C. had reacted by slapping her husband hard! J. C. was stunned by the unfamiliar and intense nature of her reaction to her husband's behavior. In the same session J. C. reported a memory, without consciously connecting her reaction to her husband's approach or her recent thoughts about her therapist's "attractive" neckties. The memory was of her father who had put his hand between her legs from behind and fondled her when she was ten years old. J. C. told her therapist that she had not thought about this episode in a very, very long time.

In the context of an evolving erotically tinged transference and a suggestion to the patient about the territory of the transference ("perhaps you are having sexual feelings about me and this is disturbing to you"), an old memory reappeared. This memory revealed to the patient that a less-than-positive perspective of her father, heretofore a man who had been idealized by the patient, existed in the memory bank of her mind. While this awareness may not have been entirely welcome to the patient, the example does represent an expansion of the patient's perspective, that is, "continuity with the past."

Another example follows:

> Mr. F, a very successful, sophisticated, and articulate lawyer, had grown up in the Midwest. In the course of his psychotherapy, Mr. F became aware of the great extent to which he yearned to know his deceased father. Simultaneously, Mr. F developed an interest in farming; this was an interest that previously would have seemed absolutely incongruent with the urbane manner and sophisticated lifestyle with which Mr. F initially presented. As time passed, another interesting phenomenon occurred. Mr. F's specific and precise enunciation began to soften, and a slight Nebraska accent distinctly appeared. At the end of the treatment, Mr. F was contemplating becoming an investor in a farming concern in the Midwest.

These events are reflective of the patient's discovery of his positive feelings about his roots. Mr. F was surprised to find out that a comforting feeling could be derived from allowing for "continuity with the past." This was a comfort that had previously been unavailable to Mr. F because his conflicted and unresolved feelings regarding his father had interfered with his fully embracing his own personal history.

INCREASE IN "FULLNESS OF EXPERIENCE"

Alice Miller (1981) theorized that the opposite of depression is not "gaiety"; the opposite of depression is "vitality," or the "feeling of being *alive*." While temperamental variables are probably a factor affecting the *capacity* for vitality, psychological factors markedly affect vitality as well. Psychological factors that figure into the ability to feel fully alive can be described simply at first (in later chapters, these factors will be described in more detail and from a theoretical perspective). These factors include:

1. the ability to achieve mutuality, that is, to be able to give and take in supportive human relationships.
2. the achievement of a stable sense of oneself and the ability to see other people as potentially whole and stable as well.
3. the ability to tolerate and identify feeling states (affects), acknowledge needs, and be aware of wishes and dreams without unnecessary restriction.

All of the above allow for freedom of thoughts and feelings, and the experience of vitality and joy.

Ralph Greenson (1962) joked that "a death wish a day keeps the doctor away." This adage seems on the surface to be a contradiction to a discussion of vitality. However, the thought acknowledges that the ability to let go of or at least be aware of and experience intense passions, including hate, within oneself, defines health. This is because the ability to be comfortable with a potentially conflicted emotion such as hate, correlates with the ability to enjoy life, have greater emotional energy, and to experience intensely other (positive) emotions. Holding back feelings requires effort. That is, repression requires energy. Therefore repression depletes the individual and leaves him or her "devitalized." Psychotherapy seeks to make it possible for people to be enriched by their feelings, as opposed to being encumbered by feelings, needing to constantly watch over or defend against feelings (affect states). This is not the same as "letting it rip." Awareness of feeling states and acting upon the feelings that arise are two entirely different issues.

It is joked that the well-analyzed obsessive is still a well-analyzed obsessive; outward appearance may change little with psychoanalytic treatment. The obsessive doesn't become histrionic, but may develop the capacity for a richer inner experience and deeper interpersonal relationships. The histrionic or hysterical individual typically sobers, having developed a broader range of authentic affects and an enhanced capacity to empathize with others.

INCREASE IN SELF-ANALYZING CAPACITY

Roughly speaking, there are two types of self-analyzing ability, that which is conscious and that which is preconscious. The capacity for both conscious and preconscious self-analyzing ability is a goal of psychotherapy because of its enormous usefulness in enabling a person to understand and make use of inner reactions to better deal with the challenges of life. Hopefully, self-analyzing capacity ultimately becomes intuitive, automatic, and not excessively labored or utilized defensively. One can analyze life, and yet in so doing, not live life. Freud once told an apropos joke about a centipede that functioned quite well until someone inquired how it coordinated its many legs. From that day on, the centipede was never able to walk again. Insight and the consequent ability to self-analyze are meant to be in the service of liberation, not further psychological restriction. Many therapists feel that the development in psychotherapy of an individual's capacity for self-analysis has positive prognostic value. Of course, as with most things obtained in psychotherapy, self-analyzing capacity develops gradually, often being most obvious and labored in its early development. An example of the development of self-analyzing capacity in the course of psychotherapy follows:

> Mr. P, a patient mentioned previously, began to quote his therapist to himself at times of stress; during these times of stress, Mr. P would begin to perceive his wife as a "persecuting bitch." Based on his growing ability to look at himself (as he began to be able to "call up" his therapist's words within his head), Mr. P was able to stop himself from acting on his distorted perceptions. Mr. P learned to hold back his angry and provocative attacks toward his wife, which of course had only invited her to be angry in turn with him, thus confirming his suspicion that she hated him. Later he was able to step back from his emotions and examine what was happening within himself. Within the context of psychotherapy, Mr. P developed the capacity to self-observe (observing ego).

INCREASE IN SELF-SOOTHING, AND THE "CAPACITY TO BE ALONE"

The capacity to comfort or soothe oneself ("self-soothing") and the ability to tolerate being alone are seemingly simple skills and yet they are vitally important. Patients who lack these abilities upon the outset of treatment and gradually develop these skills over the course of psychotherapy appreciate the value of the acquisition. Dependence on alcohol or drugs, or repetitive and self-destructive behaviors such as gambling, compulsive sexual behavior, or other risky self-stimulating behaviors are often reflective of the inability to comfort or soothe oneself (the risky behavior is intended to provide comfort, even though the intent may not be obvious in the "manifest content" of the act). Self-pity is another form of self-soothing behavior, however ineffective, destructive, or alienating to other people the self-pity might be.

The ability to self-soothe is an "ego function" (property of the ego or the regulating agency of the mind), requiring for its presence a mastery of certain developmental tasks. The achievement of a stable self-representation (sense of self and identity), and the experience of benevolent and calming caretakers in childhood that allow for the internalization of benevolent and calming internal object representations are necessary factors. Thus, Winnicott (1958) described the "capacity to be alone" as an important developmental task of childhood, and also an important but often overlooked goal of psychotherapy.

IMPROVED INTERPERSONAL RELATIONS

Many psychotherapists believe that an increase in the depth and quality of object relationships is the most important change that can come from psychotherapy. Mutually supportive relationships are enormously important in sustaining mental health. Bowlby stressed the value of close relationships and the resilience that such relationships offer to the individual in facing life and illness (Bowlby 1969, 1973, 1980; Ainsworth 1963, 1967). The ability to handle stressful situations and/or periods of time, without becoming emotionally or physically compromised, is facilitated by the ability to find and maintain mutually supportive and healthy relationships.

With psychotherapy, we hope to help our patients develop more varied and realistic expectations of other people. In accordance, we hope to help our patients learn to tolerate the mixed feelings, or ambivalence, that are part of every relationship; this includes helping our patients to find and maintain positive feelings for those people who have been significant. During psychotherapy, some patients get out of disturbed and unrewarding relationships and into more caring ones. Many patients develop a greater capacity for the mutually supportive and intimate kinds of relationships that can result in closer and more gratifying interpersonal experiences.

SEXUALITY

The ability to combine a warm, considerate, and respectful bond and sexual gratification in the same relationship is an important outcome goal of psychoanalysis and psychotherapy. Early psychoanalysts emphasized the importance of noninhibited, gratifying sexual relations (Abraham 1926) in adult development and functioning; this means having the ability to be free sexually, to be free from anxiety and guilt, and to relate to and feel for another human being. Mature sexuality then occurs in the context of an "intimate" ("essential; closely acquainted, or associated; very familiar . . . or close"; Webster's Dictionary) relationship; it is not simply "sex," a one-night stand, or a "fling."

The mature sexual relationship, as described by the early psychoanalysts, sits at the top of a broad pyramid of psychological components of "normality" (or goals of psychotherapy) including sufficient consolidation of sexual identity, ease with interpersonal relationships (object relationships), flexibility of superego functioning, and fullness of affective range. For example, mature sexuality should not be encumbered by confusion as to the gender of the sexual partner, an inability to be sexual with someone with whom one is close, or excessive prohibition or guilt.

To elaborate briefly, sexuality in relationships means having the capacity, at least in moments, to be vulnerable with and depend upon another human being. It means being able to maintain positive feelings, despite the inevitable mixed feelings that arise in all relationships. It means having a sufficiently cohesive sense of self so that sexual acts, or the opposite sex, are not threatening. It means feeling reasonably adequate about oneself as a man or woman and the ability to perform sexually. Furthermore, healthy sexuality depends upon the freedom to experience, without being overwhelmed, not only tender feelings but erotic and hostile or aggressive thoughts and feelings.

As described above, the development of mature sexuality is dependent upon and affected by many psychological factors. This means that improving sexual capacity and gratification in psychotherapy can be a slow process. Like many goals of psychotherapy, difficulty around sexuality typically does not change in isolation. And like most enduring psychological issues, sexual problems often relate to long-standing psychological patterns that are deeply interwoven with character.

INCREASE IN CREATIVITY

For many patients, psychotherapy opens up new creative avenues and/or greater enjoyment of the arts. Obviously, psychotherapy cannot and will not teach a person how to write or paint; for some people, however, psychotherapy can and does unlock the facility to see aspects of the human experience previously obscured, to access memories with greater fluidity, and to play creatively with thoughts and feelings. For others, an increased appreciation and enjoyment of art, literature, drama, and/or simply observing the human condition can follow.

Among patients who seek psychotherapy, many, if not all, have difficulty accepting the past and mourning for what is irretrievable, and struggle to integrate all the many feelings that human beings can have. Life offers many challenges; these challenges inevitably evoke internal reactions. In order to be creative, comfort with all the "stuff" that motivates and challenges humans—the good, the bad, the painful, and the joyous—must be possible. Shakespeare, for example, was able to wear many hats. Within his mind's eye, he was able to move into the mind of the murderer, the lover, the envious, the competitor, the individual who cannot love, and so on. The power to express all these possibilities artistically is an example of "sublimation," the channeling of feelings (affect) and attitudes in acceptable and constructive ways. Freud observed that Shakespeare wrote *Hamlet*, the great oedipal drama of family competition, the year following his father's death; Harold Bloom (1998) observed, in a similar vein, that Shakespeare wrote *Hamlet* following the death of Shakespeare's own son, who was named Hamnet.

Psychotherapy assists the individual to be more open to internal experience, to be curious and reflective about "why one does what one does," to gradually become aware of the complexity of the human process. Similarly, creative endeavors become opportunities to "try on" human challenges, offer others a vicarious experience, and explore and explain the themes and vicissitudes of life and of living, of mourning, and of dying.

REFERENCES AND READINGS

Abraham, K. (1926). Character formation on the genital level of libido-development. *International Journal of Psycho-Analysis* 7: 214–22.

Ainsworth, M. D. S. (1963). The development of infant-mother interaction among the Ghana. In *Determinations of Infant Behavior*, vol. 2, ed. B. E. Foss. London: Methuen.

———. (1967). *Infancy in Uganda: Infant Care and the Growth of Love.* Baltimore, MD: Johns Hopkins University Press.

Bloom, H. (1998). *Shakespeare: The Invention of the Human.* New York: Riverhead Books.

Bowlby, J. (1969). *Attachment and Loss,* vol. 1: *Attachment.* London: Hogarth Press.

———. (1973). *Attachment and Loss,* vol. 2: *Separation.* New York: Basic Books.

———. (1980). *Attachment and Loss,* vol. 3: *Loss.* New York: Basic Books.

Erikson, E. (1950). *Childhood and Society.* New York: W. W. Norton.

Freud, S. (1996). *The Oxford Dictionary of Quotations*, ed. Angela Partington. Oxford: Oxford University Press.

Greenson, R. (1962). Psychotherapy lecture series, University of California at Los Angeles, Center for Health Sciences, Neuropsychiatric Hospital and Institute. Audio–Video Library Archives.

Kohut, H. (1984). *How Does Analysis Cure?,* ed. A. Goldberg. Chicago: University of Chicago Press.

Kris, E. (1956). The recovery of childhood memories in psychoanalysis. *Psychoana-lytic Study of the Child* 11: 54–88.

Loewald, H. W. (1971). Some considerations on repetition and repetition compulsion. *International Journal of Psycho-Analysis* 52: 59–65.

McGlashan., T. H., and G. H. Miller. (1982). The goals of psychoanalysis and psychoanalytic psychotherapy. *Archives of General Psychiatry* 39: 377–88.

Miller, A. (1981). *Prisoners of Childhood*. New York: Basic Books.

Winnicott, D. W. (1958). The capacity to be alone. *International Journal of Psycho-Analysis* 39: 416–20.

———. (1965). Ego distortion in terms of true and false self. In *The Maturational Processes and the Facilitating Environment*. New York: International Universities Press.

Wolfe, T. (1929). *Look Homeward Angel*. New York: Charles Scribner's Sons.

2

INITIAL EVALUATION
OF THE PATIENT

In the initial phase of seeing a patient, the therapist must begin the process of trying to establish a connection with the patient. This is in the service of and at the same time as the therapist is trying to determine the best approach or treatment. The approach or treatment is based upon the therapist's determination about the areas in which the patient is successfully functioning or not functioning.

A therapist may not always have a choice with respect to the patients to be treated, but a choice is usually possible regarding the type of psychotherapy and the parameters utilized in the psychotherapy. The same treatment approach for every patient is probably not suitable; not all patients have identical treatment needs. A treatment should be chosen that matches the patient's psychological and practical/realistic circumstances. The latter would include concrete resources, such as finances for treatment, time, availability, etc. Sometimes, a treatment approach that does *not* attempt to understand intrapsychic meaning but is more focused on symptoms and how to remove them rapidly makes more sense. Nonpsychodynamic psychotherapies would include behavioral psychotherapy, interpersonal psychotherapy, and cognitive psychotherapy.

Nevertheless, obtaining essential information, and in a manner that is psychodynamically informed, offers significant additional advantages. A thorough evaluation is helpful in order to anticipate certain potential difficulties: for example, for the therapist to be aware of possible areas of sensitivity and conflict within a particular patient. A thorough evaluation is useful in order to predict the course of psychotherapy, as much as that is ever possible. A psychodynamically informed evaluation enables the therapist to explain to and advise the patient about treatment options and the potential usefulness of psychodynamic psychotherapy. Last, an initial evaluation that is conducted in a manner that is psychodynamically informed, serves to remind the therapist that it is always important to keep in mind the possibilities and limitations of any therapy for any patient.

The discussion to follow offers a format for the psychodynamic evaluation of a patient in the initial phase of psychotherapy.

What should the therapist be curious about when beginning to evaluate a new patient; that is, what is involved in "obtaining essential information and in a manner that is psychodynamically informed"?

1. What brings the person to treatment and why now? Is there a crisis? Is there a significant life event or new developmental challenge (which may be obvious or not so obvious)? Has a compelling feeling state or sense of urgency recently surfaced (anxiety, depression, restlessness and/or boredom, etc.)? A compelling feeling state would be a reason for the acute state of discomfort in the patient.

2. What is the person's world like and how effectively does the person function overall? Who is in the patient's life, and what is the quality of the relationships? In the patient's life, is there a partner or a special friend or a particular group of friends; what are these people like? What is the history of the patient's work life (student or professional context)? Has the patient's work life been characterized by a sound work ethic and pattern of stability or is this not the case?

3. Has there been or is there now a serious health issue?

4. Is the person functioning according to what you might judge to be full realistic capacity? What ability and what promise does the person realistically have to achieve and gain gratification from the real world? Where is the person in terms of potential life span? Does sufficient time remain to allow for meaningful change?

5. Inquire specifically about intimate and sexual relationships (as opposed to friendships): how long did relationships last, what was the depth of relatedness in any given involvement, did particular and/or specific patterns repeatedly characterize the person's relationships (for example, a woman continuously chooses men who beat her up)?

6. Watch for (or if possible, directly solicit) recollections of events from childhood (early childhood, latency, adolescence, and early adulthood): What were these developmental periods like for the person? Certain questions can be helpful. What was school like? What was the family experience like? Were separations easy for the person, or confounded with anxiety, depression, or other symptoms of distress

(starting kindergarten, going to sleep away camp, and going away to college)?

7. Inquire about special memories; of all the potential events of childhood that could be remembered, usually a certain few are retained in memory with particular clarity. These memories seem to carry psychological significance (see "screen memories").

8. Inquire about who is in the person's family, especially parents, siblings, and any other significant caretakers (grandparents, nanny). Are the parents described in a one-dimensional way, or as more complex characters? Are the parents idealized (to regard or show as perfect or more nearly perfect than is true) or are they vilified? Is or was a particular parent preferred?

9. Inquire about recent dreams or repetitive dreams. Many patients will recall a dream from the night before the first psychotherapy appointment; these dreams may reflect anticipation and anxiety about beginning a treatment.

All of the above questions can be asked of the patient directly. The therapist may also take note of important information from the initial evaluation period that is not revealed through direct questioning.

1. Take note of the person's interaction with the therapist: what is the level of comfort? Does the person seem to feel at ease, wary, or frankly frightened? How rapidly do feelings or reactions to the therapist develop? In general, the more needy or primitive the individual (as opposed to mature or neurotic), the more rapidly and intensely will reactions to the therapist develop.

2. What is the nature of the person's reaction to questions, clarifications, or feedback? Is the reaction thoughtful, with consideration given to psychological possibilities, or is the reaction defensive and what defensive style is evident? The more psychologically limited or primitive individual may have an intense reaction (such as paranoia) and evidence primitive defenses (such as splitting). In contrast, the more neurotic (or less primitive) individual will have reactions that are more subdued: higher-level defenses, such as changing the subject, answering a slightly different question, or intellectualizing, might be employed.

3. Try to search out a dominant theme or themes: often a primary concern, emotion, or pattern will become clear by the end of the first or second session. A dominant concern would be, for example,

the fear of loss of an important source of stability (job, relationship). A dominant emotion might be anxiety or depression. A dominant pattern might be repetitive involvement with people who will never become available (a woman who gets involved with married men).

While there is no ideal candidate for psychoanalytic psychotherapy, certain individuals will be more likely benefit from a psychodynamic modality than will others. How does a therapist make that determination?

An "optimum candidate" will be in need of treatment, but also possess enough coping capacity to tolerate the delayed gratification that comes with a process like psychoanalytic psychotherapy; that is, the person brings to the table sufficient "ego function" (to be explained in chapter 3, "Formulation"). Appreciable initial capacities ensure a foundation upon which to build during the process of psychotherapy. Some individuals who look like "good" psychotherapy candidates do not do well in treatment or do not stay the course or go the distance. Some patients who seem like poor or unlikely psychotherapy prospects will work diligently and grow beyond initial expectations. Sometimes the "fit" between patient and therapist can influence the possibilities, even for patients who appear to have a limited prognosis; however, this is never something upon which one can count. The following example illustrates the advantage incurred with a better "fit."

> Mrs. L was an attractive, self-possessed woman who, within minutes of meeting a male therapist for her first consultation, said to the therapist "I could never work with you, you look like my brother." Mrs. L explained that she and her brother had been intense competitors, a situation that had been created by parents who believed that competition fostered excellence. Mrs. L and the therapist both concluded that a woman therapist would allow for a more comfortable fit under the circumstances.

Some patients who seek psychotherapy simply do not have a good prognosis for staying in the treatment (not leaving prematurely) or for improving, even with an "optimal goodness of fit." A number of useful schemas for evaluating an individual's capacity to utilize psychotherapy and psychoanalysis have been addressed in the literature. Otto Kernberg has spoken about levels of character structure and the related capacity to benefit (or not benefit) from psychotherapy or psychoanalysis. Kernberg's ideas are worthy of study by clinicians at all levels of practice and expertise.

In the therapist's contact with the patient during the initial evaluation phase, the information acquired will allow the therapist to form an opinion about the likelihood that the patient will be able to get something useful out of the treatment, and remain long enough to allow that to happen.

What factors are useful to consider when evaluating a person's suitability for psychoanalytic psychotherapy? This question is closely linked to another question, which is, what would be useful to think about trying to accomplish, having decided that psychoanalytic psychotherapy is the treatment of choice?

THE ROLE OF ETHICS AND VALUES: THE "SUPEREGO"

Does the patient have a secure sense of values and morals that allows for a clear sense of what is right and what is wrong? Does the patient possess a reasonable respect for others and for the rules of human interaction that is currently present and has been enduring over time? Murray (1964), in quoting Robert Frost, reminds us of the wonderful metaphor "Freedom is moving easy in harness." Hopefully, the "inner harness," that is, the internal system of values and morals or the superego is in harmony with the realistic demands and necessities of living in the world.

Character traits and/or symptoms can result from having either too loose or too restrictive a value system (conscience), respectively. Of importance, symptoms are usually visible to the patient. However, character traits, which bring a person into conflict with the outside world, may be visible to the therapist, but not to the patient. A lack of harmony between the "self" and the "conscience" may be expressed through feelings and thoughts, and in behaviors and dreams. The following examples are in the category of a conscience that is too restrictive.

> Mr. R came to therapy because he was troubled by recurrent dreams in which a policeman had stopped him for speeding, and he was trying to defend himself. The policeman, who happened to look somewhat like Mr. R's father, wore glasses like Mr. R. The recurrent nature of the dream suggested that Mr. R was having difficulty with some aspect of his father, ingrained now in his own conscience, and represented in the dream by the policeman.

> Another patient, Mr. C, found himself frequently walking around his apartment engaged in an inner dialogue. This inner dialogue became at times so intense that Mr. C would talk out loud to himself.

He would tell himself repeatedly, "I am a good person!" In his "dialogue," Mr. C was speaking to his long-dead father, who had
viewed Mr. C as a negligent son, disloyal to the family.

In the category of patients who battle with too restrictive a conscience,
a particular pattern can sometimes be observed. As the intensity of conflict
between the person's desire and the conscience (superego) increases, the
"internalized" or "introjected" elements that have contributed to the person's conscience become "reanimated."

Internalized or introjected in this context means that the decision
about what is right and what is wrong now lives inside the person's own
mind, and to a greater (internalized) or lesser (introjected) extent is integrated as a part of the person's own value system. If these internalized or introjected elements are now *reanimated and projected* outside of the self and
onto others, the once *internal* conflicts of conscience can be converted into
external acting-out.

"Reanimation" refers to a process in which early life experiences with
authority figures, which are laid down as precursors to the development of
a person's conscience, seem to come to life and are seen more clearly in
thoughts, dreams, and fantasy. The portrayal of the cartoon character, with
the devil posed on top of one shoulder and an angel on top of the other
shoulder, each talking into one of the character's ears, graphically depicts the
process of reanimation. The patient who found himself talking out loud to
his own voice (attempting to reassure) and the voice of his dead father
(which was *not* reassuring), illustrates not only the reanimation experience,
but also the intensity with which it can appear. In the case of Mr. C, through
the mechanism of reanimation, the dead father (who in present reality had
no authority or power) had a substantial capability to torment Mr. C.
Therefore, two separate and distinct events, "reanimation" and "projection,"
can occur in situations in which the superego becomes less integrated.

Unfortunately, a conscience can also be too loose. The therapist should
consider whether noticeable "holes" exist in the patient's conscience, such
that ethical behaviors appear alongside unethical behaviors. Is the patient's
behavior consistent with the *expressed* moral code? Extreme shifts in behaviors and morals indicate impaired "superego" functioning, tend to be consistent with a less favorable prognosis and indicate more primitive types of
pathology (borderline, narcissistic, schizoid, etc.).

Mr. W worked in a financial business. He repeatedly took risks by
virtue of certain questionable business practices, which had al-

ready been questioned by his superiors. Mr. W insisted that although his behavior might be marginally ethical, it was nevertheless, legal! Additionally, Mr. W felt compelled to pursue his activities, believing that he must earn every possible cent. Occasionally, Mr. W would worry during the day and then wake up at night in a panic; he had stretched the law and done something "stupid," despite repeated promises to himself that he would stop. This panic did not, however, induce any change in his behavior. In fact, instead, Mr. W repeatedly attempted to solicit feedback from or engage his therapist (as well as others) in a debate about the "rightness" of or "wrongdoing" in his behavior. He would ask or state: "Don't you think it is wrong or stupid to push the edge and attempt to make money in this way?" Without waiting for or unable to wait for a reply, Mr. W would immediately justify his behavior, insisting to his therapist that "a man would have to be a sucker not to take the money."

Mr. W continually attempted to distance himself from any *internal* moral judgment about his behavior, and at the same time prevented the therapist from providing an *external* moral and ethical restraint. This kind of pattern can be indicative of internal ethical conflict, that is, a battle with one's own conscience: "Don't you think it is wrong or stupid to push the edge and attempt to make money in this way?" Unfortunately, this pattern can also be indicative of a conscience that looks like "Swiss cheese," that is, a patchy or poorly integrated system of values ("superego lacunae"): "a man would have to be a sucker not to take the money." The former problem would present a difficult but not insurmountable therapeutic problem. More destructive and difficult to contain in psychotherapy, however, would be the latter problem, a conscience with the texture of Swiss cheese.

In order to function smoothly, the demands and requirements of the superego must be adaptive, realistic, and allow for sufficient gratification of needs; that is, the superego should have the capacity to absorb and integrate a different or changing morality. Are the patient's moral views and behavior in conflict with the present social time? A person living in the sexually liberated 1960s would not have done well with a conscience from the 1890s. Are the demands of the patient's conscience so antiquated that success and pleasure become unduly curtailed? Conversely, does the patient have some continuity with respect to values, beyond just the fashions of the day? Sustaining beliefs, ideals, and goals help to provide stability, in the face of the inevitable trials of life.

The well-functioning superego or conscience is realistic, reasonably consistent, and enables its owner to set achievable values, while living concurrently in the real world with balance and inner harmony. Individuals seeking psychotherapy often lack such inner harmony. At one end of the psychotherapy spectrum is the individual who seems to have no morals or only gives lip service to morals, i.e., the sociopath. At the other end of the psychotherapy spectrum is the individual who is tortured by a harsh, perfectionistic, and rigid conscience. The sociopath has a poor prognosis generally and does not respond to dynamic psychotherapy. The person with an excessively harsh conscience generally has a good prognosis and response.

THE SENSE OF SELF, SELF-ESTEEM, AND IDENTITY

People who come to psychotherapy often speak of difficulties with self-esteem, and seem to present with vaguely articulated difficulties in the general arena of the "sense of self" and "sense of identity." Issues of self-esteem can run the gamut from very low self-esteem, to widely fluctuating self-esteem, to low but somewhat reasonable and realistic self-esteem. Therapists can expect to see patients who may virtually hate themselves; others may perceive themselves as a failure, inadequate, defective, or bad. Of another order, patients may describe feeling good about themselves at times but struggle to maintain well-being, and in the face of criticism or negative life events, lose the capacity to regulate self-esteem.

Healthy self-esteem is reflected in a generally positive and balanced self-experience or view of oneself, a view reinforced by realistic accomplishments and feedback from others (especially from loved ones). For these "healthy" individuals, positive self-esteem is sustaining and comforting during periods of stress and through the unavoidable failures of life. People who seem to have an inflated and unrealistic sense of self that is based on fantasy tend to have a brittle coping style; grandiosity is necessary for the maintenance of psychological equilibrium. Rapid disintegration or narcissistic rage can result when a failure is perceived or suffered, or when others refuse to share the aggrandized self-view.

Extremes of self-esteem (extremely negative or grandiose) augur a less favorable prognosis for a successful psychotherapy. Therefore, individuals with intense self-hatred and well-entrenched or intractable masochistic personality elements may be difficult to treat. The excessively grandiose individual can be prone to rapid devaluation of the therapist in the setting of an empathic failure. When the failure of empathy occurs around the subject of the patient's sense of self, without a swift and accurate correction and a good measure of luck, this type of patient may leave abruptly. Marred by serious narcissistic difficulties, these patients have fragile self-esteem and are highly dependent on approbation ("mirroring") from other people. Narcissistically vulnerable patients, who actively look for feedback or praise from the therapist, may quickly withdraw, turn off, retreat, or become hostile when the "right kind" of feedback is not immediately or fully available. In psychotherapy, a less-than-positive, less-than- "optimally attuned," or muted response from the therapist, may be unmanageable for the seriously narcissistically damaged patient; regrettably and additionally then, this type of patient is less likely to stick with or benefit from treatment generally. These patients require patience, empathy, great skill, and at times judicious modification of parameters.

Individuals with rapidly fluctuating and widely varying self-esteem may also be difficult to treat, because the instability in the area of self-esteem may be a marker for an underlying diagnosis of a more primitive disorder (for example, borderline personality disorder). The widely fluctuating *self*-esteem (wide variations in the self-perception) may be matched by widely fluctuating perceptions of *others*, that is, the tendency to quickly idealize but also to quickly devalue. The therapist may be a messiah during one hour, only to become a miscreant in the next hour. Maintaining a sustainable, working relationship with such a patient, especially in the face of repeated idealization and devaluation, can be quite difficult as well as taxing for the therapist.

IDENTITY

Closely related to self-esteem is the concept of identity. "Identity" refers to the reasonably enduring experience, perception, or understanding of oneself, which includes values, beliefs, awareness of capacities or abilities, sexual orientation and the way in which sexuality is integrated, etc. Typically, the self-concept expands and identity consolidates with input from life and reality, as new skills and new responsibilities, changing world realities, and changing bodily capacities (with growth and aging) come together.

All people tend to struggle (in greater or lesser degrees) during periods of stress, or when around powerful authority or transference figures. When confronted with a powerful transference figure, seemingly stable elements of identity can feel (and look to the observer) temporarily much less stable. When around authority figures, different degrees of (distressing) identity flux may surface; some people are much more inclined to identify quickly with an authority and forget a prior belief or system of beliefs. Even "healthy" people question themselves or notice some internal doubt when in the face of someone admired or respected who has a different or new opinion. In fact, this is a necessary requirement for *education* to occur.

Nevertheless, some people have much more difficulty maintaining an inner compass. One young man promoted himself as a right-wing conservative moralist, only to change identities several months later and begin promoting homosexual rights. Helene Deutsch termed the individual with a fluctuating identity, who seems to change with the wind, an "as if" character. This is the person who seems to adapt to each new circumstance as though no previous identity existed, adopting the persona of the new situation or people in the new situation. Woody Allen's humorously depicted character, "Zelig," changed in mirrorlike fashion to reflect the persona of those around him. An excessively fluid identity typically reflects a lack of inner stability, diminishing the likelihood of a positive treatment prognosis.

Standing in contrast to the excessively fluid identity is the defensively held, exaggerated identity that tends to come across like a caricature; Marilyn Monroe (ultrafeminine) or Rambo (ultramacho) would be prototypes. Career, talent, looks, etc., become the citadel within which to hide, thus to protect self-esteem, minimize vulnerability, and defend against conflict. Physicians who come to psychotherapy *as patients* may attempt to "protect self-esteem, minimize vulnerability, and defend against conflict" by relating to the therapist like a peer, buddy, or physician-colleague. Many defensive (characterologic) patterns can be dealt with during psychotherapy; some more entrenched patterns may prove insurmountable.

GOALS AND ASPIRATIONS: THE "EGO-IDEAL"

Goals and aspirations are an integral part of identity, essential for the maintenance of self-esteem, and as a part of the "ego ideal" (see chapter 3, "Formulation") are theoretically paired with the conscience as a companion component of the superego. The isolation of individual goals and aspirations, like the growth of a sense of self and refinement of values and morals, is informed by reality and matures through and with experience. The input of teachers and coaches, friends, and loved ones dovetails with a realistic self-appraisal of capacities and the availability of opportunities, to make up the "reality" and "experience" components of which we speak. The *ego ideal* is a theoretical concept that refers to one's wishes and aspirations (goals). Aspirations may be realistic, improbable, or nearly impossible, much like the dictates of conscience. Goals and aspirations are essential for living, but can be inspiring, frustrating, or completely self-defeating. Some people never actualize their expectations, and live with resultant feelings and reactions; these can include sadness or depression, lowered self-esteem or frank self-criticism, guilt (if the failure to actualize goals or aspirations is perceived to have harmed someone else), or shame. For the patient and the therapist, coming to terms with the discrepancy between aspirations (that turn out only to be unrealizable wishes) and real ability and achievement is a fundamental goal of psychotherapy.

Unrealistic aspirations can thwart a patient's ability to achieve realistic goals. Being able to find and identify real capacities in the patient, and the patient's willingness to develop realistic and therefore stable goals, are important indicators of treatment outcome. Patients who demonstrate an extreme divergence between aspirations and realistic capacity (the person with a low/average IQ who wants to be an astrophysicist) may be difficult, if not impossible to treat with psychodynamic psychotherapy. The presence of intensely desired yet unrealistic self-expectations tends to indicate a limited capacity to accurately perceive reality and/or accept and integrate new information. This phenomenon can be due to limited cognitive capacity, and/or can reflect a rigidly defensive psychological structure.

Insistence by the patient about the realizability of goals that are clearly out of the range of ability or possibility typically indicates a major disturbance in self-awareness and a diagnosis in the spectrum from narcissistic pathology to the psychotic disorders. If the grandiose ideals are grossly unrealistic and tenacious (winning the Nobel Prize or becoming a rock star in the absence of any notable talent in these arenas), psychodynamic psychotherapy is an inappropriate medium, and other therapeutic modalities should be considered.

ACCEPTANCE OF REALITY AND REALITY TESTING

The patient's capacity to differentiate reality from fantasy needs to be ascertained. This ability, called *"reality testing,"* may be more difficult to evaluate, and its absence less obvious than one might initially imagine. The ability to distinguish reality from unreality spans a continuum from gross abnormalities of reality testing to subtle distortions in the way others are seen and experienced. Rarely completely intact, and rarely completely absent, the strength of reality testing determines the presence or absence of psychosis.

Difficulties in reality testing are most obvious in the psychotic or paranoid individual who sees or hears things that others do not (hallucinations), or maintains beliefs that are clearly unrelated to reality (delusions). However, more subtle distortions of reality testing may be apparent only during times of stress, or in intense interpersonal situations in which the motivations of others and even the ability to see and recall factual events may be distorted. People with "primitive" disorders, such as the borderline personality, often have difficulty with subtle reality differentiation. When idealized images of the self and/or others are challenged, perceptions of others may become grossly distorted.

Patients with limited difficulties with reality testing may be treatable with a more directed but psychodynamically informed approach: the therapist serves as an auxiliary arm of the patient's self (or "ego") and assists with the assessment of reality. Individuals with more significant difficulties with reality testing are probably not candidates for psychodynamic psychotherapy. Psychotherapy, by necessity, temporarily disrupts or alters the individual's defensive style. When defensive structures are already brittle or rigid, the potential for psychotic decompensation, or exposure of a current psychosis exists.

Patients with primitive personality disorders require much skill and experience on the part of the therapist, and even in the hands of the most expert psychotherapist, may do poorly with an insight-oriented approach; obviously, it is difficult or impossible to achieve insight without reality testing! Although some analysts have attempted to expand the domain of insight-oriented work with the primitive disorders (notably, Melanie Klein and Howard Searles), most psychoanalysts have felt that psychosis was a contraindication to dynamic psychotherapy, and certainly to psychoanalysis. Therefore, caution is certainly warranted should the therapist attempt dynamic psychotherapy with a psychotic individual, especially if the treatment is conducted in the absence of the concurrent use of medication.

AFFECT TOLERANCE AND ACCEPTANCE OF VULNERABILITY

Many of us have known or observed people who will leave a room, remove him-/herself from an interaction, or exit a movie when a particular emotion or emotions arise. Specific feeling states are frightening, overwhelming, or fragmenting for certain people. What kinds of feelings does a person allow in and what kinds of feelings does a person shut out? Is a dominant emotion present in lieu of other emotions? What emotions seem to be tolerated less easily than are others?

Most people find it difficult to tolerate certain feelings or need states. Nevertheless, the avoidance of a particular feeling or need state has meaning; a person doesn't avoid what isn't uncomfortable. The need to contain or eliminate certain feelings and need states absorbs energy, blocks out a dimension of human experience, and leads to the avoidance of any experience or situation that might bring up the feeling or need state. During the initial evaluation with a new patient, what emotions are not apparent during the interview or by history?

When a patient comes for psychotherapy, dominant and sometimes powerful emotions are usually close to the surface. One person may be sad, another full of rage, another full of shame or guilt. As previously noted, the absence of a specific feeling might be the most apparent feature of the hour. When one affective state regularly prevails, inevitably it is tightly interwoven with the person's character structure, and has the potential to provide an enduring resistance. Some affective states, especially if intense and chronic, may tax a therapist's capacities. For example, intense and chronic rage can be seen in some individuals with a borderline or narcissistic personality structure, and this feature usually carries with it a poorer prognosis.

WHO IS IN THE PATIENT'S LIFE?
THE ARENA OF OBJECT RELATIONS

People need other people because "man" (generic, to include men and women) is a social creature. Therefore, psychic health includes the ability to relate to, participate and work with, enjoy, and become close to (including intimate with) other people. This is the arena of "*object relations.*" True health in the arena of object relations depends upon the presence of "*object constancy.*" Object constancy is defined as the ability to maintain a stable and positive view or representation of another person, even in the face of frustration and disappointment with that person. Thus, object constancy in any given individual denotes a capacity to recognize and yet integrate both the negative and positive aspects of significant others (family, spouse, children, etc.). Obviously, *without the capacity to recognize* that people are human and therefore sometimes disappointing, it would be difficult to maintain an affectionate, deep, and enduring relationship with anyone!

The capacity for object constancy exists along a continuum; it is never fully and irrevocably achieved. Any "factor" that fosters "regression" can disrupt object constancy. These "factors" are usually precipitants of *stress*, such as illness, trauma, depression, anxiety, falling into a transference config- uration, loss, etc. Patients with borderline pathology generally exemplify the most obvious impairment in object constancy. In the life of the person with a borderline personality organization, people and situations tend to be di- vided into the "good pool" or the "bad pool," without recognition that a "pool" can be a mixture of both positives and negatives simultaneously. The lack of object constancy in such patients can be problematic for the thera- pist. Patients with borderline personality organization may grossly idealize the therapist, yet with a seemingly minor lapse on the therapist's part, turn to a dramatic denigration of the same therapist.

"Self-constancy," the mirror twin of object constancy, is the capacity to remain aware, even in the face of shame or disappointment with oneself, that those qualities that are valued aspects of the self and identity are still present. How does the therapist evaluate the patient's "object relations," that is, the quantity (presence of) and quality (nature of) relationships in the pa- tient's life?

All people have human relationships that will vary in quantity and quality over time. Beyond the absolute number of friends that any given person might have, relationships differ in depth, from the superficial to the intimate. Relationships can last for hours: two people have a chance meet- ing on a plane—a deep connection is obvious, but no likelihood exists of meeting again. Relationships can last for years, such as the best friend that is sustaining through the "trials and tribulations" of the college years. Rela- tionships can last for decades, such as the couple who is lucky enough to celebrate, and celebrate joyously, a fiftieth wedding anniversary.

Does the individual have friends? For example, a person might have many superficial friends, or a few very close friends of long standing. Are a person's relationships predominantly gratifying or predominantly frustrating, and what is it that makes them one way or another? Are friends or partners understood to be and related to as complex human beings (with indepen- dent needs and feelings) or merely as "need-satisfying objects" (nothing is important except for the particular needs or functions that the friend or part- ner provides for that person)? Relationships should allow for mutuality and respect for differences; these are characteristics of the mature relationship.

The clinician should think about the patient's description of significant others. Are parents or children or a spouse portrayed in simplistic, black- and-white terms? Do significant others come across as three-dimensional people ("complex human beings") or as two-dimensional figures that are hard to conceptualize? Are descriptions of people muted and vague or do descriptions come across as well "fleshed-out"? Do people come across as real, with assets as well as with limitations (Kernberg 1976)? Kernberg distinguished between the two-dimensional and the three-dimensional description of people by making use of an analogy. In the "Grade B movie," characters are undeveloped and often superficial (stereotypical heroes and villains). In contrast, a great movie or piece of literature allows the characters to come alive, conveying degrees of nuance that include both positive and not-so-positive elements. In this way, characters are rendered believable and human (Kernberg 1971, 1976). The therapist should take note, however: some people are just not facile with descriptive language! As time passes, and the therapist learns more about the patient and the patient's life, it may become clear that the patient has tremendous concern for the aging parents, or the child who is struggling in school, or the spouse who is anxious about starting a more challenging job. The patient is simply not able to put the thoughts and feelings into words.

Taking into account the patient's sexual preference, the therapist will want to know how relationships with both men and women seem to work for the patient. How great is the degree of comfort with the gender that is the focus of sexual choice, and with the gender that is not of sexual choice? What is the natural history of the patient's romantic and sexual involvement? What kind of person does the patient tend to choose as a partner, and do the choices appear to be wise?

A MAJOR CONTRIBUTOR TO THE WORLD OF OBJECT RELATIONS IS THE FAMILY OF ORIGIN AND THE IMPACT OF PERCEPTIONS ABOUT THIS FAMILY

The perception of one's own family and relationships with family members profoundly influences how a person sees the world and the people in it. That is, it influences "object relations." In general, people seem to have great difficulty with the accurate perception and assessment of parents and family members; the subject matter is simply too close. Parents are so vitally important, so essentially needed, and therefore have such a great ability to produce an effect (to hurt feelings or to cause disappointment), that distortions are common, if not universal. The questions posed in the previous section are relevant here. In speaking of the family, does the patient have an appreciation for the various shades of gray? Is one parent idealized while the other is denigrated? Is the description of the parents consistent over a period of time, or does the story not quite fit together?

Mrs. B, a hard-working, somewhat masochistic woman, was urged by her husband to seek help for herself. She presented symptoms of chronic depression and fatigue, and seemed to have some limited awareness that she might have a role in creating the feeling of restraint and deprivation with which she lived.

In the second hour, Mrs. B spoke of her "wonderful and loving" mother. The therapist asked if there was anything that Mrs. B disliked about her mother, and she emphatically stated, "No!" The response was so emphatic that somewhat later in the interview, the therapist returned to the subject of the mother, choosing to inquire about the mother's circle of friends. Now, Mrs. B began to speak of her mother's "directness." Neighbors and friends were often hurt by the mother's "directness"; in fact, the mother could be so hurtful in her commentary, that over time, no friends remained. A picture of an intrusive, tactless, woman emerged.

To some extent, everyone has to grapple with the perception of the past and the family that was a central facet of the past. Only with many life experiences, distance, self-understanding, and wisdom does a person really begin to understand a parent in a balanced and realistic fashion. For many people, having children offers the opportunity to take a new look at the problem of parenthood. Therefore, the patient who comes to a psychoanalytically oriented therapy frequently paints confused and confusing portraits of parents. However, some individuals cannot or will not explore the qualities of a parent or parents, because as with a child (who is still dependent on the parents), the process is too disruptive. The following example illustrates this point.

Mrs. F had been in two prior psychotherapies, one with a female therapist and one with a male therapist; each was to no avail. She came to therapy for the third time (the therapist was again male) and announced that her father was a "vicious bastard." When the therapist asked Mrs. F to explain what it was that made her father a "vicious bastard," she said that her conclusion was beyond question and she would not discuss it further.

Over time, Mrs. F continued to allude to her father in many associations. Occasionally, and tentatively, the therapist would attempt to clarify her feelings or wonder about her reticence to talk of her father. Mrs. F would always respond in the same way. She would become angry, the subject was closed, and therapists are all overly concerned about things that are "no matter."

Somehow the therapy endured and the patient made minor strides in her life, but it was slow and limited in benefit. From what little information the therapist was eventually able to pick up about Mrs. F's father, it seemed that he probably was a "vicious bastard"; allusions to his rages, physically abusive behavior, and molestation of Mrs. F appeared in indirect associations, dreams, and specific phobic behaviors. The problem for Mrs. F was, however, that her father was the only family left to her and she felt she would be able to count on him to ensure her future financial security (he was quite wealthy).

Mrs. F knew that her father had violated her boundaries on multiple levels. Consequently, her ongoing relationship with him was intensely disturbing and filled her with shame. These feelings, and the reality situation in which Mrs. F found herself, negated any likelihood of an analytic exploration of the character of her father and its impact upon her.

In contrast to Mrs. F, the more neurotic patient may defensively idealize or denigrate a parent, but can more rapidly and with more curiosity explore the way in which the past family situation can impact the present.

Ms. X spoke in the first psychotherapy consultation about the difficulty she had with self-assertion. She spoke of her family; she had been labeled as fragile and was always overprotected. She and her mother had battled all through her adolescence. Ms. X spoke about her father and his involvement in the family. He was loyal and nurturing to the members of the family, a "real saint." He was a gentle soul, and continued to be so. As Ms. X discussed her father, he sounded almost "saint-like."

At some point, the therapist inquired what the father was like outside the home. Ms. X hesitated and then said; "He does things with money that might not be so good." Upon further questioning, Ms. X related her suspicions that her father was involved in some type of criminal activity.

Before the therapist could inquire further, Ms. X changed the subject and began to talk of the difficulty she had in expressing herself and how she had always been shy. The therapist asked if she had any difficulty in talking with or asserting herself with her father. She again seemed to change the topic, noting that she rarely got angry. Recently, however, she suspected that her anger was more intense than she might have realized, particularly when she found herself enraged with one of her senior male professors. Ms.

X reflected for a moment and wondered out loud if she had some unresolved feelings about her father. She again spoke of some of her father's business practices, which she knew to be unethical.

In the above example, Ms. X shows the ability to examine mixed feelings about a family member, even when the mixed feelings are uncomfortable. She questions whether her recent anger toward a male professor has something to do with her feelings about her father.

Some people have a very limited positive experience with parents, guardians, mentors, or authorities. The person who has had *no* significantly sustaining relationships in his/her past history may have difficulty forming a therapeutic relationship or a therapeutic alliance. One approach the therapist can take in the exploration of a patient's history of previous attachments is to inquire: was anyone (a teacher, coach, religious figure, or neighborhood friend) an emotionally available or sustaining figure, who could be turned to for support? With little or no familial support, psychological survival is quite difficult. Some individuals, because of luck or because of remarkable temperamental capacity, manage to find someone to whom they can turn and upon whom they can rely. Unfortunately, this is usually an exception to the rule.

For many years, a man frequented the emergency room at a local hospital. He would present with a crisis and often with self-destructive ideation, but never of sufficient magnitude to warrant hospitalization. So regularly would he come to the hospital ER, that eventually all of the resident psychiatrists knew him.

In spite of his frequent visits to the emergency room, and all late at night, the man was persistently resistant to follow up. He would not see any therapist for a more in-depth and planned assessment and treatment. The man actually had a series of small computer-related businesses, and with these, he had achieved a modicum of financial security. Yet, despite his success, the man lived in a series of changing motel rooms and sometimes in his car.

The man's pertinent history was the following. From the age of two-and-a-half to seven, this man had lived in and miraculously survived a prison camp. Once he was freed, he lived in an orphanage until adoption by a family, when he was ten years old. As a result of his early life experiences, this man was unable to form attachments or maintain enduring relationships. Psychological survival had been based on his capacity to detach, a capacity that became a defining element of his character. It was impossible for this man to engage in psychotherapy.

MOTIVATION

Motivation is perhaps the single most important prognostic factor of success in psychotherapy; motivation is also sometimes difficult to assess. Of the various precipitants that create the condition of "motivation," psychic pain is probably the most significant factor. Without psychic pain, a person becomes one of the many people who might benefit from psychotherapy, but have little desire to seek help. On occasion, a difficult life event or a rocky transition through a new developmental phase creates a temporary discomfort, but once the event is sufficiently distant or the transition less unfamiliar, the motivation is forgotten.

How does one determine the level of pain that a potential patient might feel? Of course, sometimes the patient simply reports the experience of pain directly, because pain is the conscious driving force that brings the patient to treatment. Frequently, the stories that the patient tells us are obviously painful, such as the inability to attain a deeply desired goal (for example, to get into medical school). On occasion, the story is so difficult to listen to that the factor of pain is unmistakable (for example, a parent who speaks of losing a child to acute leukemia). Sometimes, only a "feel" or intuition, which is derived from the therapist's empathy, indicates that pain is present in sufficient quantity to secure the patient's attachment to the treatment.

Emotional pain is idiosyncratic. Even when the patient's history is not clearly striking, the sensitive therapist may be able empathetically to appreciate the patient's sorrow, and with that understanding, help to facilitate a therapeutic resolution over time. The therapist should never forget that if a patient comes to treatment, a reason exists for having done so. On occasion, a person comes to treatment who seems to "have it all together"; the reason for consultation is initially unclear. Only with time and effort directed toward understanding does the patient's suffering become evident.

The following story of Mr. J reminds us that, in addition to the clinical reality that emotional pain is subjective, personal, and idiosyncratic, patients frequently have only a vague awareness that something is wrong.

Mr. J was a high-functioning professional person. His own reason for coming to psychotherapy was obscure. He had arranged for a consultation only at his wife's urging, because she was concerned that he was losing interest in her and feared that he might have an affair. Mr. J insisted that his wife's concerns were unfounded. However, he showed no resistance to attending the consultation hours, during which time he described a life story that appeared remarkably positive.

Mr. J was handsome, athletic, articulate, urbane, witty, and poised. Having achieved remarkable academic success, he then went on to travel the globe as he rocketed to corporate success. While still in his thirties, he became head of a large company. He described his wife as beautiful and supportive, and his young children as adorable. Although he did acknowledge some minor struggles with his wife about how much money she spent, Mr. J expressed no significant dissatisfaction with his wife.

Several meetings passed, and the therapist felt no closer to an understanding of the reason(s) that Mr. J might feel compelled to seek treatment. Was Mr. J coming to therapy only to appease his wife? It seemed unlikely that a man such as Mr. J would continue to waste his time for only this reason. The therapist was just beginning to feel that he might have no insight to offer at all, when to his surprise, he noticed that the patient's hands were trembling!

With time, hidden behind the mask of Mr. J's achievements and abilities, his deep sadness emerged. Unearthed by his father's recent death, for the first time Mr. J began to experience an intense sense of loss about the poverty of his relationship with a father he had little known. The yearning for closeness and mutual respect that he had not had with his father, and now would never have (with the event of his father's death), became funneled into a dimly recognized wish to "sink" into his wife for comfort and nourishment. These wishes were frightening to Mr. J, and opposed his sense of dignity. Mr. J believed that self-reliance and self-containment were the only true qualities of value; neediness and dependency could and would only be disdained.

In a sense, his wife was right to have been concerned that Mr. J was moving away from her. She was wrong, however, about the reason. Mr. J was not having an affair, but he was preoccupied, distant, and very afraid that his wife would be as disgusted as he, were he ever to reveal to her the depth of his vulnerability and uncertainty. With psychotherapy, it became clear to Mr. J that the value system he imposed upon his wife was really *of his own making* and *belonged to him* alone. In fact, Mr. J's wife was more than willing to respond to his vulnerability, and be a helpful partner in the event of his uncertainty.

Motivation that is derived from another party, who urges or insists that the patient seek psychotherapy, may be no motivation at all. This "patient" comes at the insistence of a partner or a wife/husband or a parent/parents.

If the other party's insistence or urging is truly the dominant motivation, rarely is this sufficient to push the "patient" through the difficult and at times painful aspects of psychotherapy. The therapist has to be attentive, however, to the possibility that the patient is merely making use of another person's request/requirement/ultimatum to come to treatment in order, consciously or unconsciously, to prevent exposure yet fulfill a desire to secure help. Teenagers in particular may insist that succumbing to therapy is simply a measure to appease a parent or parents; the desire to have someone to talk to, or the acknowledgment of being in distress, is difficult to admit for many adolescents.

In the example of Mr. J, although the *expressed* motivation to seek treatment was not the most positive prognostic indicator (that is, Mrs. J wanted Mr. J to get help), the *hidden* motivation (Mr. J's pain) was an important reason to seek and pursue a psychoanalytically oriented psychotherapy. Unfortunately, not all hidden motivations for seeking pyschotherapy are likely to result in positive outcomes (as the example above). A primitive and tenacious desire to make use of the treatment to enact rather than to resolve an old conflict or pattern, is one such poor hidden motivation. The fulfillment of a "masochistic" need (or needs) would be an example of this. In this situation, the individual derives some pleasure or gain from psychic suffering (pain); therefore, the examination of intrapsychic conflict and subsequent relinquishment of the same is exceedingly difficult and at times impossible for the patient. People with profound masochistic character elements may need longer treatments and have less robust results.

> Ms. T, a middle-aged woman with a long history of seeking attention from medical doctors for certain physical symptoms, sought treatment after circumstances made it impossible for her to continue living with her mother. The patient and her mother had an enmeshed relationship; they had provided constant companionship for each other.
>
> The *pathologic* nature of the closeness between mother and daughter was sequestered behind a rationalization, which was that the relationship was justified because the daughter (Ms. T) had a "disabling" medical condition (the cause of her "certain physical symptoms"). Many physicians had suggested to the pair that the medical condition was minor (not major) and possibly even self-induced. Doctors who failed to confirm the mother and daughter's belief that the medical condition was severe and had resulted in a severe disability were summarily dismissed.

Ms. T had a self-defeating character style. She frequently fantasized about hurting herself. Over time, it appeared that the fantasies, or actual self-defeating behaviors, seemed to appear or be enacted when Ms. T was about to take a step toward actualizing independence and self-sufficiency.

Ms. T's early life was characterized by physical and sexual abuse at the hands of her father. The actual abuse ended with the disappearance of her father at some point in her teen years. However, the father's presence was *replaced* by the adoption of a favorite and secret fantasy, with which Ms. T pleasured and tortured herself. In the fantasy, Ms. T had the possibility of escaping from a "dreary" life, to enter a wonderful life that offered unimaginable possibility, only to be derailed at the last moment by some event that involved physical trauma (a car accident, a mugging). In response to this trauma, Ms. T would submit to her fate. She would then adopt a saint-like attitude, while all the while, privately and simultaneously, she would feel great self-pity. In fact, Ms. T felt herself "bathing" in her sense of victimization, the consequent anger, anguish, and despair.

The etiology of Ms. T's medical condition remained unclear throughout her entire psychotherapy, leaving her therapist to wonder frequently how much of Ms. T's symptomatology was hysterical or really self-induced (as previous doctors had speculated). This question remained unanswered and was perhaps unanswerable; however, over time it did become clear that Ms. T's symptoms worsened consistently and predictably whenever she began to master a task that clearly indicated her competence and capacity for independence. Ms. T would then cling to her mother ever more tenaciously, seemingly irreversibly entrenched in her desire to be helpless and dependent. This was really what Ms. T wanted from the treatment as well ("hidden motivation"). She wanted a place to be helpless and dependent, to "swim" endlessly in her self-pity. Her therapist, a reedition of both father and mother, would have to watch her suffering but also be consigned to take care of her forever, the only acceptable restitution (in Ms. T's mind) for the crimes committed against her (her father's molestation of her; her mother's failure to protect her).

With much long and difficult work over many years, Ms. T improved somewhat. She remained with significant limitations in her overall functioning, and achieved less insight about her own motivation than one would have hoped.

Sometimes motivation occurs in the context of a transient stress; motivation precipitated in this manner may lessen as the stress diminishes. It could be argued that short-term, crisis-related treatments would be more suitable in this kind of situation, especially with a person who is only in need of a short-term intervention. For another type of person, the transient stress is a harbinger of the longer-term appearance of deeper and more enduring difficulties; however, the ability to tolerate anxiety or to develop a working relationship is lacking. Often, the inability to maintain motivation is implied by the individual's history: an exploration demonstrates the inability to tolerate a close relationship, or the inability to tolerate anxiety, or a pattern of flight from previous difficult situations, etc.

The wish for financial gain can be a motivation to engage in psychotherapy. Referrals to a therapist/psychiatrist may occur in the context of a lawsuit in which "pain and suffering" is a component of the claim, or in a case that involves workers' compensation. These kinds of situations are rarely sufficient to fuel a useful therapeutic process.

RESPONSE TO FEEDBACK

Feedback, in the form of a clarification or a tentative interpretation, is frequently part of the process of an initial evaluation. The manner in which a new patient responds to feedback from the therapist provides important information. "Feedback" takes the form of a variety of different kinds of comments that can be offered during an evaluation. Emotions can be identified and underlined for the patient: "You seem depressed." Perceptions can be clarified, and the contradictions between perceptions can be explored: "You tell me that your mother is the most wonderful person in the world, but you also tell me that your mother drove your father away." More complex interpretations regarding motivation or transference can be made: "You describe your husband very much as you describe your father, and both seem to frustrate and upset you enough to seek some help."

The most common initial feedback or intervention used during an evaluation is the clarification of a dominant emotion the patient seems to have (sadness, anger, fear, etc.). This type of clarification may be combined with a comment about the arena in which the emotion most seems to manifest itself; this arena could be in a professional context, a romantic relationship, in relationship to family. An example would be: "What you have told me about today seems to be most dominated by your sadness about the death of your father last year." The current emotion often echoes a prior area of difficulty. An interpretation in this regard might be: "It seems as though you were missing your father *throughout* your life, even before his death, because you saw him so infrequently after the divorce." A focus on the present and current emotions initially may be more tactful, especially if the patient is quite anxious about the consultation. An interpretation about the potential connection between the current emotion and a past emotion or perhaps its precipitant allows the therapist to investigate the patient's responsiveness to the psychotherapy experience.

When interventions of this variety are made, what occurs in response? Do interventions on the part of the therapist lead to further associations, memories, or observations on the part of the patient? The individual with greater maturity may become mildly uncomfortable or defensive, but will also and for the most part demonstrate some capacity to explore different perceptions. This kind of response suggests that psychotherapy can be made use of by, and therefore should be useful to, the patient. In contrast, do interventions on the part of the therapist lead to defensive reactions, regression, or negativity on the part of the patient toward the therapist? This latter response is not necessarily a poor prognostic sign, but depending on its intensity and magnitude, may portend a more difficult course.

When the patient has an intense initial reaction to the therapist, with the development of rapid and obvious transference reactions, the therapist should consider the presence of more serious pathology. Rapid and intense transference reactions can suggest intense dependency needs, seen in some very dependent, "oral" individuals. Rapid, intense, and oscillating transference reactions with defenses that are more dramatic (such as projective identification and splitting), are also often seen in borderline and narcissistic personality types. With the even less integrated individual, a loss of reality testing and evidence of psychotic features may be manifested.

DEFENSIVE STYLES

Many authors have examined levels of defensive operations. Kernberg (1966, 1970, 1971, 1976) has studied the relationship between defenses and character pathology. Vaillant (1977, 1992; Vaillant, Bond, & Vaillant 1986) has studied the prognostic value of different types of defensive functions: that is, do "levels of defense" correlate with how a person will fare in life, love, work, health, etc.? Defenses can be ranked (levels of defense) as mature/ neurotic/primitive or as upper level/middle level/lower level.

While it seems clear that level of defensive function says something about a person (and thus, a patient), just what it is that might be said may not be precise or absolute. As a generality, individuals with mature and/or neurotic defenses are easier to treat and have a better prognosis than people with more primitive defenses. The probability that any person's defensive style can be changed is somewhat dependent on the initial level of defensive style. The person who has primitive defenses may develop neurotic defenses, but may never develop mature defenses. The individual with neurotic defenses is likely to develop more mature defenses with successful psychotherapy. Defenses are often difficult for the beginning therapist to conceptualize and identify (see chapter 5); actively looking for a person's defensive style and accurately identifying particular defenses is essential for assessment.

Countertransference reactions (on the part of the therapist) may add further information to the assessment of a patient's defensive style. Individuals with lower-level defenses often evoke more intense and uncomfortable countertransference reactions in the therapist. The psychotic individual often evokes a distinct sense of discomfort and disquiet.

TRAUMA

Trauma overwhelms a person's capacity to tolerate the associated affects and to integrate the experience. Childhood traumas vary in degree, ranging from the early loss of a parent or sexual/physical abuse, to having difficulty separating from the mother to start kindergarten or breaking an arm playing soccer just before the final championship game.

Some traumas become successfully integrated into an individual's character. These traumas may be of a lesser order, which although traumatic at the time, could be overcome without long-lasting or permanent consequences. Traumas may also be of a greater order, but the surrounding circumstances mitigated against some of the potential damaging impact. An example would be the following:

> Dr. B was a successful neurosurgeon who *never presented to treatment.* No particular reason for his seeking psychotherapy seemed to exist.
> As a child, Dr. B had an encounter with a terrifying head injury, the result of a dive into a too shallow pool. Dr. B spent several days in a neurosurgical intensive care unit, a longer time in a rehabilitation wing of the hospital, but recovered with no sequela! He recalls that the experience was very frightening, but his stronger memory is of the staff and doctors who were attentive, calming, and always responsive to his needs. The impact of this experience

upon Dr. B's character is best illustrated by the professional reputation he later developed in the community in which he practiced, and with his colleagues. Not only did Dr. B develop an enduring interest in medicine and neurosurgery, but he was also known as the "only neurosurgeon you really want to have if you're in trouble" because of his skill, his deep dedication to his patients, and his empathy for his patients' pain and suffering.

Unfortunately, a positive outcome doesn't necessarily evolve from an earlier trauma. Trauma can also have a very negative effect. Traumas of a more severe nature leave deeper imprints on a person's character. Interestingly, many therapists have endured traumas, and these traumas may play a meaningful role in the choice of profession. Very significant early deprivation or trauma, such as the early loss of a parent, a parental suicide, severe abuse, etc., often leave profound scars. While most individuals with childhood trauma benefit from treatment, the rapidity of change and the magnitude of change possible varies and is dependent upon several factors. These factors would include:

1. the extent of the insult
2. temperament and constitutional endowment
3. possibility for restitution, which is partly dependent upon temperament and constitutional endowment
4. prevailing environmental factors, such as financial situation, support systems, realistic possibilities for gratification in the patient's current world, etc.
5. the age of the patient; the younger, the better.

Significant childhood traumas should be noted in an evaluation and the role of the trauma in the person's development considered. Occasionally childhood traumas will lead to insurmountable difficulties, making psychotherapy impossible. The earlier example of the man who had spent his early years in a concentration camp, and later frequented the emergency room but would not accept a referral to a therapist is such a case.

INTELLIGENCE AND PSYCHOLOGICAL MINDEDNESS

Intelligence is of assistance in the understanding of the process of insight-oriented psychotherapy and low intelligence can be a hindrance. "Emo-

tional intelligence" or psychological mindedness is a strong positive prognostic variable, often shortening the time involved in bringing a course of
psychotherapy to a successful resolution. Conversely, "pseudo" psychological-
mindedness can serve as a resistance. "Pseudo" psychological-mindedness
looks like psychological-mindedness, but what is really present is a familiarity with the "lingo" of psychotherapy, with no integration of the ideas or
true interest in employing the process in the service of change.

> A very intelligent and psychologically sophisticated woman
> dragged her despairing husband into a couples' treatment. Al-
> though this woman had had many years of psychotherapy and
> talked a "good game," she clearly had no interest in changing her-
> self. She was only interested in making use of her psychological
> savvy to undermine the validity of her husband's (legitimate) com-
> plaints about her in order to ensure that she would continue to al-
> ways get her way.

The treatment of a fellow mental health colleague deserves a special
category. Intelligence and psychological-mindedness are often a given. Of
more concern is the therapist's ability to create an atmosphere of dignity and
respect, so that the colleague is free to relinquish the analyzing posture and
engage in an experiential and personally meaningful process.

ADDICTIVE BEHAVIOR

Significant drug use or alcoholism is very difficult to treat with insight
alone. In fact, some mental health authors have adopted strident stands
against using dynamic psychotherapy for these individuals. Perhaps most
pertinent is to understand the potential difficulties of this group of people, establish workable parameters, and not overestimate the power of
psychotherapy to deal with addictive behaviors. In this vein, most patients
with drug or alcohol problems will need supplemental treatment. For
substance users with less severe problems, supplemental treatment can
come in the form of a structured support system, such as Alcoholics
Anonymous or an outpatient drug or alcohol treatment program. For
substance users whose problem is more severe (outpatient measures alone
are not sufficient to curtail the drug-seeking behavior), an inpatient re-
habilitation program that offers containment may be the only workable
measure.

SOMATIZATION

"Somatization" (from the word root "soma," which means "body"), or somatic preoccupation, is the tendency to unconsciously translate emotions into body sensation and body concerns. Somatization has both cultural and familial determinates. In some cultures and in some families, somatic concern is sanctioned, whereas direct expression of emotions and needs is not. Cultural and familial factors can add to a particular individual's tendency to focus on body observations or body sensations, the endpoint of which can be a tenacious throng of somatic preoccupations. Somatic concerns and preoccupations can be understood, worked through, and alleviated in the course of psychoanalytically oriented psychotherapy. However, somatization can also be a difficult resistance to overcome. The somatic focus limits the area of concern to the physical, thus effectively restricting the awareness of feelings and the acknowledgment that bodily concerns can interfere with successful insight. Additionally, the therapist may find empathy difficult with these kinds of patients.

DIAGNOSIS

When it comes to the prediction of who is likely to commit to and benefit from psychotherapy and who is not, diagnosis is an important but sometimes surprisingly limited prognostic variable. A schizoid individual, or a person with a diagnosis of borderline personality disorder who is *obstreperous*, may face a very complicated road to improvement. Patients with a narcissistic personality disorder can be challenging, but the therapist (road crew) probably can find the material to fill in the deep potholes in the road. Depressive or dysthymic individuals comprise a broad group, many of whom can benefit greatly from an insight-oriented treatment that is aimed at understanding the root of the depression or dysthymia (medication can be, of course, an adjunctive treatment). Obsessive and high-functioning histrionic individuals typically may be the best candidates for dynamic psychotherapy.

It should be stressed, however, that diagnosis might say little about the level of functioning of any given patient, within any given diagnostic category. Within any diagnostic category, great variation may exist.

REFERENCES AND READINGS

Bean, M. H., and N. E. Zinber, eds. (1981). *Dynamic Approaches to the Understanding and Treatment of Alcoholism.* New York: The Free Press.

Deutsch, H. (1942). Some forms of emotional disturbance and their relationship to schizophrenia. *Psychoanalytic Quarterly* 11: 301–21.

Kernberg, O. (1966). Structural derivatives of object relationships. *International Journal of Psycho-Analysis* 47: 236–52.

———. (1970). A psychoanalytic classification of character formation. *Journal of the American Psychoanalytic Association* 18: 800–822.

———. (1971). Prognostic considerations regarding borderline personality organization. *Journal of the American Psychoanalytic Association* 19: 595–635.

———. (1976). *Object-Relations Theory and Clinical Psychoanalysis*. Northvale, NJ: Jason Aronson.

Khantzian, E. J. (1980). The alcoholic patient: an overview and perspective. *American Journal of Psychotherapy* 34: 4–19.

MacKinnon, R. A., and R. Michels. (1971). *The Psychiatric Interview in Clinical Practice*. Philadelphia: W. B. Saunders.

Mahler, M. S., F. Pine, and A. Bergman. (1975). *The Psychological Birth of the Human Infant: Symbiosis and Individuation*. New York: Basic Books.

Moore, R. A. (1962). The problem of abstinence by the patient as a requisite for the psychotherapy of alcoholism. *Quarterly Journal of Studies on Alcohol* 23: 105–11.

Murray, J. M. (1964). Narcissism and the ego ideal. *Journal of the American Psychoanalytic Association* 12: 471–511.

Rosenfeld, H. A. (1952). Transference-phenomena and transference-analysis in an acute catatonic schizophrenic patient. *International Journal of Psycho-Analysis* 33: 452–64.

Searles, H. F. (1976). Psychoanalytic therapy with schizophrenic patients in a private-practice context. *Contemporary Psychoanalysis* 12: 387–406.

Vaillant, G. E. (1977). *Adaptation to Life*. Boston: Little, Brown.

———. (1992). *Ego Mechanisms of Defense*. Washington, DC: American Psychiatric Press.

Vaillant, G. E., M. P. Bond, and C. O. Vaillant. (1986). An empirically validated hierarchy of defense mechanisms. *Archives of General Psychiatry* 43: 786–94.

3

FORMULATION

Conceptualizing a dynamic formulation of a patient unites clinical observation and psychodynamic theory, each of which the beginning therapist has relatively little of when he or she begins training. In the following, the essentials of psychodynamic theory, insofar as these essentials provide a schema for organizing an understanding of a patient, will be delineated. What is offered is a brief and therefore necessarily limited description of the fundamentals of important theoretical ideas. Nevertheless, this introduction to theory offers a method for imposing order, so that the therapist is not overwhelmed by the chaos of seemingly contradictory theories. Clinical practice, supervision, didactic training and professional reading are necessary in order to gradually develop a fluid capacity to think about different theories and develop something more than a rote formulation.

WHAT IS A FORMULATION?

Broadly speaking, a formulation tries to explain "what makes a person tick." A formulation is not just a description of what one sees in a phenomenological way, such as the symptoms and characteristics of a person as described in DSM-IV (1994). A formulation allows us to form ideas about what motivates people to do what they do, and provides a "road map" with which to begin to understand why a person becomes who he or she becomes. How does a person manage to find what is needed or wanted, or become unable to do so? How does a person protect him- or herself in life, or fail to do so? How does a person maintain his or her self-esteem, or adapt to the surrounding world? How does a person make choices about relationships, who to spend time with and who to pass by?

50   *Chapter 3*

DO WE NEED A FORMULATION?

Commonly asked questions are: Do we really need a formulation or a theory to explain a person's behavior? Does a formulation, which makes use of a theory (or theories), really help us to understand a person, or does it hamper or limit our ability as a therapist? One has only to look at the fervor with which therapists tend to defend a favorite theory, or theories, in order to provide suspicion that allegiance to theory can potentially be blinding, restricting one's ability to understand the multiple meanings of human behavior. So how is it then, that theory can be useful? Every therapist is both therapist and human being; each therapist has a favorite theory or theories that necessarily involve personal points of view. Additionally, every therapist has an investment in the particular ideas that allowed that therapist to arrive at self-understanding. These ideas can be held onto defensively. A particular theory may be useful for the understanding of one patient or one behavior, but may constrain a therapist's capacity to see other elements fully.

Theory is extremely useful when the therapist is able to consider human behavior from multiple points of view, and to have varied and flexible formulations that incorporate different perspectives. Patients are different and predicaments are different. How a patient is best understood—that is, the theory that might be the most useful at any given time—will vary with the situation, phase of the treatment, problem that is currently being addressed, or problem that needs to be addressed in the future.

We have now returned to the original question: Does a therapist really need a formulation or a theory in order to understand a patient? The question is actually misleading, because it implies that a therapist doesn't have to have a theory, or could operate without a theory. In fact, all therapists (and people) have biases and beliefs about human beings and explanations about why people behave as they do; therefore, a therapist always has an idea about why a person does what he or she does, or why a patient is who he or she is, and what might help. Some therapists have a simple, "one-size-fits-all" understanding; other therapists have many layers of complexity to their understanding. Studying the well-described psychoanalytic theories about the structure of the mind and the self, the motivations of behavior, the formation of character, etc., enables the therapist to question and refine personal theories; hopefully, this allows for an expansion of the therapist's ability to understand patients, as well as expands the therapist's personal awareness and/or self-understanding.

Having a theory is also useful because theory helps to minimize the feeling of being overwhelmed by the material or the patient's situation, thus allowing the therapist to think clearly and begin to understand the patient. Remember that a formulation seeks to explain how a person comes to be in terms of symptoms, character traits, etc. A formulation explains something about how the patient's personality structure is organized along a spectrum and what upsets the patient's (psychic) equilibrium. How one understands a patient depends upon what spectrum one uses. Spectrum implies that one has a theory, and the technique and practice of psychoanalytic psychotherapy is based on and depends upon theory: All therapists must, on a day-by-day basis, whether range of experience is limited or extensive, listen to, organize, and do something with a complex array of information and feeling states. It is often useful to start simply, search for several broad areas of concern, and then gradually (always returning to these concerns) elaborate further. If a therapist can decipher several broad elements of human concern, which have the character of general themes, the development of an initial formulation has begun. Broad areas to consider might include, for example:

1. The quality of the "sense of self" is of concern; this category includes issues around self-esteem, "narcissistic sensitivity," and susceptibility to experiencing states of shame (see section on self-psychology).
2. Concerns about the quality of interpersonal relationships in the workplace, in friendships, and in love relationships are a central issue (see section on object-relations theory).
3. Ineffective methods of coping are evident, or ineffective defensive styles are maintained (see section on ego psychology and the structural model).

Each of the above areas could be expanded upon or defined, depending upon the theoretical school of thought.

THE ROLE OF TEMPERAMENT

Before further exploring the formal psychodynamic theories, the contributing role of temperament, and its impact and influence, should be briefly addressed. Many psychoanalytic writers have referred to temperament, including Freud, Klein, Sandler, and Stern; however, psychoanalytic theories have not attempted to assimilate the problem of temperament in any systematic fashion.

Even in the casual observation of infants, temperamental differences are often obvious to the observer (some babies cry a great deal, and some don't). By adulthood, however, temperamental differences are difficult to distinguish from other developmental and/or psychological contributions. The use of psychotropic medication, with the attendant and sometimes surprising consequent changes that can occur in a person's reactivity, capacity to cope, ability to perceive and assess reality, etc., suggest the power of temperamental influences (as affected and influenced by biologic, that is, "pathophysiologic factors").

The interaction between psychology and temperament, and the effect that temperament has on any individual's development, should be a consideration in any dynamic formulation. Temperament colors perception. Therefore, temperament and biologic givens play a powerful role with respect to the way in which life experience is assimilated. Frustration tolerance, the ease or difficulty with which developmental tasks are mastered, the comfort with which one meets new people or adapts to new surroundings, is to some extent "prewired" or built in (temperament), and significantly influences each individual's trajectory.

Chess and Thomas (1986) described several categories of temperamental differences, having examined certain variables. Their variables included activity level, rhythmicity, approach or withdrawal, adaptability, threshold of responsiveness, intensity of reaction, quality of mood, distractibility, and attention span and persistence. Based on the above variables, children clustered into three basic groupings.

The "easy child" is characterized by regularity, a positive approach to new situations (stimuli), a high adaptability to change, and a predominantly positive mood of moderate intensity. The easy child sleeps and eats with regularity and easily responds to school and the frustrations of life without commotion. Needless to say, the easy child is "easy" to deal with, for parents and other adults alike. In their study 40 percent of children fit into this category.

The "difficult child" is at the other polarity. This child manifests irregularity in biologic functions, reacts negatively to new situations (stimuli), and is slow to adapt to change. The difficult child has intense mood expression that is often negative and as an infant, sleeps and feeds irregularly. Adaptation to change or to new routines and people is slow, but this child can do well with time and environmental constancy. Parents and adults find this type of child quite challenging. In their study 10 percent of children fit into this category.

The "slow-to-warm-up child" is in the middle of the spectrum. A combination of negative responses of mild intensity to new stimuli, with slow adaptability after repeated contact, characterizes this child. Mild intensity of reactions and more regularity with biological functions is present. Some difficulty can occur with new situations, such as meeting new people or adjusting to a new school. With time this child warms up and becomes involved, although is more likely than the easy child to accept a "side-line position." About 10 percent of children fit into this category.

The remaining children, who do not fit cleanly into one of the above temperamental categories, demonstrate some less clearly demarcated combination of the above.

How should the therapist integrate information about temperamental categories into a dynamic formulation? The focus of psychodynamic formulation includes, fundamentally, the exploration of a person's childhood experience; the child's subjective experience of childhood can never be separated from the temperamental foundation. Temperamental givens make some tasks more difficult, not only for the child, but also for the parents; the parents have to make a greater effort and have more empathic capacity, the more temperamentally difficult the child proves to be. An "easy" child is, simply, easier on the parents than a more temperamentally difficult child will be. A parent's struggles and frustrations with a more difficult child will result in an interpersonal experience (object relation) that is taken inside (internalized), then to become a part of the child's experience of him- or herself ("I am not likable, something is wrong with me, I'm the one who is always blamed when things go wrong," etc.; self-representation) and other people (object representation).

Chess and Thomas (1986), Stern (1985), and others have suggested that the manner in which the child's temperament is understood and dealt with by caretakers will greatly influence the child's eventual outcome. The child who can be guided carefully through and around limitations that arise by virtue of temperamental givens is the child who will be more likely to find ways over time of optimally utilizing his or her capacities, finding self-acceptance, and maintaining optimism regarding the world and the future.

THINKING ABOUT A FORMULATION: A BEGINNING FRAMEWORK

Momentarily leaving aside the issue of temperament and various inherited predispositions, we still assume that the adult's behavior is greatly influenced by what the adult experienced as a child. As William Wordsworth said, "the child is father to the man." The *subjective* experience of early childhood is modified throughout life by ongoing interactions with the surround. In looking at a person's development, some things go well and some things do not go well (for example, a poor "fit" between parents and child), leaving each individual with areas of strength and areas of vulnerability. These vulnerabilities can be exposed or brought to the surface in the course of life if certain circumstances arise. When someone gets into trouble, the immediate precipitant is usually in the present. However, the current precipitant typically exposes a prior area of weakness or vulnerability; that is, the immediate precipitant unearths an "Achilles heel." This is what brings our patients to our doors for help!

WHAT CONSTITUTES AN "ACHILLES HEEL"?

When we speak of an "Achilles heel," we are referring to an old "fracture line." What is a fracture line? A fracture line might be the weakest place in the structural framework of a building, or the place that the structural engineer looks at first when examining a building after an earthquake. A fracture line might be the thinnest area on the pot you just made on the potter's wheel; the place you are sure will be the most likely to crack in the kiln, ruining all the hard work that you just put in to make the most beautiful pot you've ever made in your life.

Now let's talk about people and how they are psychologically made. What would we call a fracture line, which constitutes an "Achilles heel" and brings our patients to us for help? The following are places to look for fracture lines in people:

1. An old conflict that was never adequately resolved is revived. A conflict might exist around wishes, desires, feelings, or impulses.

Mr. D, a man in his early thirties, came to therapy because he was disturbed by a recent response to his young son. Mr. D's son had just turned four. In the context of the recent birth of a second son, Mr. D's first son had become noticeably regressed, manifested by an overly needy and demanding manner. Surprisingly to Mr. D, rather than being empathetic with this son and able to be supportive and set reasonable limits, he found himself feeling disgusted and contemptuous and wanting to avoid the boy. Mr. D was dismayed by his reaction. He sought help because his feelings about his son did not correspond with his desire to be a good father and the intensity of his negativity was frightening to him.

The psychotherapeutic setting allowed Mr. D to explore the "conflict" that stood in the way of his empathizing with the struggling little boy. Mr. D came to understand that his response to his son had something to do with his own childhood, and the way in which unresolved feelings (fracture line) had been reawakened (revival of unresolved old conflict) in the current circumstance.

Mr. D was the oldest of nine children. Each time a new sibling had been born into the family, Mr. D was expected to become that much more an adult, and that much less a child. With each successive birth, Mr. D felt that his childhood and his mother were farther and farther away, eventually lost to him forever. In the home in which Mr. D grew up, there was a no-tolerance policy for "self-pity," "whining," or neediness.

In the midst of his wife's involvement and preoccupation with their second son, Mr. D felt acutely the loss of his wife's attention, affection, and nurturance; this situation revived old feelings about the loss of his mother's attention, affection, and nurturance consequent to the arrival of his siblings. These feelings, however, were completely unacceptable to Mr. D's conscience. Thus, the inner conflict that Mr. D experienced traced its origin to his belief that needy, and therefore childish, wishes (to have his wife back for himself alone, to have his mother back for himself alone) were absolutely prohibited. This conflict expressed itself in the disdain that Mr. D directed toward his son.

2. An old but unresolved psychological trauma is reawakened by something in the current circumstance. This occurrence—that is, the revival of the trauma—may or may not be obvious.

Dr. Q, a male physician in his late thirties, sustained a minor injury while backpacking and rock climbing with friends. While on a relatively easy climb, Dr. Q slipped and hurt his ankle. Initially, Dr. Q thought that he might have broken the ankle, but within a few minutes, he and a friend (who happened to be an orthopedic surgeon) surmised that he had only sustained a sprain. The pain subsided quickly and Dr. Q hiked back to his car without assistance.

Over several weeks Dr. Q completely recuperated. However, several months later he began to have recurrent pain in his leg and ankle. This pain was persistent and troublesome, consequently limiting the athletic activities that were so important to him. Dr. Q consulted many doctors and engaged in lengthy physical therapy in an attempt to deal with the pain. His long-time girlfriend, whom he had been planning to wed, became the frequent target of his frustration and anger; Dr. Q felt that his girlfriend was unsympathetic and unconcerned in the face of his obvious distress.

Dr. Q was eventually driven to consult a psychiatrist after several years of continued pain, a gradually escalating but significantly increasing level of anxiety, and a concern that his long-term relationship was seriously threatened by all that has been described.

During the initial session, the "patient" described himself as active, macho, always "pushing the edge" by physically challenging himself. Dr. Q had long been active in many sports and rugged outdoor activities including mountain climbing. He talked of his exploits and adventures in a way that implied that he was tough and fearless. Paradoxically, however, during the initial interviews he seemed anxious and somewhat childishly demanding. This was the mood and attitude to which, in recent history, his girlfriend had been subjected. Although it seemed that Dr. Q's girlfriend had attempted to understand his situation, she was clearly perplexed and increasingly frustrated with his behavior.

Dr. Q's early childhood history was notable. He was born with a congenitally deformed leg, requiring a series of four surgeries to correct before he was the age of five. Despite the corrective work, he was still left with one leg slightly shorter than the other. Several of the operations to which Dr. Q was subjected were extensive procedures requiring prolonged hospital stays; for these stays Dr. Q had little memory, and no recollection of pain, fear, or ever feeling vulnerable. He did know, but only from family stories, that this time had been very difficult for his mother, who had had great difficulty watching her son suffer; consequently she had often absented herself from the hospital when her anxiety became too great. Following the corrective work, the little boy (Dr. Q) appeared to bounce back well, but he did become exceedingly hyperactive subsequent to the events of this period.

On initial consultation, in response to his therapist's questions, Dr. Q reported that he had never wondered about any relationship between his early experience and his current predicament. In fact, it was not until well into the second year of psychotherapy, that it began to dawn upon Dr. Q just how significant the events of his early life had been. Dr. Q began to have frightening dreams of pain and bodily damage; with the onset of these dreams, at first dimly, and then more distinctly, memories of his mother and his experience of being abandoned by her in the hospital came back to him. He remembered his terror, later on his rage, mixed with a confusing conglomeration of shame and guilt about being who he was—"defective" and a source of burden to his mother (and later on, to his girlfriend).

The insight achieved in his psychotherapy allowed Dr. Q to understand the psychological dominance of his need to master the trauma of his early childhood. His character style, choice of career, and relentless pursuit of physically challenging activities was directly related to and intended to serve this end.

A minor trauma in this patient's adult life revived an old concern about "bodily integrity" (the quality or state of being complete; whole). Therapy revealed however, that the precipitant for this patient's anxiety was not only his rekindled fear of being damaged (fracture line) and unable to reassure himself through strenuous and "macho" physical activity that he was intact. Additionally, the anticipation of marriage to a woman (the girlfriend), whose response to his injury had not felt demonstrative enough, rekindled the patient's memories (fracture line) of a time of feeling helpless and alone (in the hospital), in pain and frightened (the surgeries), with no reassuring and calm presence that he could count on to comfort and reassure him (mother).

3. Brittle (easily broken or shattered) self-esteem or confusion about identity constitute the fracture lines in this category; one or the other or both become evident within the context of some stressful current event or situation.

A break up with a significant other, a "narcissistic injury" (a blow to one's sense of oneself), a career setback, or a failure of some variety (real or subjectively perceive) would be examples of the kinds of precipitants that could unearth this category of fracture line. The Marilyn Monroe story would be an example of this situation: that is, a character type that may have required the adulation that stardom provided but was also sufficiently psychologically unstable (brittle self-esteem and confusion about identity constitute the facture lines) to be unable to manage "life in the fast lane."

As a consequence of any of the above (revival of an old conflict or trauma within the context of a current situation, exposure of brittle self-esteem or identity confusion), coping styles and/or "defenses" that had previously been employed in order to manage become less useful, less resilient, or the individual simply fatigues in the course of using them. As defensive capacity begins to fail, a cascade ensues; regression to an earlier level of adaptation, with the employment of less "mature" defenses and/or defensive maneuvers, opens the door to symptom formation, such as anxiety or depression, derealization or dissociation, loss of identity consolidation, etc.

THE DEVELOPMENTAL TRAIN RIDE

Normal development, even in adulthood, is an "open system," capable of continuously growing, changing, and adapting to present-day life. Life offers a person opportunities and challenges; when an individual's psychological capacity is rigid—that is, the system is "closed" rather than open—the possibility for adaptation is thwarted and symptoms arise instead. As we have said before, a formulation attempts to provide a *road map* that includes a hypothesis about what shut down the system. That is, it attempts to explain where a given person (patient) got into difficulty along the developmental line. With a road map at hand, it is much easier to put the patient back on the path to healthy development.

Development is analogous to a long journey by train. The *"developmental" train* stops at many *"train stops"* on the way to a final destination (maturity). Each train stop is in a town; the train stops long enough for the passengers to get off the train, walk around for a little while, and then get back on the train. To follow the metaphor, the *passenger* is our *patient*, and each *town* at which the train stops equates with a developmental "hurdle," that is, an essential adaptation or achievement to master in order to proceed along the road to maturity (learning to walk or talk, learning to read, negotiating separations from home, learning to respect and care about a suitable partner, accepting the change in role necessitated by becoming a parent, etc.). The negotiation of this journey can go well (normal development) or not well (pathologic development). Pathologic outcomes might include:

1. Deciding to stay in a particular town forever, which means, not getting back on the developmental train (developmental fixation).
2. Although not staying in a particular town forever, staying in that town *too long*; that is, past the time that would be developmentally appropriate (developmental delay).
3. Getting *back on the train* but *longing* for the past town so desperately and/or indefatigably that future towns are never fully appreciated or may be never fully recognized (mourning for the unfulfilled losses of childhood).

Life circumstances or vicissitudes, like "developmental hurdles," also require change, thus demanding an adaptation that can expose a prior area of difficulty along the course of the developmental train.

What kinds of circumstances, which can and do arise in a patient's life, have the capacity to reawaken or expose a prior area or areas of vulnerability (fracture lines)?

1. *Biologic maturation* necessitates parallel psychological growth. The prime example of biologic maturation is adolescence. The teenager has to adapt to bodily changes and rising levels of hormones in the context of expanding cognitive capacity. Psychological growth or psychopathology can result.

2. *Changes in expectations or demands from the environment* (demands or events outside of the self) such as going to kindergarten, college, medical school, starting a new job, etc., require increased flexibility or adaptability. The ability to be flexible or adaptable can result in the positive acquisitions that accompany mastery of new undertakings with consequent psychological growth; the inability to be flexible or adaptable can result in the failure to master new undertakings with consequent psychopathology.

3. *A loss or other traumatic experience*, such as the death of a loved one, or exposure to violence or physical trauma, tests the strength and durability of the self. Any prior area of difficulty is likely to reappear when the self is stressed by a traumatic occurrence. To follow a physics analogy, "whenever one object exerts a force on a second object, the second object exerts an equal and opposite force on the first object" (Newton's third law of motion). That is, if a person is not able to bend and adapt when a force in the form of a traumatic experience or loss is exerted upon the person, psychopathology can (and often does) ensue.

4. *Illness or aging* similarly tests the strength and adaptability of the self. Growth, in the form of new wisdom or understanding, or other higher-level forms of coping, can become incorporated into the self. The other possibility, however, is that a failure to adapt occurs, with resultant psychopathology.

5. *Disappointment in one's ability to accomplish perceived life goals* can reawaken weaknesses in the narcissistic integrity of (ability to love) the "self," as a person finds him- or herself unable to rebound from an assault to self-esteem.

6. *A self-initiated desire* to change or develop, because of recognition of the possibility for a better adaptation (for example, the wish to go back to school, or find a new job, or move on to a more fulfilling

relationship), requires an expansion in the domain of the abilities of the self. If the attempt to expand the self to allow for a new possibility is unsuccessful, a pathologic reaction can occur.

7. *A life event, circumstance, or defeat that results in a narcissistic injury with consequent loss of self-esteem* tests the tensile strength of the evolving self. The fragile self can crumble, with resultant psychopathology.

Gathering a History Is an Essential Requirement
in Order to Develop a Dynamic Formulation

The therapist collects information about the patient's life (history) in order to elucidate the interplay between past experience and present difficulty in the context of temperamental givens, which has resulted in the circumstances that bring the patient to the therapist's office. In order to accomplish this task, theory is utilized; the use of theory may include one specific and well-articulated theory, some combination of various theoretical points of view, or a therapist's own theory based on the coalescence of experience, intuition, and knowledge of preexisting theories.

With knowledge of theory, the therapist is better equipped to recognize and identify what can be done, needs to be done, and is possible to do. Theory guides and organizes a therapist's thinking, helping to predict transference, consider future areas of conflict, and choose the time and place for interpretations. Importantly, theory helps decrease the therapist's anxiety, by allowing more comfort in the domain of the mind. Countertransference reactions are therefore more easily managed.

With this preface, various psychoanalytic models will now be examined. All models have something to offer; at the same time, all models have limitations. We believe that the greater facility with which a therapist can move among models and use multiple models simultaneously, the more able a therapist will be in conceptualizing and dealing with a diversity of psychological difficulties.

MODELS OF THE MIND

An attempt to answer an essential question underlies all theories that present possible models of the mind. What is it that motivates mankind? What is it that makes people get up in the morning, move through the day, and try to live life? Is it hunger, aggression, sexual desire, curiosity, the need to find and affiliate with others, or the desire to attain mastery? Each theory encompasses a theoretical position that emphasizes particular motivations or needs, as opposed to others.

1. Impulses or urges, conceptualized as the "drives," and the conflicts that can arise in relationship to these "drives," are emphasized in "Drive (psychology) Theory."
2. Coping styles or mechanisms, conceptualized by the individual's defensive organization, and the ability to adapt and test reality, is most emphasized and elaborated by Ego Psychology.
3. The perpetual repetition of old relationships and experiences, whatever the new form, is most emphasized and elaborated by "Object-Relations Theory."
4. Properties of self-boundaries, self-experience, self-esteem, and the nature of its regulation are most emphasized by "Self-Psychological Theory."

Each theory understands psychology and psychopathology by providing a model that attempts to explain the structure of the mind and motivation. Each theory, either implicitly or explicitly, tries to address what creates psychological safety, what creates psychological danger, and what is curative. Most theories were derived from the treatment of certain prototypical patients or arose from an attempt to describe patients incompletely understood by previous theory (self-psychology hoped to understand the narcissistic personality, incompletely understood by ego psychology alone).

At one end of the theoretical spectrum is drive theory, emphasizing the power of the drives (libido and aggression) as the primary human motivation. At the other end of the theoretical spectrum are the relational theories, including self-psychology and object-relations theory, emphasizing the need for relatedness to others as the primary motivation. This "black-and-white" description is oversimplified. Drive theory does acknowledge the "object" and the relationship to the object; human relationships just are theoretically less imperative than the pressure of the drives (libidinal desires and aggressive strivings). Similarly, aggressive and even libidinal desires are not unacknowledged in object-relations theory, but may be considered secondary to the need to search for and relate to like objects (Greenberg and Mitchell 1983; Pine 1988, 1989).

The contrast between these theoretical perspectives may be more understandable in the context of the following example. The example, and particularly the explanation of the example, is caricatured; an artificial distinction between drive and relational theory is made in order to illustrate the interrelationship and differences between the two ways of understanding human behavior and motivation.

> Barbara first came to therapy when she was six years old, and her parents were immersed in the aftermath of an angry and bitter divorce. Barbara's difficulties seemed to resolve, and after a year of treatment, her parents decided that she didn't need therapy anymore. During this period of treatment, Barbara's play was wild and chaotic, leaving her therapist to feel frequently that there was no sense to make of it at all, other than that this was the way in which Barbara was experiencing her then-current life.
>
> At age ten, Barbara returned for further treatment. Her parents complained that she was unmanageably and unbearably "aggressive" much of the time. Barbara would fight with her friends at school and at home on play dates. She was sassy with her parents, and especially cruel to her infant brother. Additionally, Barbara would preen in front of the mirror endlessly and in a fashion that made her parents uncomfortable; she would display herself in sexually provocative ways that were certainly inappropriate for her age and often inappropriate in general (such as lifting up her skirt and displaying herself, or turning upside down in a chair while wearing a skirt and similarly displaying herself in a social situation).
>
> In her therapist's office, after an initial honeymoon period, Barbara began to display the behavior that her parents had described. Barbara would taunt her therapist with how destructive she could be. In fact, Barbara seemed to have a sixth sense about identifying the objects in her therapist's office that the therapist most loved; Barbara would threaten to destroy these objects, watching with glee while her therapist tried to contain her growing discomfort or distress. Barbara would play games in which a trap would be set; she would then insist that the therapist walk into the trap again and again and again.
>
> How are we to understand Barbara's psychopathology? Is this a child with constitutionally strong sexual and aggressive drives (drive theory), aggravated by her parents' failure to contain the aggression in a timely and developmentally necessary fashion, and stimulated further by the example of her parents' continuous battling? Or was Barbara's aggression heightened, by the way in which she was made use of as a tool (relational theory) through which the parents were able to attack each other, and by the intense frustration and disappointment engendered by and associated with her parents' narcissistic preoccupations? Does a simple

formulation derived from the drive model work well enough, or would a relational model enhance our understanding?

On one occasion, Barbara's mother called the therapist after the mother and father had had a particularly nasty fight over the telephone. Barbara's mother reported that the shouting had become loud enough so that Barbara could hear every word. Barbara became not subdued nor distressed, but wildly excited. Actually, Barbara had been involved in the instigation of this particular parental fight, as she was frequently. Barbara would tell her parents stories, reporting that each had said something uncomplimentary about the other; she would continue to tell tales until her parents were sufficiently inflamed with each other that an explosion between them could occur.

In a simplified drive/conflict model, Barbara's aggressive and sexual drives were roaming wild. Without the restraint of an externally supplied and internally developing conscience that could rein in her behavior, and without a clash between her actions and external reality sufficient to stop her behavior, a fertile ground was provided for Barbara to elaborate her "nature" as an aggressive, sexually provocative little creature. She was dominated by the "pleasure principle" and saw little use in learning to employ the "reality principle." In Barbara's mind, no reason existed that would give her pause before putting her little brother at risk, and she thought nothing of her exhibitionistic behavior at a time when other girls her age might have been more modest. From a drive model standpoint, Barbara was an example of unmodified aggression and libido, with inadequate superego development (as described above) to manage the strength of her drives.

How might relational theory be applied to Barbara's circumstance? First and foremost in the relational model, people attempt to maintain ties and define themselves within the context of relationships. Barbara's parents hated each other. Each had sufficient legal restrictions on the other to prevent much direct contact, so they used Barbara to communicate their venomous barbs to each other. Barbara's relationship with her father was defined by enacting his wish to get revenge on her mother. Barbara defined her relationship with her mother by becoming the vehicle by which mother could express her disgust toward her father. In a relational model, the glee that Barbara derived from watching her parents fight would not be viewed as the direct and simple expression of and gratification of the drives and the experience of power derived forthwith. In a model that defines motivation through and around the need to seek out and maintain ties in human relationships, Barbara, as the vehicle of communication, the messenger between, had at least a special role. It was a role that, however pathologic, bound her to each of her parents; as a small child she could not survive without them.

Paralleling the drive/relational theoretical continuum is the conflict/deprivation continuum. Most clearly addressed by drive theory and ego psychology is the individual torn by mental (inside the mind) conflict; driven by desires and unfulfilled longings, conflict comes in the form of corresponding prohibitions given voice by the conscience. Simplistically, this is the neurotic, guilt-ridden, inhibited individual who struggles with assertion, sexuality, and authority, and has grown up in an enmeshed, intense but reasonably caring environment. At the other end of the theoretical spectrum, most clearly addressed by object-relations theory and self-psychology, is the deprived and internally devitalized person; subjectively "empty," this individual has had limited experience with a suitably stable and empathic parent or partner, under the umbrella of which a stable sense of self could have been achieved. Different theoretical positions imply different treatment approaches. For the individual burdened with conflict, clarification and interpretation are essential. For the individual who has a sense of self akin to an empty house, structure building (to be discussed below) in the context of an empathic presence is necessary.

The attempt to understand different "types" of patients and diverse kinds of problems drives the development of theory. With any one individual and in any one psychotherapy process, many dimensions overlap. The endless combination of arrangements, the possibilities of which are suggested above, make psychotherapy and the theory of psychotherapy challenging and endlessly interesting.

Historically, theory has evolved from drive psychology to ego psychology to object-relations theory to self-psychology. We will return to the available psychodynamic theories of the mind, looking at each one in some detail. Before doing so, however, a few of Freud's ideas should be reviewed because they are essential; others are historically important because they allow the evolution of the different theories and current theoretical trends to be more understandable.

PSYCHIC DETERMINISM

Freud (1901) postulated that thoughts do not occur in the mind randomly or by chance, meaning that each psychic event is determined by the ones that preceded it ("causality"). If any given thought seems random, it is only because the preceding thought, from which the current thought followed, was unconscious; "Discontinuity . . . does not exist in mental life" (Brenner 1957, 2). A conclusion could be drawn from this premise: every thought, idea, fantasy, dream, slip of the tongue, etc., however trivial it may seem, has meaning. This is an indispensable concept, because it implies that the patient's words (spontaneous associations) are almost always worth something (sometimes words serve the purpose of resistance; see chapter 5). While the concept of causality is a simple one, making use of the idea in practice is something else. It may not immediately be clear why the patient is talking about a specific person or theme. Actually, sometimes it is quite difficult to ascertain the meaning of the patient's communications. By assuming that no idea is likely to be random, psychologically pertinent meaning is more likely to be uncovered.

CONSCIOUSNESS IS THE EXCEPTION

A complement to the above, Freud's second fundamental hypothesis is that "consciousness is the exceptional, rather than a regular attribute of psychic process" (Brenner 1957, 2). This means that much of thought and response, particularly around emotionally significant issues, occurs without conscious awareness. For example, a person might develop a terrible headache, only later to appreciate the impact of an earlier phone call that had warned of a turn for the worse in the illness of a close family member. The worry about the potential consequences of the new information had resulted in a tension headache. A parapraxis, commonly known as a Freudian slip (1901), also allows us a window into an unconscious process—that is, a process that otherwise would not be visible. A sadistic plaintiff's lawyer clearly enjoyed hunting down his prey (the defendants) and doing his best to make his victim squirm. An honorable and well-reputed surgeon was being sued in the case of a patient who had died well after the successful resolution of an elective surgery. The patient's relatives tried to manufacture a case that the patient had died from an infection cultured from the surgical wound. The sadistic plaintiff's lawyer, when referring in court to the organism cultured from the wound in question, made a slip of the tongue and instead referred to the "orgasm" growing in the cultures. This parapraxis, revealed the erotic excitement the lawyer experienced when he thought (fortunately, erroneously) that he had trapped his victim.

PRIMARY AND SECONDARY PROCESS

In the process of analyzing the dreams of his patients, Freud discovered a type of thinking that he called "primary process." Thought to be characteristic of the id and unconscious thought, primary process thinking is irrational and illogical. Opposites or contradictions can coexist without being of distress to the person who is thinking in this manner. Parts or symbols may stand for the whole, or vice versa; several thoughts can be represented ("condensed") by a single thought or image. Words may be subserved by visual or sense impressions. Time sense does not exist (past, present, and future are perceived and represented as one). In a similar fashion, rejection, abandonment, and death seem indistinguishable. Primary process thinking is fluid (that is, boundaries and demarcations are indistinct) and wish driven.

Secondary process thinking, in contrast, is rational and makes use of the "reality principle" to invoke reason. Reason allows for and enhances the capacity to tolerate frustration; judgment can prevail; and the presence of a sense of time permits future paths and potential gains to be envisioned, resulting in the delay of discharge. The ego functions according to secondary process.

"SIGNAL ANXIETY": A THEORY OF ANXIETY

Freud (1923) postulated that anxiety acts as a signal through which the ego warns the person who is experiencing the anxiety signal, of danger(s) to come. In the real world many dangers exist, such as a runaway car barreling down a street or the enemy army advancing over the hill. These kinds of situations stimulate fear, which in turn activates the reasonable person, who is in the path of harm's way, to take flight, fight, or respond by some other protective means. What distinguishes fear from anxiety is that with fear, the stimulus is external and real; with anxiety, the stimulus is coming from the internal world of the individual (inside the mind, a "product of the imagination").

When the ego perceives an "internal" danger, such as unacceptable or disturbing desires, impulses, thoughts, or perceptions, a "trial" amount of anxiety is released. Anxiety then becomes, in Freud's model, a "signal" that warns the ego of danger to come; this mechanism is intended to avoid stepping on the landmine. It should be noted that the effect described above is not immune to malfunction. A misfiring can occur, resulting in anxiety of overwhelming proportions; this overpowering anxiety state in turn triggers defensive operations of a more massive nature, with ensuing less adaptive solutions. Hopefully, however, the anxiety signal is made use of to invoke a useful defensive strategy, which then allows our subject effectively to sidestep the problem in question before it evolves. An example follows:

> Dorothy, a married woman who exploded into an erotically charged affair, became increasingly indiscriminate about the places in which she had sex with her lover and lax about her method of birth control. She then became preoccupied with and eventually panicked about the danger of contracting HIV. She began to fantasize about having to tell her husband of the affair and of her death sentence; she would die a miserable and horrifying death from the AIDS virus and she would die alone, because her husband would leave her when he discovered her betrayal. Dorothy immediately broke off the affair.
>
> The fantasy of contracting HIV and contemplation of the potential consequences that could evolve as a consequence of her actions caused this woman to have an acute panic attack. The panic attack served as an "anxiety signal," warning this woman of the possible consequences to come if she were to fail to rein in her "unacceptable desires and impulses."

Dorothy's story and the path that she followed as a consequence of receiving the "anxiety signal" is only one possible scenario. A number of possible responses to a danger signal can occur:

1. The whole situation is successfully repressed. The desire or inclination is erased from consciousness. In the example above, this unconscious course of action could not occur, because the woman had already taken the path of becoming involved in the affair and in an indiscriminate way. This situation could apply in the following case:

> Mildred had been fantasizing about having an affair with a man who was clearly pursuing her and available. She knew that her husband had a strict moral code and would leave her immediately and without looking back were she ever to be unfaithful. Mildred successfully repressed the whole idea and temptation. Some time later, Mildred's best friend, who had had suspicions about the flirtation, asked her friend if she had ever been interested in this man. Mildred had no idea what her friend was talking about. She loved her husband absolutely and would never cheat on him; in fact, she never even thought about it.

2. Discharge of the impulse is rechanneled along an acceptable path. An example of this would be sublimation. For example, Harold wanted to punch his boss for humiliating and demeaning him in a public way at work, but decided instead to go for a workout at lunchtime in the gym across the street. Another example of this way of discharging the impulse would be that Mildred, who repressed her fantasy about having an extramarital affair, instead recalled the fantasy in delicious detail and wrote a successful romance novel about the idea.

3. A compromise formation is erected. That is, the drive and consequent anxiety is not successfully repressed. An intrapsychic conflict occurs, with resultant symptom formation. For example, Harold, the same man who wanted to punch his boss for humiliating and demeaning him (as had his father historically), instead of being able to repress his feelings or go to the gym at lunchtime, developed chronic headaches and nausea, which prevented him from being able to perform at his job. Another example would be that Mildred, who fantasized about the affair with the man who was pursuing her, didn't successfully repress her fantasy or write a romance novel, but became so afraid of being attacked by stray dogs in the street that she became unable to leave her house at all.

FIVE TRAUMATIC DANGER SITUATIONS

Now that we've defined the concept of signal anxiety, what is it that can trigger the kind of anxiety that the "ego" will then respond to with the danger signal? Freud defined five traumatic danger situations that can either trigger signal anxiety or bypass signal anxiety altogether and go on to trigger anxiety as a symptom beyond control (the anxiety signal misfires). When a therapist is sitting with a patient for whom anxiety is the chief complaint, or for whom the manifest symptom on any given day of therapy is anxiety, the following is a useful way in which to begin to understand the problem.

A. Fear of being overwhelmed is often conveyed in statements such as "I can't take it anymore" or "I'm not sure I can cope." Sometimes, this fear is expressed quite directly and literally: "I feel so overwhelmed." The fear of being overwhelmed means that a person is being bombarded with an excessive amount or array of fear and/or anxiety-producing stimuli. A newborn baby would be overwhelmed by excessive sensory input in the absence of caretakers who serve to protect the infant from the external and internal environment.

Another example (dramatized for the sake of demonstration) might be the following: A man's son has been skipping school to mainline heroin with his friends who happen to also be gang members. The man has just found out that his wife has an incurable form of breast cancer, and that he has been laid off from a job at which he had worked for the past twenty-five years. This man might be afraid of being overwhelmed; that is, he might fear that his usual coping mechanisms will fail in the face of the "overwhelming" nature of the events that have befallen him.

B. Fear of loss of the object concerns the fear of the loss of a person, who is considered to be essential to the survival of the self.

> Beth, a young girl with a history of "separation anxiety," became "unglued" shortly after receiving word that she had been accepted to the college that had been her first choice. This particular, somewhat immature young woman had an overly strong attachment to her mother. She had often felt (and verbalized) that she couldn't imagine a single day passing without being able to see or speak to her mother. When Beth found out that she had been accepted to college, a thought suddenly occurred her (a thought that she had defensively held out of her awareness) that she would now be physically separated from her mother; this was a situation that she could not imagine surviving.

C. Fear of loss of love of the object is best captured by the look on the face of the child who has been caught with a hand in the proverbial "forbidden cookie jar." The child fears that having committed an unacceptable act, the mother will consequently withdraw her love. Developmentally, fear of loss of love of the object is a higher-level form of anxiety (farther along on the developmental continuum); it is not the object that is feared lost, but the object's love for the subject (self) that is feared lost.

D. Fear of castration, or "castration anxiety," is defined in Webster's Dictionary as "the act of castrating . . . to geld; to remove the testicles of; to emasculate." However, Freud noted in 1923, "It is remarkable . . . what a small degree of attention the other part of the male genitals, the little sac with its contents, attracts in children. For all one hears in analyses, one would not guess that the male genitals consisted of anything more than the penis." The possibility of castration was concretely expressed in the

Lorena Bobbit case. Lorena Bobbit cut off her husband's penis; a retaliation for his infidelity. This case was frequently addressed subsequently through the innumerable jokes that followed.

If the concept of "castration anxiety" were extended and broadened, the reactions that people tend to have to disfiguring surgeries (such as a mastectomy or an amputation of a limb), or the concern that a teenage girl has about the perfection of her young body, might be explained. Therefore, a less literal and more clinically useful way to conceptualize the concept of "castration anxiety" would be to think about the fears that people have about harm to the body; that is, concerns about "bodily integrity."

In the popular novel, *The Horse Whisperer*, Annie Graves travels to the distant and seemingly foreign territory of Montana in hopes of repairing the physically and emotionally "castrated" states of her daughter and her daughter's horse. Annie's daughter had lost a leg and the horse had been gravely injured in a terrifying accident. In Tom Booker, Annie finds a man who she hopes has the power to heal the soul of her daughter, and the body and soul of the horse (undo or partially undo the castration).

E. Fear of loss of love of the superego has to do with the fear of the loss of the love of the self. It is a consequence of the perceived inability to live up to one's own inner expectations. An example of this follows:

> Jeremy was in his senior year of high school. He had achieved a very high GPA, excellent scores on his SAT exams, was a star athlete, and was on the debate team. He became seriously depressed after sending out his application for early decision to Harvard University.
>
> Analysis revealed that Jeremy lived in fear of how he would feel about himself should he not be admitted in the early-decision pool; in other words, it was not enough to be admitted to Harvard—he had to be admitted in the early-decision grouping. Jeremy knew that he would feel that he had failed himself were he not to achieve this lifelong goal; he also knew that the pain of this perceived failure would be unbearable. It had always seemed to Jeremy that every male in his family had gone to Harvard (in fact, Jeremy's father, uncle, grandfather, and older brother had all graduated from Harvard), and the only way to match this trend, and then to surpass it, was to be accepted early decision. He could not be at all certain that this was actually going to happen.

METAPSYCHOLOGY

With respect to the science of mental processes, Freud developed a series of ideas that he labeled "metapsychology," meaning "beyond psychology" or beyond the realm of conscious experience. These ideas were seen as fundamental; psychoanalytic theory could then be built on top of this foundation. The dynamic, topographic, and economic viewpoints could be directly credited to Freud; the genetic viewpoint was implied by Freud's theory of infantile sexuality. The adaptive viewpoint was elaborated at a later time by authors such as Hartmann (1952) and Erikson (1980). At first, these concepts may seem arcane and dated; don't be fooled. Conceptual frameworks such as these are extremely useful and important, because they lay down fundamental hypotheses that describe how things might work in the mind.

THE DYNAMIC VIEWPOINT

Freud postulated the existence of directed psychological "forces" within the mind, each of which has an origin, a magnitude, and an object. These forces (or needs), which drive the motor, possess persistence (the drive) and power, and are represented in a mental form (that is, symbolically, as in dreams). "Force," a physics concept, means "the cause of motion, or of change or stoppage of motion of a body." Therefore, mental forces, as with all physical forces, can assist each other or inhibit each other, or enter into compromises with one another; that is, needs can work in synchrony or be dissonant. The need for nurturance and the need to satisfy sexual desire might be synchronous; the need to sleep and to satisfy hunger at the same time might not. This viewpoint provides the basis for a theory of "conflict" because conflict is a result of opposing forces. Opposing forces could be love versus hate or dependency versus independence. Opposing forces could also be gratification versus frustration/deprivation, that is, the desire to have one's cake and yet have it available for later—*id versus ego/superego*!

THE ECONOMIC VIEWPOINT

Freud hypothesized that psychological energy exists within the mental apparatus. Furthermore, he postulated that the mental apparatus seeks to keep excitation low by promoting free flow of these psychological energies. In other words, the mental apparatus does not want energy to be blocked, for example, as water is blocked behind a dam. This assumption provides the basis for understanding Freud's assumption that the "pleasure/pain principle" governs mental processes: pain increases excitation, pleasure decreases excitation, therefore low excitation is desirable. Along the course of normal development, a shift must occur from sole governance by the "pleasure principle" (in which gratification or the obtainment of pleasure is the only goal) to embracing a mature form of government, otherwise known as the "reality principle" (which allows for postponement of gratification or immediate pleasure in the service of future gain).

A considerably indulged ten-year-old girl (who was old enough to know better) said to her horrified mother, with an air of absolute conviction, "When I grow up, I'm going to get a job from nine to eleven in the morning so that I can have the rest of the day to relax!" Clearly this young lady's governing body was not yet up to the reality principle!

The economic principle is, of course, oversimplified; it proposes (once again) a concept of the mind that is based on opposing physical forces. However, the economic viewpoint finds its clinical correlate in a balanced economy between pleasure/play/love and reality/industry/work. When an internal economy does not prevail (and internal economy might be substantiated by the ability to find or create sufficient stimulation, joy, connection with other people, or whatever else is needed) symptoms arise; symptoms might be manifested by a sense of emptiness, joylessness, or lack of vitality, anxiety, or frank depression.

THE TOPOGRAPHIC VIEWPOINT

Here the mind is divided into a "depth psychology": a fixed set of conscious and preconscious structures, which are shielded from the unconscious by the censor. In the topographic model, the censor prevents unacceptable impulses or thoughts from attaining entrance to consciousness. In 1923, the more sophisticated structural model replaced the topographic model (also called the "tripartite model"). Freud abandoned the topographic model when he began to realize that it contained inherent limitations and contradictions. Not only the drives but also factors that interfered with the expression of the drives (the resistances and the defenses) were unconscious. In the structural model, the concepts of id, ego, and superego provide for a more organized and internally consistent model of the mind. The structural model is reviewed here in greater detail.

THE GENETIC VIEWPOINT

A genetic point of view is implied by Freud's theory of infantile sexuality (1905); the sexual drive (or child) progresses through a series of stages or "phases." By reversing this assumption, one can infer that the adult is a synthesis of all that has come before. Therefore, knowledge of the circumstances of any given person's childhood, and an awareness of the personal meaning of those circumstances (for that given person), is an essential requirement for psychological understanding. From a historical standpoint, Hartmann, Kris, and Loewenstein came closer to actually defining a genetic point of view than did Freud. They wrote, "genetic propositions describe why, in past solutions of a conflict, a specific solution was adopted—why the one was retained and the other dropped, and what causal relation exists between these solutions and later developments" (1946, 34). The "genetic" viewpoint was relatively novel at the turn of the century when Freud wrote his great works, but this viewpoint has become widely accepted. For example, a newscaster reports about a serial killer who has finally been caught; various experts then comment about the killer's terrible childhood and the way in which certain childhood events or circumstances could contribute to a personality that commits ghastly acts.

THE ADAPTIVE VIEWPOINT

In the historical sequence, Hartmann and Erikson elaborated the adaptive viewpoint only at a later time. The adaptive viewpoint refers to the interpersonal, societal, and environmental phenomena that influence the individual's mind, and vice versa. How does mind (the psyche) adapt to the environment in which it finds itself? How does the ego modify the environment, such that harmonious existence within the world is possible? The adaptive viewpoint implies recognition that successful psychological solutions include an acknowledgment and integration of the demands, requirements, and realities of the external world. This is "adaptation" in normal development.

Let us now proceed with the basic theories of the mind.

PSYCHODYNAMIC THEORIES OF THE MIND: DRIVE THEORY

Early psychoanalysis was constructed on the premise that "instinctual" or "drive" energy impelled or powered the psychic apparatus, and therefore was the motivational factor for human behavior. Recall that ideas or ideologies are always reflective of and limited by what is known and understood about the physical world. Freud's intellectual development paralleled a scientific era that was based in physical science. Forces come in pairs of polar opposites, and so, therefore, must the instincts. Freud's attempts to find a suitable duality for the instincts took him through several permutations (self-preservative instincts versus sexual instincts, ego libido versus object libido, life/"eros" instincts versus death/"thanatos" instincts) before he eventually settled on a final form. Freud's final formulation took him and early psychoanalysis to an "id psychology," which proposed the final duality of the libidinal instinct versus the aggressive instinct. These "instincts," or drives, or forces, as contents of the "id," were unconscious.

The word "id" appealed to Freud; the term was evocative of an idea developed by Groddeck that "what we call our ego behaves essentially passively in life . . . *we are lived by unknown and uncontrollable forces*" (LaPlanche and Pontalis 1980, 197). Or, to quote Freud himself, "An instinct [Trieb] . . . appears to us as a concept on the frontier *between the mental and the somatic*, as the physical representative of the stimuli originating from within the organism and reaching the mind, as a measure of the demand made upon the mind for work in consequence of its connection with the body" (Freud 1915, 122 emphasis added).

Freud's first attempt to delineate a theoretical model for drive development began with the vicissitudes of the libidinal drive. The libidinal drive was the fundamental need; from this, ultimately, all other needs were derived. Freud used the term "libido" from the 1890s on; the word came to possess a variety of meanings, which led to a variety of usages with the development and unfolding of psychoanalytic theory. Ultimately, however, Freud described a maturational tract for the developmental of the sexual drive, in which libido becomes directed toward a series of "erotogenic zones," or the oral, anal, and phallic zones.

Detailing the historical development of the term "libido" is not the focus of this summary; suffice it to say, however, that libido is a form of mental energy, including all or parts of affection, erotic desire, and loving attachment directed toward another person. To quote Moore and Fine, "The most important feature of libido theory . . . is the idea of a causal factor common to a variety of pleasure states and personal attachments throughout life" (1990, 113). It was only later that Freud finally settled upon and added a second and opposing drive to his libidinal drive; perhaps in part influenced by his own illness and the First World War, the aggressive drive found its place in Freud's formulation. Importantly, however, Freud never elaborated a developmental model for aggression, as he had done previously with the libidinal drive. An argument could be made that Klein (1931; Spillius 1994) did elaborate a developmental paradigm for aggression with her description of the paranoid-schizoid and depressive positions.

This leaves us faced with an important question, deserving of an answer. What is aggression anyway? A theory that is half-based on the motivational drive of aggression, without a definition of aggression, and especially, in the absence of a developmental model for aggression is not of much use to the clinical practitioner. An array of thoughts and behaviors could be considered aggressive, ranging from reasonable assertiveness to overt aggression. The following example would illustrate reasonable assertiveness.

> A frustrated but reasonably successful actor, who had not had an audition for a long period of time, called his agent and manager and told both that it was time to talk. He reminded his representatives that they would not earn income from having him as a client if he did not work, and that he saw no advantage in an ongoing affiliation if it was not to be of benefit to all.
>
> The next week, the young man received a call from his agent that three auditions for parts that were "just perfect" for him had suddenly become available (where none had been available just the week before); auditions had been arranged for him. The young actor auditioned successfully, then to find that he was being sought after for not just one wonderful role, but two wonderful roles.
>
> The employment of reasonable assertiveness on this man's part paid off!

Overt aggression, in contrast, does not have the above self-preservative, self-enhancing, or forward-thinking characteristics described in the above example. Overt aggression appears on the continuum of an attack upon or violence against the self (masochism) or an attack upon or violence against someone else/other people (sadism).

Freud's notion of the drives has stimulated intense debate since his initial contributions. It has often been suggested that his drive concept is overly mechanical, reductionistic, and specifically does not integrate sufficiently the human need and desire for interpersonal interaction and relationships (that is, man is a "herd animal"). Therefore, many have directly or indirectly challenged Freud's assertion that man is instinctually driven by libido and aggression. This leaves us to speculate: Could there be other factors that might account for the privileged position in which Freud placed libido and aggression in his theory?

Freud's ideology was deeply affected by his personal psychology, dictating a need to view himself as autonomous and not ruled by convention and societal beliefs. He felt a strong commitment to the construction of a scientific model that would appear logical to the medical establishment of the day, and he was influenced by the prevailing philosophical debates of his time (as he was influenced, as above, by the scientific climate of the time). Greenberg and Mitchell (1983) have pointed out that social and political philosophy continues to struggle with the dialectic between viewing man as an individual animal and viewing man as a social animal.

It would be difficult to practice psychotherapy for any extended period of time without being struck in the clinical setting by the frequency with which people struggle over issues that have to do with desire (nonerotic affection or frank eroticism), aggression, or some combination of the two. Freud was struck as well by the frequency with which people grapple with these issues, and the potential consequences of failure to come to grips with a strong impulse to act (sexual or aggressive). Freud developed a model that described a sequential cascade, beginning with the wish/desire to pursue some impulse and ending with anxiety and/or symptom formation. In between these two poles, the sequence went from impulse, to "taboo," to conflict, to defense, to failure of defense, to the pole of anxiety and/or symptom formation (or impacted the development of character, the formation of character traits, or the choice of character "armor," a contribution of later theorists).

Whether or not a therapist decides to make use of or reject Freud's theory, inescapably Freud introduced with the drive model a basis for understanding conflict. People live with internal thoughts that can have great influence and power, generating wishes and desires that then somehow have to be managed. This observation is not original to Freud; artists and philosophers (think of Shakespeare!) have long recognized that mental conflict exists. However, Freud formalized and therefore made clinically useful observations about mental conflict. Consequently, he has bequeathed a model within which to comprehend the nature of conflict and its resultant psychic torment.

Let us return now to the cascade of impulse (drive) to symptom formation. From a clinical and theoretical standpoint, a problem exists with a theory that speaks only of a motivational factor (in this case the id). A drive doesn't think, doesn't learn, doesn't make decisions, doesn't adapt, and doesn't feel guilt or resulting conflict. Ego psychology and structural theory thus were born.

EGO PSYCHOLOGY AND STRUCTURAL THEORY

Ego psychology concerns the study of the structure that we call the "ego": what is the ego, what are the ego's functions, how does the ego interact with other structures of the mind, how is an understanding of the ego and its functions clinically applicable? Structural theory was an attempt to explain mental functioning by means of the construction of a certain model of the mind. The model included the establishment of certain "structures," the structures being defined by their functions; these structures were organized and interrelated, and possessed endurance over time. The ego is one of those structures.

Freud first formally described his structural model in 1923 with his publication of *The Ego and the Id*. While this model is constructed on the substrate of the drives, it is a much more complicated theoretical system because of the description of various and different agencies of the mind and the importance of their interrelationship. Anna Freud's (1938) study of the ego's defenses and Hartmann's (1952) elaboration of ego adaptation followed, helping to usher in the reign of dominance of ego psychology from the 1930s to the 1960s.

What is important to know about the conceptual idea, which we call "structure"?

1. A structure is a mental construct; it has no organic substrate. We infer the properties of a structure based on our observation of the way in which people behave and think.
2. A "structure" is only a name for a group of mental processes or functions.
3. Interactions can take place between structures; therefore, a possibility is created that conflict will also occur between structures.

An important assumption of ego psychology is that while many of the functions of the various structures occur at an unconscious level (the individual has no conscious awareness of the function), the three structures—id, ego, and superego—do have "internal psychic representation." This means that these structures have some awareness of each other, the demands and power that each possesses. The three structures or agencies of the mind that are defined by the structural model are the id, the ego, and the superego. The utility of ego psychology and delineation of the various ego functions is to allow the clinician (and then, the patient) to understand the workings of the mind in order (hopefully) to facilitate adaptive change.

WHAT DOES THE EGO DO?

The ego coordinates and organizes all behavior. Therefore, the ego has as its task a complicated job. The ego must mediate among the demands of the id (drives/needs), the external world (realistic parameters that are determined by the world in which we live), and the superego (conscience). The end result of this effort is to achieve maximum gratification and at the same time be self-preservative, achieve increasing mastery, live according to an inner set of ethical standards, and attempt to realize personal goals.

The capacity to weave together all of the above is called the ego's "synthetic function." In Freud's words, "The poor ego serves three severe masters and does what it can to bring their claims and demands into harmony with one another. No wonder that the ego so often fails in its task. Its three tyrannical masters are the external world, the super-ego, and the id" (1923, 56).

WHAT ARE THE EGO FUNCTIONS?

1. Recognizing, assessing, and adapting to reality: The world, fortunately or unfortunately, changes over time. Successful people are able to perceive reality, take reality into account before acting, and can accept and adapt to changing external circumstances when necessary. The ability to master all of this described is the job of the ego.

2. The ability to allow and at the same time contain affect states: This means the ability to withstand anxiety, frustration, depression, and disappointment. It also means the ability to postpone satisfaction, even when times are difficult. For Freud there was a maturational hierarchy from indulgence of the pleasure principle to integration of and postponement of gratification in accordance with the demands and obligations of life.

3. The ability to form positive (affectionate/friendly) object relationships: The development of gratifying object relationships is related to the healthy solidity of the mental representations of objects that any given person might have. Remember that mental representations (elaborated more fully below) are the "more or less consistent reproduction, within the mind, of a perception of a meaningful thing or object" (Moore and Fine 1990, 160). It is the purview of the ego to evaluate current relationships by making use of the lessons learned from experiences with people from the past.

4. Thought processes: The ego is the agency of the mind that possesses the capacities that result in many abilities; these include the ability to make sense of perceptions, to think and arrive at conclusions, to detect similarities and differences, to remember previously acquired information, to concentrate when necessary, to learn and eventually to take the information learned to make reasonable judgments, to plan for the future.

5. Synthetic, integrative, and organizing function: As described above, the synthetic function refers to the ego's capacity to integrate the various agencies of the mind in the service of future gain.

6. Autonomous functions: Characterized by Heinz Hartmann (1952), the autonomous functions of the ego initially seem to be relatively immutable; consequently these autonomous functions would not be easily affected by conflict. Described as "conflict free," the autonomous functions include perception, motility (movement, walking, use of hands), intention (planning, anticipation, purpose), intelligence, speech, and language. Of course in practice, many of these functions are not immutable; emotional states (especially anxiety and/or depression) can and do influence the capacity to make use of even these ego functions.

7. Defensive functions: These are mechanisms utilized by the ego, in order to force out of awareness thoughts or impulses that are unacceptable and thus arouse anxiety. When the ego senses an unacceptable thought or impulse, a small amount of "anticipatory anxiety" is released ("signal anxiety"), instituting the cascade of defense(s) that serve to protect the self. (The many common defenses are defined in chapter 5.)

All of the above is the explanation for our ability to speak of certain aspects in the dynamic formulation. We talk about "ego strengths" (the above properties are sufficiently in evidence), "ego weaknesses" (some or all of the above properties are missing), "ego-syntonic" (seamlessly fits with one's image of oneself, and therefore seems acceptable), and "ego-dystonic" (the property feels alien to the self).

The many ego functions have a substantial genetic, and therefore constitutional, and therefore temperamental component. However, the sequential development of ego functions is also profoundly affected by the nature of any given person's interactions with significant early figures (parents or primary caregivers). While ego capacities expand throughout a lifetime, the first five or six years of life is a critical period; it is a time of developmental plasticity, during which time the ego has the ability to grow with greater ra-pidity, and influential interactions with primary objects have more impact. For an example, we turn to the development of language; language devel-opment has a critical period or window when assimilation of vocabulary and inflection occurs with relative ease (ages two to ten). After this critical period ends, the development of new language becomes substantially more difficult. Many ego functions are likely to have a similar, developmentally critical period or window, during which time the evolution of a new ego capacity occurs with greater ease; the implication is that change occurring past the critical period happens only with difficulty or not at all.

SUPEREGO

The "superego" as a theoretical concept refers to a person's values, morals, and ethics (conscience), as well as to a person's aspirations and goals. Like the ego, the superego is simply a name for a group of functions. These func-tions are really a set of guidelines that serve to protect the individual (in or-der to survive, a child must learn not to run in front of a moving car) and ideals that serve as signposts along the way (ideas about who one wants to be in life). The set of functions that make up the superego become solidi-fied during the oedipal period of development. At a time when, in the con-text of great cognitive development a significant upsurge of sexual and ag-gressive impulses occurs, a system of internal rules and regulations becomes of greater significance.

Freud speculated about the observation that during the oedipal period, the child desires to possess the parent of the opposite sex and eradicate the parent of the same sex (oedipal complex). A confounding variable is that at the same time as these feelings exist, the child loves the parent of the same sex, and still very much needs that parent. The resolution of this dilemma and the internalization of a more complete set of values sets the stage for the child to begin the process of formal education that is a central organiz-ing facet of the latency period.

The superego is the voice that determines what one should or should not do (the ego provides the motor apparatus to carry out the act). What is taken into the superego is the authority of the parents. Once that authority is taken into the superego, the authority derives its power from the drives. This has clinical and not just theoretical implications. The more powerful is the aggression that the child feels during the oedipal period, the harsher the superego will be. The child's aggression is projected onto the parents and then redirected against the child in the form of a punishing superego; the effect is that the child will fear punishment commensurate with his or her own (self-perceived) aggression. Most psychoanalytic theories acknowledge pre-oedipal contributions to the superego, but also emphasize the role of the oedipal period. Melanie Klein (1932), however, focuses primarily on the pre-oedipal period.

The "ego ideal" is also a part of the superego. While the superego dictates what one should do or should not do, the ego ideal dictates what one must be. The ego ideal contains an individual's wishes and aspirations; in that sense it is a gratifying agency. Fulfilling the expectations of the ego ideal results in an experience of mastery and consequently generates a feeling of pride. On the other hand, the superego (conscience) is a restricting and prohibiting agency. The ego ideal is theorized to originate in one's own childhood sense of omnipotence, projected onto the parents, and then taken back into the self through identification. This means that, "If my parents are big and capable (even omnipotent), when I am with them or if I become like them (identify with them), I will feel big and powerful too."

Ideally, the ego ideal matures as time passes. A person's expectations are supported or refuted by the reality within which a person lives; a growing awareness of capacities and limitations accompanies confrontation with reality. If the aspirations of the ego ideal are not in accordance with realistic abilities and possibilities, psychopathology is a potential consequence (a perfectionist or unreasonable superego can become an internal tormentor). The hypertrophied ego ideal can be the end result of multiple pathways: inability on the part of parents to help the child accept realistic capacities and limitations, and/or narcissistic needs on the part of parents to which the child endlessly and perhaps hopelessly tries to mold, are two examples.

OBJECT-RELATIONS THEORY

Freud built his early concept of psychoanalytic theory around the concept of the drive, and then the conflict that can occur between the drives (id) and other structures of the mind. In his famous paper on mourning and melancholia (1917), for example, Freud spoke of the object and the conflict that can be focused around an internalized object image. Nevertheless for Freud, the "object" was still secondary; the object was "a thing through which the instinctual drive is able to achieve its aim" (Moore and Fine 1990, 160).

With Freud's theory of the instinctual drives as the focus, the field of psychoanalytic theory evolved and diverged in the decades following

Freud's first major theoretical statements. Jung and Adler departed in radical ways; Fromm and Horney departed in less radical ways. Of those who continued to regard themselves as Freudian, several groups evolved. The ego-psychological school was initiated by the work of Anna Freud and Heinz Hartmann. Melanie Klein and her followers—Bion, Segal, Rosenfeld, and many others—led the Kleinian movement. The "British Middle School" (less pure in theoretical viewpoint) was represented by Winnicott and Fairbairn. Fairbairn, Klein, and Winnicott have all influenced the development of object relations theory; Winnicott has continued significantly to influence self-psychological theory.

There have been two major theoretical strategies for dealing with the motivational factor that drives object relations; which one is espoused, as suggested above, depends upon whether one thinks the horse drives the cart or the cart drives the horse. Hartmann, Mahler, Jacobson, and Kernberg work from the standpoint that object relations are derived from the drives. Sullivan, Fairburn, Guntrip, and Winnicott work from the point of view that relations with others constitute the building blocks of mental life and therefore modes of relatedness are the force that drives human behavior. Melanie Klein was a transitional person between the two schools above. She remained loyal to Freud's vision of the drive; however, Klein conceptualized an entire psychology predicated on the internalization of object representations as a constant force in both illness and health.

WHAT IS OBJECT-RELATIONS THEORY ABOUT?

Object-relations theory attempts to provide a theoretical explanation for the observation that people seem to serve two masters simultaneously; that is, people can live in an external world and at the same time respond to and be guided by an internal world. The relationship between the internal and external worlds can be fluid, meaning that the experience from the outside and perception from the inside can be easily integrated (differ little). Alternatively, the relationship between the internal and external worlds can be sharply delineated so that internal images do not match with external reality; the result is a confusing and disorienting experience of people, various situations (in which the dichotomy is evident), and the world.

Object-relations theory understands the individual in terms of the various images of objects that are represented within the mind ("internalized"). These images or representations are the culmination of an amalgam of early experiences (emotional, sensory, intellectual, physical) with significant people. Taken inside the mind, these internal object representations later influence perceptions of and consequently experiences that any given individual will have in the world. Old stories can be played out, or repeated, in action as well as in fantasy. This means that an internal drama can greatly influence a person's choices in life. A person who bears an internal image (object representation) of a hateful, punishing authority will move through the world in a very different way than the individual who carries an internal image of a powerful but warm and supportive authority.

Internal images serve certain important functions. They conjure up an *anticipatory image* that serves the function of providing some measure of what one might expect from people in the real world; this expectation is intimately intertwined with the individual's experience of people in the past (as above). Internal images serve as personal guides and guardian angels, providing emotional security in times of stress or isolation: "My parents believed in me . . . they must have had good reasons for believing in me . . . therefore I can believe in myself . . . I will get through this." Edith Jacobson (1961, 1971; Kernberg 1979) came up with the wonderfully descriptive phrase, "peopling the internal world." Greenberg and Mitchell said, "Internal images constitute a residue within the mind, of relationships with important people in the person's life. In some way, crucial exchanges with others leave their mark; they are 'internalized', thus shaping subsequent attitudes, reactions, perceptions, etc." (1983, 11).

In summary, object-relations theory explores the following:

1. The motivation for forming relationships; that is, the search for object relatedness is a fundamental driving force for human beings.
2. A developmental continuum exists, in which the infant progresses from childhood to maturity laying down constellations of mental images.
3. These "constellations of images," once laid down, help to explain the complexity of choices and points of view that we possess as adults.

PART OBJECTS

An important contribution of object-relations theory is the concept of the "part object." An image or representation can be divided into contradictory images. Remember that object representations or mental images are an amalgam of experiences of a person; therefore, contradictory impressions of the same person can exist and in fact do coexist side by side; that is, not fully integrated. The "Madonna-whore" constellation exemplifies the part-object relationship. One encounters this constellation in the themes of movies. The "sex object," usually a woman (although not necessarily), is viewed only as an object of sexual desire, a body, or even body parts— breasts, legs, etc. (the porn star); all other attributes are dismissed. One comes across this constellation in the treatment of certain male patients who have had difficulty in forming lasting relationships with women. The problem in this case lies in the man's inability to coordinate two split-off part-object images of women. One group of women is seen as warm, selfless, and almost motherly (Madonna). These women are either not sexually interesting or the man is *unable* to think of this kind of women sexually (even if the woman is attractive). Another group of women is seen as intensely erotic, but the intoxicating sexuality of these women, although captivating, feels "whorish" to the man.

Looking at normal development, the boorish behavior toward girls of the late-latency and early-to-middle adolescent (and too often, the late-adolescent) boy, demonstrates the inability to pull together contradictory (repressed) internal images of the mother. Thus the latency and teenage girl becomes the unhappy recipient of the unpleasant treatment that can be delivered by boys in the midst of this developmental struggle. With psychological maturity, the overidealized and denigrated internal images of women move closer together, allowing the boy, who will someday be a man, to love and be turned on by the same woman.

SELF-PSYCHOLOGY

Self-psychology involves the delineation of the concept "self" and the study of the vicissitudes of the development of the self. Historically, self-psychology takes its cue from an elaboration upon the psychoanalytic concepts of the self and narcissism by Kohut (1971; Kohut and Wolf 1978) and his followers. Kohut has been criticized for not acknowledging prior contributors (from whom his work does follow), such as Fairbairn, Winnicott, Guntrip, Mahler, Jacobson, and Fromm-Reichman.

Essential definitions in self-psychology include the following: The "self" as described by Brandschaft and Stolorow (1990) has to do with the attempt to organize experience. This definition, although somewhat abstract, captures the clinical usefulness of a concept of the self. Many patients seek treatment because they are unable to discover and/or to solidify a "sense of self."

In contrast, we speak of the person who seems "so sure of him- or herself" (a solid sense of self). Therefore the healthy self, as a psychological structure, provides a sense of well-being or self-esteem. The "self" includes the totality of a person's physical and psychological organization. Similar to the manner in which experiences with people are laid down in a series of object representations, the self is characterized by an amalgam of self-images that coalesce in any given person's "self-representation." The "self-object" refers to a person whose value is contained in the function that that person (object) provides for "the self." Assistance with the integration of frightening (disintegrating) or disorienting affective states is the primary function that the self-object provides. The self-object is not experienced as a separate person in his or her own right.

It is very important to have experiences with people (self-objects) who are sources of certain attributes. These attributes include the ability to be strong, confident, and calm; all told, the summation of these qualities provides for the person who possesses them a feeling of internal security. These experiences eventuate in the ability to make sense of situations, people, and internal feelings and then to soothe oneself, especially in the face of difficult affective states. Anxiety and depression are two primary examples of "difficult affective states." It is essential to be able to tolerate various affective states, in order to both survive these states and make use of the experience of them in the service of the enlightenment of the self. This is what we call the "ability to integrate affect."

Therapists serve self-object functions. Many terms have been used to describe this affective integrating function of the therapist as self-object: "stimulus barrier," "protective shield," "holding environment," and "container." The solidity of the "self" and the ability to make use appropriately of self-objects when necessary, are essential, contributory factors to the sense of vitality with which any given person traverses life. Interactions with others can lead, at one end of the spectrum, to a sense of excitement, enrichment, and vigor. Unfortunately, at the other end of the spectrum, interactions with others or experiences that lead to a sense of personal failure can result in varying degrees of "fragmentation of the self." Manifested by depression, anxiety, panic, derealization, or depersonalization, "fragmentation of the self" implies a feeling of "falling apart."

The infant (because it is helpless and dependent) requires the actual physical and emotional presence of a person (mother, father, or other protective person), who provides life-sustaining care. As time passes, more and more parental functions are taken in ("internalized") and taken over by the growing child to adolescent to adult. Maturity requires an evolution to a point at which the ability to restore the "integrity" of the self (the opposite of a "feeling of falling apart"), when necessary, is achieved by evoking "symbolic representations" (mental representations) of important experiences or "nodal" moments with an important self-object or self-objects.

> One young woman said to herself, in the midst of a course frighteningly called "Multivariable Calculus," and in the face of an upcoming examination: "My parents have always believed in me and told me that I would prevail no matter how challenging the circumstances; I will somehow get through this examination as well."

Certain kinds of behaviors and/or addictions, such as gambling, repetitive sexual behaviors, and drug and alcohol use, can be viewed from a self-psychological perspective. In a person with a vulnerable "self-structure," stressful life events can overwhelm the ability to cope. In the absence of adequate self-objects or a "good enough" self-representation, addictive behaviors become a substitute form of self-soothing. Alcoholics Anonymous is an organization that seeks to offer itself as an alternative "self-object" to the ravages that the cruel self-object master of addiction unleashes.

INTEGRATING AND MAKING USE OF THEORY
IN THE DESIGN OF A DYNAMIC FORMULATION

One of the never-ending challenges in psychodynamic psychotherapy is the proper use of theory in the service of cementing an understanding of a given person's (patient's) character, personality, and psychopathology. Many therapists align themselves with a particular theoretical viewpoint; often the viewpoint that is chosen was at one time personally helpful to that particular therapist. For some patients, one theoretical viewpoint may explain the problems at hand; for many patients, one theoretical viewpoint does not permit sufficient understanding to resolve the issues or dilemmas that brought the patient to treatment. Pine's (1988, 1989) perspective on the use of theories provides a model for the integration and utilization of multiple theories. Pine has observed that all personalities have hierarchies of motivation and correlating psychologies that would best serve the understanding of that particular person.

Understanding theory, and then further making use of theory and multiple theories in clinical practice, can be a daunting task. This is especially true for the beginning therapist. The capacity to integrate theory into clinical work is a gradual process; it develops during the multipronged educational approach that makes use of didactic education, supervision, and particularly the psychotherapist's personal psychotherapy.

The following is an example of the integration of theory into the development of a tentative formulation. By focusing on a few select ideas, a formulation was developed after only a few sessions.

> Edith was a thirty-eight-year-old businesswoman and mother, who had quit her full-time job two years before coming for treatment. She complained of fatigue, depression, and an annoying indecisiveness about whether to be a stay-at-home mother or return to the full-time work at which she had previously excelled.
>
> In the first hour, Edith spoke of the pervasive restlessness and unhappiness that invaded her current life, even though by any objective criteria she felt she "should be" happy. Edith had two lovely children. Her husband, although somewhat obsessive in style, was kind and supportive. The family was financially secure and had a bright future.
>
> Edith had been very successful in a former business career, which had only been set aside when the duties of parenthood intervened. She missed the feeling of competence that had come so easily in her work life, but felt that being a "mom" was "where it was at." Actually, being a mother was very important to Edith; she applied herself with a diligence that not infrequently led to resentment and fatigue. In this context, Edith quietly mentioned that she often found it difficult to connect with her youngest child, the only girl.
>
> In the initial hour, Edith oscillated between speaking of her wonderful family and her inescapable sadness. She mentioned that her husband's frequent business trips had caused her increasing distress and anger. At one time, she had also traveled frequently and felt important. In fact, her style was one of energy and determination and always being on the go. This style carried over into her social and recreational life. She was an avid sports enthusiast and skier, a real tomboy. This was a description with which her appearance matched.
>
> It seemed as though Edith never slowed down.
>
> In the second hour, Edith turned to speaking of her childhood and especially of her mother. Growing up had been chaotic. Many moves, many different individuals living in the house (as her mother had changed lovers) and ongoing poverty had characterized this woman's developmental years. Edith's mother was bright,

able, and attractive when well; however, the mother was subject to manic episodes, at which time she was often psychotic. Even when she was not psychotic, spending sprees and periods of promiscuous behavior drained and frightened the family. In spite of her childhood situation, Edith had survived. A remarkable resilience, aided by her innate "constitutional endowment" (including her capacities as an athlete and her tenacity as a student and professional) had probably saved her.

Stability, tenderness, and nurturing were clearly not a part of Edith's childhood. Consequently, she spoke of a desire to be a different parent and a different person from the person and parent that her mother had been. She also spoke of a long-time pattern of never thinking about the homes of her past. Only recently, in fact, had she thought much of the past at all. This was in the context of recognizing the difference between her own childhood and the childhood that she had attempted to provide for her children. Edith was visibly sad in speaking of this recognition.

What Would a Beginning Formulation Look Like if We Were to Use Edith's Story as a Point of Departure?

Edith had a conscious conflict regarding her business career and her role as a mother. Edith's business career made use of the enormous capacity (ego strength) that had enabled her to survive in the dysfunctional world of her childhood (reality) and at the same time, consolidate a positive self-representation. However, in order to fully approximate her ego ideal, Edith felt deeply that she needed to provide a kind of attention and security for her own children that had never been an aspect of her own experience. These superego demands (the successful professional and involved mother aspects of her "ego ideal"; the attentive and selfless mother component of her "conscience") were mutually exclusive at times.

Additionally, Edith had her own deep dependency needs. She assiduously attended to her own needs by displacing them onto her children and then trying to attend to the children as she wished someone had attended to her. Unfortunately, Edith then ended up resenting the children for getting what she had so desired for herself; clearly a partial explanation for the distance that she sometimes felt from her children.

The therapist also wondered if Edith was conflicted about her feminine identity. Her style of dress was distinctly unfeminine, and Edith had mentioned that relating to her daughter (as opposed to her son) was particularly difficult. The therapist speculated about

Edith's internal object relations. Edith's mother was not a person that Edith wanted to be like. Actually, Edith tried very hard not to be like her mother in every way. Perhaps Edith's positive feminine identification got swept away in the tide of her attempt to "disidentify" with her mother. Edith tried to be a "supermother," and she viewed herself as full of energy and always in control. Unconsciously and fundamentally, however, Edith clung to a secret and more appealing image of herself: tomboyish (masculine) and a bold professional, she was a fearless and gifted athlete who could certainly match any man in the sports that she had mastered.

Ideally, a therapist must always remember that the task is to "locate" the patient. This means that the therapist must try to understand the way in which the patient thinks, ascertain the problem or problems that the patient is facing, and try to figure out how the problem or problems originated. As described in the story of Edith, all of this was done as a necessary prelude to the attempt to visualize a solution. How can this be done without a framework and a game plan? This is what we have tried to explain with the concept of a "dynamic formulation."

REFERENCES AND READINGS

Bowlby, J. (1969). *Attachment and Loss*, vol. 1. New York: Basic Books.

Brandshaft, B., and R. Stolorow. (1990). The borderline concept. *Bulletin of the American Psychoanalytic Association* 38: 1117–19.

Brenner, C. (1957). The drives and the psychic apparatus. In *An Elementary Textbook of Psychoanalysis*. New York: Doubleday Anchor Books.

Chess, S., and A. Thomas. (1986). *Temperament in Clinical Practice*. New York: Guilford Press.

Diagnostic and Statistical Manual of Mental Disorders (4th ed.). (1994). Washington, DC: American Psychiatric Association.

Erikson, E. H. (1980). On the generational cycle: an address. *International Journal of Psycho-Analysis* 61: 213–23.

Fairbairn, W. D. (1952). *An Object Relations Theory of Personality*. New York: Basic Books.

Freud, A. (1938). *The Ego and the Mechanisms of Defense*. New York: International Universities Press.

Freud, S. (1901). The psychopathology of everyday life. *Standard Edition* 6: 53–105. London: Hogarth Press, 1960.

———. (1905). Three essays on the theory of sexuality. *Standard Edition* 7: 135–206. London: Hogarth Press, 1953.

———. (1909). Analysis of a phobia in a five-year-old boy. *Standard Edition* 10: 1–144. London: Hogarth Press, 1955.

———. (1915) Instincts and their vicissitudes. *Standard Edition* 14: 111–40. London: Hogarth Press, 1957.

———. (1917). Mourning and melancholia. *Standard Edition* 14: 237–58. London: Hogarth Press, 1957.

———. (1923). The ego and the id. *Standard Edition* 19: 3–107. London: Hogarth Press, 1961.

———. (1926). Inhibitions, symptoms and anxiety. *Standard Edition* 20: 77–178. London: Hogarth Press, 1959.

———. (1933). Introductory lectures on psycho-analysis. *Standard Edition* 15: 13–80. London: Hogarth Press, 1957.

Gedo, J. E., and A. Goldberg. (1973). Freud's clinical theory of 1923: the tripartite model. In *Models of the Mind*. Chicago: University of Chicago Press.

Greenberg, J. R., and S. A. Mitchell. (1983). *Object Relations in Psychoanalytic Theory*. Cambridge, MA: Harvard University Press.

Hartmann, H. (1952). The mutual influences in the development of ego and id. *Psychoanalytic Study of the Child* 7: 9–30.

Hartmann, H., E. Kris, and R. M. Loewenstein. (1946). Comments on the formation of psychic structure. *Psychoanalytic Study of the Child* 2: 11–38.

Jacobson, E. (1961). *The Self and the Object World*. New York: International Universities Press.

———. (1971). *Depression: Comparative Studies of Normal, Neurotic, and Psychotic Conditions*. New York: International Universities Press.

Kernberg, O. F. (1979). The contributions of Edith Jacobson: an overview. *Journal of the American Psychoanalytic Association* 27: 793–819.

Klein, M. (1932). *The psycho-analysis of children*. London: Hogarth Press.

Kohut, H. (1984). In *How Does Analysis Cure?*, ed. A. Goldberg. Chicago: University of Chicago Press.

Kohut, H., and E. Wolf. (1978). The disorders of the self and their treatment: an outline. *International Journal of Psycho-Analysis* 59: 413–25.

LePlanche, J., and J. B. Pontalis. (1980). *The Language of Psychoanalysis*. London: Hogarth Press.

Lichtenberg, J. (1983). *Psychoanalysis and Infant Research*. Hillsdale, NJ: Analytic Press.

———. (1988). A theory of motivational systems in psychic structure. *Journal of the American Psychoanalytic Association* supplement 36: 57–73.

Moore, B., and B. Fine. (1990). *Psychoanalytic Terms and Concepts*. New Haven, CT: Yale University Press.

Nagera, H. (1970). *Basic Psychoanalytic Concepts on the Theory Instincts*. London: George Allen & Unwin.

Ogden T. H. (1983). The concept of internal object relations. *International Journal of Psycho-Analysis* 64: 227–41.

Pine, Fred. (1988). The four psychologies of psychoanalysis and their place in clinical work. *Journal of the American Psychoanalytic Association* 36: 571–96.

———. (1989). Motivation, personality organization, and the four psychologies of psychoanalysis. *Journal of the American Psychoanalytic Association* 37: 31–64.

Stern, D. N. (1985). *The Interpersonal World of the Infant.* New York: Basic Books.

Stolorow, R. (1978). The concept of psychic structures: its metapsychological and clinical psychoanalytic meanings. *International Review of Psycho-Analysis* 5: 313–20.

Stolorow, R., B. Brandchaft, and G. Atwood. (1987). *Psychoanalytic Treatment: An Intersubjective Approach.* Hillsdale, NJ: Analytic Press.

Spillius, E. S. (1994). Developments in Kleinian thought: overview and personal view. *Psychoanalytic Inquiry* 14: 324–64.

4

LISTENING

At its foundation, pyschodynamic psychotherapy requires that the therapist listen to the patient and attempt to discern the meaning of the patient's story; change occurs in psychoanalytic psychotherapy at least in part by virtue of achieving an understanding of the patient's thoughts, symptoms, character traits, repetitive dysfunctional patterns, etc.

To listen therapeutically is to have the ability to "read between the lines," that is to detect or ascertain meaning beyond the patient's words. This is in the service of beginning the process of dissecting threads of significance from the maze of associations and concerns that bring the patient to therapy in the first place. To listen in a manner that is "psychodynamic" is a multidimensional task. This task involves clarifying the patient's issues, identifying the most pressing issues, remembering that communication occurs on many levels simultaneously and that associations and responses can have multiple meanings, and all the while, keeping an eye on the patient's vulnerabilities and pain. All of this is a complicated task for any therapist; it is an especially difficult task for the beginning psychotherapist.

DREAMS AND FREE ASSOCIATION:
PASSWORDS TO THE UNCONSCIOUS

What do dreams and free association have to do with psychodynamic listening, and the search for understanding the meaning of the patient's difficulties? Dreams and free association express or reveal "unconscious material." By "unconscious" we are referring to "the sum of all thoughts, impulses, desires, feelings, etc., of which the individual is not conscious but which influence his behavior." By "unconscious" we refer to "that part of one's psyche which comprises repressed desires and other matter excluded from but often tending to affect the consciousness" (*Webster's New Twentieth-Century Dictionary*). Unconscious material can help to explain the meaning of the patient's thoughts, symptoms, character traits, repetitive dysfunctional patterns, etc., and unconscious material is not helpful to a patient unless it is made accessible.

Both dreams and free association operate according to what Freud (1900) labeled "primary process." Primary process is a style of thought. Revolving around infantile wishes and needs, and dominated by certain characteristics that include a lack of concern for logic, cause and effect, or an appreciation for time (the unconscious is "timeless"), primary process thought is always egocentric. In contrast, secondary process is a style of thought that is *not* based on infantile wishes and needs; secondary process thought obeys the "master of reality." Secondary process conforms to logic, has an understanding of the factor of time, and obeys the rules of reasoning that involve cause and effect.

Most adults assume that their own thought process is logical and rational, and are unaware of or minimize the degree to which less mature thinking can predominate. The thought process of adults is still subject to "ego centricity" (significantly oriented around the needs of the self) and to a greater or lesser extent can be highly colored by childhood wishes, perceptions, and experiences. A goal of psychodynamic therapy is to explicate the elusive, silent, and disruptive interference of primary process thought within any given person, in the service of self-understanding and self-acceptance, and in order to facilitate greater ability to make rational choices.

THE TECHNIQUE OF FREE ASSOCIATION

Free association is the fundamental language of psychodynamic psychotherapy. The ability to free associate is a cultivated achievement, because the patient has to be able to feel free to share spontaneous thoughts, without being overly concerned at the time about the reason for the content or the logic of the thoughts. This means that whether thoughts seem important or meaningless (the reason for wanting to share the thought is apparent or not), are flattering or embarrassing, refer to personal issues or refer to others including the therapist, no thought should be censored.

Freud (1912) had the following way of explaining free association. Free association is akin to looking out the window while sitting on a train and trying to describe the scene that is passing by outside the train. With free association, however, as opposed to a description of the external scenery, it is the "landscape" of one's own thoughts that is described. While this idea may not be a difficult one to grasp in the abstract, some patients find it difficult to allow thoughts to come to mind freely, and/or find it difficult to report the thoughts (or some of the thoughts) that do come to mind. Patients who have had previous insight-oriented therapy are usually aware that it is not helpful to censor thoughts, and that perhaps the very thoughts that one would like to leave behind could be the most important. Individual differences, which are based on personality type, culture of origin, intelligence, ability to think abstractly, or the particular psychopathology at hand, will also affect the relative difficulty or ease with free association. For example, the obsessive individual may have difficulty with spontaneous thought.

Nevertheless, free association as a therapeutic medium is vital to the psychotherapy process. As a therapeutic medium, free association can be defined (as above) and explained to patients (Freud 1912). Although educating patients about the utility of the therapeutic modality of free association may be useful occasionally, most patients do not need specific instructions, and specific instructions may be experienced as intrusive. Patients come to psychotherapy needing to talk and hoping to feel consequently unburdened; therefore, what a patient chooses to tell a therapist is already a form of free association! At such time as the free flow of material seems to be impeded, or expression becomes effortful, explaining the process of free association can be useful, and therefore more likely to be welcomed by the patient.

Once the patient is educated, interference with spontaneous thought could be considered a "resistance" (an impediment to the free flow of material, the determinant of which is unconscious), and resistance cannot be commanded or educated away. The reason for the difficulty must be tactfully explored with the patient, always remembering that the process of free association usually becomes labored when there is something that the patient does not want to talk about. It is important to remember that to *not* want to talk about something is to "resist"; that is to oppose, withstand, or strive against. In psychoanalytic terms, a "resistance" carries the additional connotation that the resistance and the determinant of the resistance are unconscious.

Free association, for the patient and as a therapeutic medium, is a "tool" to make use of in the service of understanding. Once this tool is understood and appreciated, first by the therapist and then by the patient, a vast and fascinating window into the patient's intrapsychic life becomes available. Freud's fundamental rule of "psychic determinism" postulates that every thought follows the preceding thought; if this seems not to be the case in any particular situation (that is, thoughts do not seem to follow, but rather, seem unrelated), it is only because the preceding thought was unconscious. Thus nothing in the mind is arbitrary or capricious. It follows then that the technique of free association provides a window into the intervening and unconscious thoughts ("reading between the lines") that would otherwise escape us all.

DREAM ANALYSIS IS A MODEL FOR PSYCHODYNAMIC LISTENING

To listen past or avoid becoming distracted by a patient's narrative can be a strain; the easier task is simply to listen to the patient talk about real-life events. The dream teaches the therapist temporarily to dismiss concern with reality per se, and wonder instead what the dream conveys about an individual's inner experience. Therefore, dream analysis is a model for psychodynamic listening. Dreams are emotionally evocative and frequently illogical; therefore dreams require the listener to pay more careful attention to abstract or "primary process" elements. It is more difficult to be distracted by the story line when listening to a dream; sometimes it seems as though there is no story line to the dream at all. Consequently, dreams facilitate and even require the therapist to concentrate on and try to conceptualize how a person thinks, and to contemplate what might be the function of the creation of any particular fantasy.

> A patient complained in an hour of the following: her boss favored another employee and picked unfairly on the patient.

In listening to the patient's account, the therapist could easily have come to the conviction that the patient's boss posed a significant problem for the patient, perhaps the major problem in the patient's life.

> The patient again felt that her boss was picking on her, but this time a blue parrot happened to be sitting on the shoulder of the boss and the patient was dreaming. In the dream, the boss seemed to be favoring an unknown person.

In the face of such an odd dream, it is not likely that the therapist would accept the patient's problem with the boss at face value, but rather would be drawn to speculate about what the interaction/experience with the boss meant to the patient. That is, the therapist would be curious about how the story was informative about the patient's inner life. The line of questioning would be relatively easy. Who is the unknown person? What was the feeling in the dream? Why is the patient bothering to dream about the boss anyway? Does the boss have a particular significance for the patient, or remind the patient of anyone else (transference figure)? Does the dream have a historical reference for this particular patient (transference figure)? Why would someone "dream up" such an unappealing script? The image of the blue parrot must have come from something/somewhere (the patient's inner life, recent or past experience). Otherwise, the "odd element" in the dream (blue parrot) could just as easily have been a purple toad or a red fish or a yellow elephant. What ideas might the patient have about this?

When a patient tells a story that is *not* a dream, listening and the line of questioning that follows should still be directed at trying to unravel underlying meaning. For example, in the case of the same woman above who was struggling with her feelings about her boss, the therapist might have considered certain questions. What does the boss represent for the patient? What is the meaning in this particular patient's life, of being (or feeling) poorly treated, while someone else is favored? When self-protection becomes necessary, is the patient able to be assertive in an appropriate manner? The story of the boss and the patient's feelings about the situation could have been told at other times, and any story could have been selected for the telling. Why was this story selected and at this time?

By making use of the dream, Freud elaborated a whole theory of psychic functioning. Although ideas about dreams have evolved since Freud's time, many of his ideas are still useful and help to provide a road map for organizing the content of a therapy session. Freud found the dream so useful that he elegantly labeled it the "royal road to the unconscious" (Freud 1900). Later generations of analysts have tended to diminish the role of dreams in psychotherapy, and elevate the role of transference. Nevertheless, the method used for deciphering the dream is more than a complement to the method for deciphering free association. The understanding and interpretation of a dream or dreams can be a profoundly useful resource in the service of illuminating what might be bothering a patient; that is, in order to elucidate the patient's state of mind.

The following is an example of the use of a dream to further a patient's understanding of herself as well as an illustration of the meaning of the "manifest dream," "associations" to the dream, "day residue," "latent content," "displacement," "condensation," and "symbolism":

> Tracy, a female patient, was very capable, competitive, and in constant motion. She appropriately prided herself on her remarkable

capacity to be effective, an important aspect of the competence displayed in her career. Unfortunately, she felt that little else about herself was of value. Although Tracy was quite attractive and very able, she felt that she was physically unappealing and viewed herself as a "fraud" (unworthy of the impression she made on other people).

Questioning her motivation about almost anything and worried about who she really was, Tracy would often speak about her fear of "what was inside her." She viewed herself as different, especially with respect to her perception of herself as a woman, and wondered if she were a latent (dormant, yet to be revealed) homosexual. Manifested in a variety of ways, Tracy was significantly conflicted about her identity as a woman ("feminine identity"). She had difficulty in allowing herself to be in any situation in which she might feel vulnerable and dependent (particularly in relationship to her husband). She hated being referred to as "a mother" because she felt the reference carried with it the implication that she wasn't first and foremost a "career person." She had considerable difficulty with her attitude about sexuality and her own experience with sexuality, manifested by the fact that she was completely anorgasmic and avoidant of participating in sexual activity with her husband.

In treatment, Tracy gradually became more aware that she really felt "less put together." Moreover, she learned of the possibility that antecedents could exist, which would help to explain the way she felt about herself; that is, an explanation was available that would help to explain why she "felt less put together." In the session prior to the reported dream, Tracy's therapist had specifically suggested an interpretation. The interpretation was that Tracy made use of hard work and competence to counteract a feeling of vulnerability and degradation, and that the latter feelings were part of the "less-put-together self." Furthermore, the therapist suggested that Tracy associated "vulnerability and degradation" with her "pathetic" mother (now deceased), who had been a chronically depressed woman, dependent upon tranquilizers and "low-life" men. In contrast, the therapist went on to suggest that Tracy preferred not men necessarily, but "masculine" characteristics, because in feeling herself to have "masculine" characteristics, she protected herself against feeling "female"/like a vulnerable and "pathetic" woman.

Within the psychotherapeutic process, Tracy had begun to feel (and become aware of) a desire to rely upon her male therapist, whose presence revived (stimulated) in her an underlying desire to be able to depend upon a safe, strong, and reliable object. However, these desires were also confusing to Tracy. She experienced them not as desires for comfort and stability, but as uncomfortable erotic feelings (the feeling of being "stimulated"), which strongly activated her self-contempt (to be attracted or feel dependent upon a man was to acknowledge her femininity and risk becoming a "pathetic woman"). Additionally, the feeling that a therapist who was "male" could appear strong and reliable, only further increased Tracy's "hidden" belief (the belief was reasonably conscious, but the determinants of the belief were *not* conscious) that men were invulnerable to the "pathetic" state. In this context Tracy had the following dream:

> She was driving down a highway in a "superfast" and expensive sports car, when she saw a woman hitchhiking at the side of the road. She contemplated picking the woman up, but then noticed that the woman looked familiar. While still within the dream, she noted that the "woman" had features of "two women" that she knew in a limited fashion. Disturbed by this realization, she pretended not to see the woman and drove on.

Tracy had seen on the street the day before her dream, one of the women whose features appeared in the dream woman. However, both women (who shared the features of the dream woman) had had psychiatric difficulties, but one was doing very well now and the other was not. The former woman (who was doing well) was small and dark, quite attractive, and had become very successful in a business after recovering from her difficulties. Tracy noted that she herself was small and dark. The other woman was not attractive, and Tracy thought of her as particularly desperate, "at times like a beggar, going door to door in need of help." Tracy also spoke of her associations to the car. She spent so much time in the car pursuing her business. Tracy liked cars and prided herself on knowing a lot about cars. Having a fast, sporty car was very important to her. "Cars are masculine; they go together with a buff man, a hard man who works out all the time, like a macho man driving fast."

Day Residue: A seemingly innocuous event from the day before the dream is incorporated into the body (manifest content) of the dream; that is, seeing one of the two women who was "featured" (no pun intended) in the dream on the street the preceding day. Freud felt that when an event of the day or previous few days ("day residue") appeared in a dream, the event (which under other circumstances might have been trivial) had provoked an increase in an underlying current, then to be expressed in the dream. Modern psychoanalysts have emphasized the importance of understanding the meaning of the "day residue." The day residue is not just an artifact, but a highly meaningful "symbol" (something that stands for or represents another thing, especially an object used to represent something abstract) because it has the power to evoke an old "theme" (recurring "melody") or "paradigm" (example or model).

Manifest Dream: The manifest content of the dream (or the manifest dream) is the actual dream recalled or reported. Freud minimized the significance of the manifest dream because he felt that the manifest dream did not convey unconscious meaning. Later authors have reevaluated the importance of the manifest content, and suggested that while the manifest content may not represent preexisting unconscious strivings, it does serve the purpose of alluding to or highlighting the dreamer's significant conflicts and concerns (Pulver 1987; Spanjaard 1989; Lowenstein 1961).

Latent Content: The meaning of the dream is not obvious from the manifest content of the dream alone; therefore, meaning must be ascertained from associations to and analysis of the dream. In the example of Tracy's dream above, a deeper level of meaning (latent content) could be inferred, even though the manifest content of the story line seems innocuous and meaningless. The most interesting element is the image of the woman on the side of the road, who wasn't just one woman, but was a distillation of two women. One woman had overcome her difficulties and was successful and attractive. The other woman had not overcome her difficulties and seemed degraded, vulnerable, and "pathetic" ("going from door to door like a beggar"). Tracy was quick to say of the two women who were condensed into the dream woman: "I could accept being like the small and dark woman; she looks so much like me anyway and she is successful. But the other woman, I would die if I had to be like her!"

The latent content of the dream confirms the therapist's suggestion to Tracy about the meaning of her "less-put-together self." In the dream, the woman is split into two images, Tracy's images of woman. On the one hand, a woman can overcome her difficulties and become an attractive and successful person. On the other hand, a woman is "pathetic," vulnerable, dependent on men, degraded, and even so degraded that a woman (like Tracy's mother) will accept dependency on a "low-life" man rather than to have to be alone! Men, however, are like a "fast car." They are inherently "invulnerable" to dependency or degradation, and therefore are invulnerable to being or becoming pathetic. Thus, even though a woman can overcome her difficulties and become attractive and successful, she is not invulnerable because she has to overcome her difficulties. The state of being well "put together" is not a given, as it would be for a man or a sleek sports car.

Censor: The censor is an unconscious mechanism, the function of which is to assess/judge and prevent/prohibit disturbing or unacceptable thoughts, wishes, perceptions, or realizations from reaching the conscious awareness of the dreamer. Thus the censor serves as a "filter," sorting out what will or will not reach consciousness. In order for a disturbing or unacceptable thought, wish, perception, or realization to be expressed in the dream, a disguise must be assembled or constructed that is sufficient to elude the censor. In his later writings, Freud attributed this function to the superego.

Generally, the effects of the censor will only become visible through an exploration of the latent content of the dream. In Tracy's dream above, the effects of the censor disguise and therefore keep hidden the anguish of Tracy's fundamental conflict. She was unable to identify with her mother as a positive role model of femininity (because her mother wasn't a positive role model), an identification that would have allowed her to see herself positively as a woman. This resulted in a deep wish to shun the evidence of her femininity (permit an "interdependence" with her husband and respond to him sexually, and to enjoy her motherhood) and be "invulnerable" like a man.

Dream Wish: The underlying wish that motivates the dream seeks expression; this motivation is labeled the "dream wish." The dream wish is not easily visible in Tracy's dream, because this dream has more the quality of a "self-state" or a "communication" dream (see the dream models below). However, it could be inferred that an early attempt to reconcile conflicting images of women (pick up the woman on the side of the road) in order to embrace her femininity fails; instead, Tracy drives off in her car. Thus in the end of the dream, she and the car are one; she is like an "expensive sports car," having rejected femininity (failed to pick up the woman on the side of the road)—perhaps the dream wish.

Condensation: Condensation is a process that describes the combining of separate themes into one idea or symbol. These "composite images" are formed by blending multiple features together to represent a theme. Freud likened condensation to a house of parliament: issues receiving the most votes are placed forward. Similarly, symbols or images, or "composite images," are represented in the dream (provided they can evade the censor) because they offer the greatest possibility of expressing the underlying content. Most people can think of a dream in which a composite image appears. In Tracy's dream, the woman on the side of the road represented a composite image; two distinct images are fused together, a woman who was repugnant to Tracy (a woman she would never want to be like) and a woman whom she could almost find a way to appreciate. Another example of condensation in the dream was the car, which represented her desire to be masculine, powerful, and invulnerable to being or becoming pathetic.

Displacement: In displacement, a more distant but acceptable thought replaces the original unacceptable thought. Therefore, in displacement, a thought, impulse, or wish holding high psychic or emotional valence is stripped of intensity, and substituted with another "symbol" that has less intensity. In Tracy's dream, the wish to be like a man is displaced onto the car. The disturbing and unflattering perceptions of what it means to be a woman are displaced onto the composite woman.

The concept of displacement is visible in the free associations of a therapy hour as well. An example of this was evident with Mr. T, a man who was normally excessively nice to everyone, overly polite, "a gentleman to the core." In psychotherapy, Mr. T began to criticize his wife's dog. In fact, he became obsessively focused on the "miserable little creature." Finally, after speaking endlessly about the "creature" for several weeks, Mr. T ultimately realized that he cared very little about the dog and must in some way be talking about his wife. Shortly thereafter, Mr. T began to criticize the magazines in his therapist's waiting room, and soon after that, began toying with the possibility of actually sharing his criticisms of his therapist *with* his therapist.

Symbolism: Freud thought that interpreting a dream based on analysis of symbolism was an unreliable technique; to paraphrase Freud, "sometimes a cigar is just a cigar." In spite of his caution concerning the reliability of symbols in dreams, however, Freud frequently relied on interpretation of symbols in order to determine unconscious meaning.

Freud described the workings of a vast unconscious process from his diligent study of dreams; he laid the groundwork upon which later analysts were able to build. A number of potential methods for looking at a dream are available; several are worth describing. These methods are applicable to the process that occurs in a psychotherapy hour as well. In each of the five models or perspectives discussed below, a particular paradigm is given priority over other paradigms. In practice, the model that is made use of for any given dream or in any given hour, depends upon a choice that is made by the therapist. Ultimately, the only correct interpretation is the most useful interpretation for the patient at hand. In the final analysis, what is most useful for the patient in question will depend upon multiple factors. Where is the patient in the treatment: is the patient in the early phase, middle phase, or end/termination phase? What are the patient's major themes and what is necessary to do in order to further delineate those themes? How intense is the transference and will that intensity interfere (or not interfere) with the patient's ability to understand the interpretation? Finally, how significant is the potential for the patient to integrate the interpretation? The therapist should never fail to remember that any interpretation, however clever, will mean nothing to the patient if that patient is not in a position to make use of what is said in order to procure deeper understanding.

DREAM MODELS

Wish Fulfillment

In Freud's (1900) classic model, dreams are understood to be representations of forbidden or disguised wishes, so that in the manifest content of the dream, a wish exists to be extracted. When considering a dream or associations to a dream from the perspective of wish fulfillment, the therapist must identify the disguised wish, and also ask why this wish is unacceptable or "conflict-ridden" for the patient. For example, the therapist was aware that a male patient had a deep longing for dependence upon his wife, yet the patient was clearly quite uncomfortable with any image of himself that did not involve independence and self-sufficiency. Guilt or shame often accompanies wishes that feel unacceptable. This patient had a dream in which he was in the living room in the home of his childhood, lying on the sofa with his head in his mother's lap. In the dream, however, this man's mother was wearing a dress hat that he clearly recognized as belonging to his wife!

Wishes, desires, and needs creep into all aspects of life, as does the judgment of those wishes, desires, and needs. Litigation is full of people who often believe in their respective causes so ardently that reasoning becomes biased and the ability to see clearly is compromised. In any legal dispute, volitional and conscious lying may play a role; however, motivated by underlying desires, unconscious wishes often play a powerful role in perception. A strong desire to believe in something can cloud judgment and alter the capacity to accurately assess the facts. Prominent trials or public disputes, such as the O. J. Simpson murder trial or the sexual harassment dispute between Anita Hill and Clarence Thomas, reveal the way in which powerful preconceived beliefs and underlying desires shape opinion. Some simply know that O. J. was guilty; others are sure he was framed. We believe what we want to believe, yet most of us think our beliefs are objective and our decisions rational. The task of the therapist is to listen nonjudgmentally and try to understand why "wishes" (as in the wish–fulfillment dream) have become unacceptable and therefore repressed.

Interpretation in the wish–fulfillment dream focuses on the recognition of the dream wish, along with an attempt to help the patient understand the meaning of the wish and why the wish must be buried or denied (resisted). Understanding is made possible because of the safety and boundaries provided by the therapeutic experience, and because of the therapist's interest, curiosity, and neutrality.

> Early in his therapy, Ross dreamed of a former boss. The dream was very simple. In the dream, a former boss had purchased a very nice present for him. Actually, the former boss was no longer a boss but was now an equal, because Ross had ascended in the company. Recently, Ross had been assigned to a project that was out of his usual division, and so had had cause once again to run into the former boss. This taciturn, remote, former boss was a man who gave nothing, so it would have been out of character to be a bearer of a nice gift, as appeared in the dream. Later in the same session Ross spoke of his father; his father (who was no longer alive by the time this patient had sought treatment) had been an uninvolved and difficult man, with whom Ross had had little desire to communicate, and in whom Ross had little conscious interest.
>
> For this patient, the dream represented an old and deep "wish," rekindled by his feelings for (transference wishes toward) his therapist, to have a warm and involved father. In the dream, a man who was distant and difficult to engage (the boss) gave Ross a present, representing a "resistitutive" fantasy or wish fulfillment. That is, Ross no longer had an uninvolved and difficult father/boss; he had a warm and involved father/boss, a man who would think to bring him a present.

Sometimes dreams represent a wish fulfillment, but the wish is not as clearly and succinctly visible as it was in the dream just described.

> A male patient, Mr. G, described himself as always reasonable and polite; in fact he was so polite that even in his psychotherapy, it was difficult for him not to be deferential to his therapist. Therefore, Mr. G found it quite distressing when he began to dream of guns.
>
> In the first "gun" dream, Mr. G found himself in a state of great anxiety, walking around a house with a gun in his hand. He was afraid that someone might have been killed. In his associations,

Mr. G noted that the house was his childhood home. He remembered that he had always been fascinated by but yet fearful of guns.

The gun represented a fusion of Mr. G's hostile impulses and the wish to feel potent and proud. Hostility, potency, and pride were all sins in Mr. G's eyes, his rigid perspective a consequence of a very stringent religious upbringing. The anxiety in the dream reflected Mr. G's reproach against himself for having hostile wishes, and his fear about the potential destructiveness of allowing hostile wishes to creep to the surface. Mr. G came to understand that his hostility was in part connected to his feelings about the rigidity and hypocrisy of the religiosity with which he was raised. His father was a "religious man" and his mother a "religious man's wife." Mr. G felt that this upbringing had squashed his potency and pride. The disguised wish in the dream was to "possess the gun himself, and not be afraid to use it."

As patients progress in psychotherapy, dreams that carry an important theme such as the fulfillment of an intensely desired wish, tend to evolve as well. Mr. G continued to report dreams with a similar theme, allowing the underlying wishes or strivings to become more clearly elaborated. In addition however, the character of the dreams began to change. The gun dream was no longer just about the fulfillment of a desired wish, but began to have the character of the "self-state" or the "self-object" dream, the models of which will be described below.

Mr. G reported a dream in which he had another gun. He was with his wife, and the gun was for protection. He went to a store, but the store was a library. He got the wrong ammunition the first time, went back a second time and got the right kind of ammunition; the ammunition was like that used in a particularly deadly weapon that was once used in Vietnam. The bullets were in a deep blue box, "like the color of the ocean," and it was marked with the number "76." The dream shifted to a dinner party, and Mr. G was trying to hide the gun. He couldn't get it back into the box. He put the gun in his pocket, but it kept pointing barrel up so that it could be seen through his pants. Mr. G was anxious.

By this time in his treatment, Mr. G had a familiarity with the usefulness of understanding dreams. He also knew that the "gun" dreams were serving to elaborate a theme and he wanted clarification for himself now, whatever that clarification might be. He easily supplied associations to the above dream.

Mr. G had begun his treatment in the year 1976.

Mr. G loved the library. It was a place that had provided a haven for him in his youth, as well as a place that represented many hours of enjoyment during that difficult period. Additionally, the library represented for Mr. G the sense of empowerment he later found in his career, because he had made a professional choice that was inspired by his time immersed in books and admiring great writers.

The gun was something his father had owned, and in the town in which Mr. G had grown up, it represented being a tough guy, a "man" who wasn't afraid to hunt. The contradiction in his father's character was one that Mr. G couldn't fathom. His father was a religious man who preached morality and the consequences of sin at every opportunity, and yet he owned a gun and hunted with the men in the town

The reference to Vietnam was clear to Mr. G. He had escaped going to Vietnam because he had been fortunate enough to be assigned a high lottery number. He was, however, ashamed and terrified whenever he contemplated what would have happened to him had he been drafted and put in a position in which he would have had to shoot a gun.

The image of the gun, "like an erect phallus in his pocket," reminded the therapist of a painful incident that Mr. G had once described. Mr. G was seventeen years old, and had asked out a girl whom he had had a crush on for some time. The evening was surprisingly lovely; she looked beautiful, her eyes a deep blue color, "like the color of the ocean," and it was so easy (and exciting) to be with her. At the conclusion of the evening Mr. G took the young woman home, walked her to the door and in the darkness of her front porch leaned forward to kiss her, a moment that he had imagined for a long time. Just as his lips touched hers the porch light went on, and the front door opened. The young woman's father, who happened to be the police chief in the small town in which they all lived, was staring down at Mr. G with daggers in his eyes! The moment was ruined. The young woman rushed inside; Mr. G left feeling profoundly self-conscious and embarrassed; it was the last date the two would ever share.

On one level the dream could be understood to declare the wish to be powerful and aggressive, as well as to allow expression of sexual and exhibitionistic wishes, all symbolized by the gun. However, the dream does not end with the fulfillment of these wishes. The dream ends in a state of discomfort with Mr. G feeling anxious. What if alternatively, the dream represents Mr.

G's attempt to reconcile conflicting images of himself in order to determine what feels acceptable to him and what does not (superego function)? Is it moral to kiss a girl or be aroused by a girl (the gun in his pocket), especially a girl with eyes a deep blue, like the color of the ocean? If his father could be a religious man and yet like to hunt, then why couldn't Mr. G be a good man and still be assertive (not deferential)? What if the dream reflects Mr. G's attempt to consolidate an experience of himself ("self-representation") that would be less fragile than the experience of himself that he had carried before? Are words power (his literary gift) or are guns power? What is the right kind of ammunition in order to feel like a man?

Traumatic Dream

In a traumatic dream, the content of the dream reflects a previous traumatic experience or experiences (Dowling 1982; Pulver 1987). Traumatic experiences that have not been worked through and assimilated into the traumatized person's psychic life have enduring psychological power. The effect is manifested by a continuous reappearance in thought, fantasy, creative endeavors, and especially in repetitive dreams of the traumatic event and its impact upon the psyche.

Trauma is not necessarily defined by apparent pain; the individual's experience of being overwhelmed and left psychologically helpless by the situation is a far more important indicator of a traumatic response. A number of factors contribute to a person's reaction to a traumatic event; these include level of emotional and intellectual development, availability of environmental support and empathy, and breadth of previous trauma.

When listening to and identifying trauma in a dream, the therapist will find emphasis placed on a specific event or series of events in which the overwhelming nature of the stimulus or pain cannot be contained and/or assimilated. The trauma that reappears in the dream or associations may be an obvious trauma that anyone would recognize, or the event that is experienced by the individual as traumatic may be much subtler. In the later case, the "trauma" is "traumatic" for reasons idiosyncratic and unique to the individual. A dream or an association that refers to a trauma is often stimulated by a current-day event or by feelings that become activated in the oscillation of transference that occurs with the therapist. Memories surface and experiences are reconsidered as, in some associative way, the person is reminded of the trauma.

The trauma dream (which is often repetitive) represents an attempt by the patient to master the trauma (overcome the fear stemming from the trauma) through revisiting and reliving the trauma. Elaborated by Freud and others, this formulation forms a powerful, explanatory model that differs from wish fulfillment (Blum 1983). Freud's (1920) simple yet brilliant observation of his eighteen-month-old grandson, playing the same game endlessly in his crib whenever his mother would leave him for a time, offers an insight into many repetitive behaviors. In the game, the toddler would throw a wooden spool attached to a string over the side of crib; he would then pull it back to him, repeating the sequence again and again. Each time the small tot threw the spool over the edge, he would say, "gone"; each time he would retrieve the spool, he would happily say, "there." The observation of this sequence led Freud to deduce that his grandson dealt with the "traumatic" separation from his mother by creating a symbolic game of the experience of being abandoned. In this way the child tried to master his anxiety at having been left and his helplessness to bring his mother back, though a repetitive act that placed the "trauma" of a separation (throwing away the spool) under his active control (reeling it back in).

The above model has since become an important means of understanding many repetitive dreams, fantasies, behaviors, interpersonal relationships, and seemingly immutable character traits, which at first glance appear illogical or even self-destructive. Instead, the dreams, fantasies, behaviors, interpersonal relationships, and immutable character traits can be understood to reflect enduring scars and the attempt to remaster the trauma(s) that resulted in the scarring. Freud said that repetitive dreams serve a distinctly different purpose from the simple wish fulfillment model (which adheres to the pleasure principle). These dreams "help carry out another task, which must be accomplished before the dominance of the pleasure principle can ever begin" (1920, 32). The need to master trauma through repetition in dreams was, according to Freud, an "independent" and more "primitive" function than the gratification of pleasure through fulfillment of needs and wishes. Thus, the need to master trauma is a compelling and necessary prerequisite that must be achieved, superseding the pursuit of pleasure and the need to resolve conflict.

The trauma that appears in dreams can be narrowly or broadly defined; the distinction from wish fulfillment correspondingly can be distinct or the edges quite blurry. Trauma can be viewed across a continuum, from massive physical or emotional trauma such as war or a life-threatening rape to more subtle emotional traumas that occur in the setting of intense desire or early childhood wishes and disappointments. De Saussure (1982) suggested that the intensity of desire often plays a role in producing the overwhelming aspect of the trauma. She specifically noted that the overt content of the dream, especially the fear element relating to the trauma, is remembered; on the other hand, the latent content that reflects the "satisfaction of the forbidden wish," is repressed. De Saussure's conceptualization points out the difficulty encountered in attempting to differentiate the traumatic dream from the other models (especially, wish fulfillment). Nevertheless, considering the traumatic dream to be a repetitive attempt to achieve mastery over helplessness is a compelling hypothesis in its own right. Dreams portray trauma in a relatively undisguised fashion. Pulver (1987) proposed that these undisguised dreams tend to be accompanied by intense anxiety or dysphoria. The dreamer may experience him- or herself as a child within the dream, the dreams tend to be recurrent since childhood, and the clear presence of a physical space may appear in the dream (as seen in the examples offered below). Some self-psychologists have observed that a failure occurring in the arena of empathy and nurturing can be experienced as traumatic (Stolorow, Brandchaft, and Atwood 1987; Wolf, Gales, Shane, and Shane 2000). Since most people probably experience some degree of failure in the department of empathy and nurturing, whether this becomes of primary psychological importance probably depends on variables that include individual differences in experience and innate constitutional givens and temperament.

When psychodynamic listening includes attention to trauma, with respect to a dream or the content of a therapy hour, the particulars of what was overwhelming to the patient and why it was overwhelming (which may be obvious) are always on the therapist's mind. The following is a vignette about Sandra; her trauma was unmistakable.

> Sandra was forty years old when she came to treatment. She had recurrent dreams about being alone in a dark, cold, and dingy place and feeling petrified. She sought treatment following the unexpected death of her lover. Sandra's adult sexual experience was limited and constrained. She experienced her first consensual intercourse when she was thirty-eight years old, and the lover she had lost before coming to treatment was only the second man with whom she had been involved.
>
> In the context of her therapy, a variety of feelings surfaced that included her desire for as well as fear of trusting a man. Erotic feelings came up as well, and during this time period, the meaning of the repetitive dream gradually crystallized in a series of recollections that were confirmed by her older siblings.
>
> Sandra was aware at the outset of therapy that a male relative at some point had sexually and physically abused her during her

childhood. As time went by and the therapy progressed, Sandra reported many bizarre and graphic dreams, which offered intense sexual and sadistic themes. With time it became apparent that the dark place, appearing so often in her dreams, was a part of her own childhood home; this was a home in which she, her siblings, and her parents had lived in the early part of her life before her parents divorced. Over time, the initial repetitive dream began to change. Graphic scenes of being forced to masturbate herself and perform fellatio and a variety of other acts reflected frank abuses, that were perpetrated upon her by her father and which took place in the wine cellar ("dark, cold, and dingy") of that early childhood home. Sandra now knew that these and other events were not just dreams, because a sibling had confirmed having being subjected to similar horrors.

Traumatic elements that are not easily ascertainable can be conveyed in a dream as well. Only with time does the traumatic element become apparent, or is it possible to figure out what it must have been.

Ann Marie was a woman in her late thirties when she came to treatment. She had numerous recurrent dreams of being alone in various places. When she actually began to contemplate in her therapy the places reflected in the dreams, she realized that the majority of the locations visualized were places she had been at some point in her life. The dreams were quite vivid, so that Ann Marie was able to describe the locations in minute detail. Typically she found herself focusing on specific elements; sometimes these were design or architectural elements.

The following is an example of one of the early dreams. Ann Marie dreamed of being in a motel room. She described the interior of the room and the old-fashioned plumbing in the bathroom. The bathtub had no shower attachment; she hated taking baths. Later on in the therapy another dream was set in winter. It must have been on the East Coast because the buildings were old and the trees were bare of leaves. The scene was at an old hospital or a sanitarium; the place was cold and sterile, and made of reddish-colored bricks.

Although often full of inanimate details (as in Ann Marie's dream), until late in her therapy when the character of the dreams began to change, all of Ann Marie's dreams were stark and devoid of people.

The presence of many descriptive details in Ann Marie's early dreams actually served to distract the dreamer (and the therapist) from the absence of something else, which is that there were no people in Ann Marie's early dreams. The absence of people was the only subtle reference to trauma; this is something that would be very difficult to uncover at first glance. What was the trauma in Ann Marie's life and how was the trauma revived by current circumstance?

Ann Marie took great pride in her ability to move from relationship to relationship, job to job, and place to place. She couldn't understand the feeling of "nostalgia" because she never experienced it. Surprisingly then, Ann Marie appeared to have an inexplicable reaction whenever her therapist would take time off time for a holiday. Each time the therapist would tell her about an upcoming vacation, Ann Marie would shrug with indifference. Within a short period of time, however, she would announce that she had had a change of heart about the treatment, no longer felt positively toward her therapist, and wanted to stop coming to therapy. This pattern occurred a number of times before Ann Marie was able to contemplate that some relationship might exist between her therapist's leave-takings and her own reactions. With time it became more evident that the anticipation of a separation from the therapist was the "current circumstance" that had "revived" the previous trauma, and the previous trauma involved psychological loss and human failure that was overwhelming.

Ann Marie's early life was characterized by chaos. Frequent physical fights between her parents often necessitated nighttime runs to emergency rooms in order for one or both parents to receive medical treatment. Ann Marie would be woken in the middle of the night to accompany her bloodied parents on these runs (she was too young to stay home alone). Additionally, more than one bankruptcy forced a number of moves, the changing of schools, the leaving of friends and the making of new friends, and wondering when the next move would come. Another move always did follow. Ann Marie even recalled, on more than one occasion, living for a few weeks out of the family car.

Eventually, Ann Marie learned not to attach herself to anything at all. Homes became just scenes, as though in a painting (the scenes in her dreams!). People became like two-dimensional figures, and then didn't exist at all. Ann Marie learned to keep to herself, make books her friends, and pretend not to see the looks of pity she read on the faces of the families whose children went to school with her. Ann Marie once calculated that by the time she left home at age seventeen, she had attended at least eighteen different schools!

Ann Marie's dreams were a chronicle of her trauma and the way she had felt inside her traumatized self. Visually depicted in the depersonalized dream scenes was a revisitation to the "scene of the crime"; she was drawn back again and again to many times of overwhelming stress and chaos, as she struggled in her dreams to rework and attempt to master years of awful loneliness, fear, and desperation.

As time passed in the treatment, and Ann Marie was able to understand her terror of the pain of attachment and subsequent and inevitable loss, the character of her dreams began to change. The following is a dream from much later in the treatment, demonstrating the change in quality and content of Ann Marie's recurrent dream.

> She was driving a car and a female friend was with her. The two decided to stop in order to explore the inside of an interesting building. A guard stood at the doorway, but smiled and waved them through when they asked to look around. Upon entering the building, to their delight, a rich old interior with many interesting features was laid out before them. They ascended an old staircase to a balcony, which looked out over a sunny field on which people were strolling.

To follow Edith Jacobson's concept of the "peopling" of the representational world, Ann Marie is no longer alone in her dream; "people" now are present within the dream. Slowly and painfully, she now began to recall some of the friends of her childhood, so many connections that she had had to leave behind. In one particular series of similar dreams, the "female friend" in the dream above evolved to clearly remind Ann Marie of a long-ago and very best friend. Ann Marie had met this girl during her time at the only school she had been able to attend for more than one year. The "sanatorium on the East Coast" in the early dream turned out to be the place at which her mother was eventually permanently institutionalized, after many shorter stays throughout Ann Marie's childhood. Her mother's diagnosis turned out to be paranoid schizophrenia.

Self-State Dream

The self-state dream is exactly what it sounds as though it would be. The primary motivation for the dream in this model is to define and encapsulate an internal experience of the self, contain the associated feelings, minimize the possibility of psychological fragmentation (the feeling of "falling apart"), and bolster sagging self-esteem. All of that is probably a tall order for a dream. However, in the self-state dream (or in the content of a psychotherapy hour that is about the state of the self), an aspect of or feeling about the self is depicted, and an effort to maintain self-esteem or to integrate an emotion is attempted (Kohut 1971). The intent of the dream may fail, leaving behind for the dreamer simply a heightened awareness of some aspect of the self. Consequently, all of the elements and objects within the dream represent elements of the dreamer's internal experience.

A dream or a psychotherapy hour that is understood from the vantage point of "self-states" may reveal shame, the loss of self-esteem, an experience of internal fragmentation, or the feeling of being overwhelmed. Alternatively, self-state dreams (or a psychotherapy hour understood from the vantage point of a self-state) may reflect a desired state for the self. Flying dreams, for example, may express an "above-it-all" quality that permits independence from others; conversely, the flying dream may convey to the "self" the danger of "flying too high," as a symbolic expression of becoming too grandiose (Kohut 1977). Thus in the Greek myth, Icarus (the son of Daedalus) escaped from Crete by flying with wings made by his father. Icarus ignored Daedalus's warnings about the danger of asking for too much; Icarus wanted to "fly higher" despite his father's imploring. The sun's heat melted the wax by which his wings were fastened, and Icarus fell to his death in the sea.

The following is the story of Mark, a young man whose repetitive self-state dreams became the key to understanding what brought Mark to the place in which he found himself at the time he sought treatment.

> Mark was a seventeen-year-old boy who was encouraged to seek psychotheraputic intervention because his parents were concerned about his excessive drug use and the fact that Mark was sleeping twelve hours a day. Mark came to treatment deeply reluctantly; psychotherapy was to him only a confirmation of his "pathetic" situation.
>
> Mark took pride in his pacifism. In tenth grade he had become a "Jesus freak." In eleventh grade this affiliation seemed to fail him and his self-esteem plummeted. He was left with little he could find of value within himself, except for his belief in the value of a nonaggressive (pacifist) posture. At home, Mark lived with an envious and narcissistic father whose own self-esteem was deeply and chronically threatened by his very bright and handsome son's early talent and magnetism.
>
> Mark loved to dream and he was a prolific dreamer. In his dreams, Mark was always "Robin Hood." As the central figure in

his dreams, he would do many daring and aggressive things, such as fighting off multitudinous adversaries in order to carry out his "mission."

Mark's dreams expressed a wished-for state of the self, a desire for greatness and power that he was otherwise not able to feel. Although the dreams could easily be seen as simple wish fulfillment, what made them not so were a few crucial details. Mark had been a childhood "fencing" prodigy. He gave up this sport as he was becoming more heavily involved in becoming a "Jesus Freak." Although Mark's father initially had been quite proud of his son's athleticism and speed with a sword, the father later became quite threatened by his son's ability. On some level Mark sensed his father's antipathy. Mark loved to fence, but he was justifiably fearful of the consequences of his father's hostile and retaliatory behavior and he clearly sensed the danger in his father's envy of his ability.

Mark actually was incredibly talented and capable; he longed to have permission again to be strong, powerful, proud, and admired, rather than the pathetic mess he had allowed himself to become. The dreams revealed the depth of his wish as Robin Hood to "steal" from the "rich" (his father) that which he felt was taken from him. He wanted to give back to the "poor" (himself) his right to be the swordsman he could have become, a representation of his vital self. Therefore, in addition to fulfilling a wish, Mark's dream was an attempt to restore (in fantasy) his vitality and power, to rescue himself from the painful loss of self-esteem.

> In the hours with his therapist, Mark gradually revealed his aspirations and learned about the way in which he had sabotaged his "true self" in order to protect his father's fragile self. In the context of a positive relationship with his male therapist and armed with an understanding of what had happened to him, Mark came alive again. He returned to actualizing his love of fencing; he joined the school team and was named "most valuable player" in his senior year.

The dreams ceased. Mark no longer needed to sleep twelve hours a night in order to dream of Robin Hood. Mark no longer felt that he had to sacrifice his vital self in order to protect his father, and thus protect himself. Armed with the "bows and arrows" of understanding "meaning," the meaning of his own symptoms, Mark was now in his own actual existence, a living "Robin Hood."

Self-Object Dream

Another example of the self-state model, which ultimately is really a self-object model and exemplifies a self-object dream, is visible in a dream and a psychotherapy hour that occurred during a very stressful period in Dr. R's life. Dr. R, another patient, returned to psychotherapy in the context of a tortuous malpractice lawsuit.

Dr. R was a diligent and responsible physician, and a devoted husband and father. He had come to psychotherapy some years previously in order to work on his pattern of excessive worry and his vulnerable self-esteem. Dr. R felt that he had benefited greatly from his treatment, although the therapy had ended with Dr. R still experiencing occasional bouts of doubt about his capacities. These doubts appeared entirely unfounded. Dr. R was extremely well-respected in the community in which he practiced; in fact, Dr. R's therapist had heard about his professional reputation long before Dr. R appeared as a patient.

Dr. R was the last of seven children, born many years after his older brothers and sisters. He had known for as long as he could remember that he was an "accident." At some point in his adolescence, Dr. R inadvertently discovered that his mother had unsuccessfully tried to abort him with a "home remedy" that a friend who was a midwife (evidence that his mother had serious intentions) had told her about. Consequently, Dr. R had always felt himself to be a burden to his much older and exhausted parents. Throughout his childhood and young adulthood, Dr. R had striven to be a good son. Despite his efforts, however, Dr. R felt that no amount of "good enough" or "successful enough" could really engage his parents, particularly his mother, who seemed "wasted" and disinterested in him. Dr. R had hoped that his parents would finally be pleased when he decided to go to medical school and become a doctor. Sadly, an eventuality of their older age at the time of his birth, both parents were dead before Dr. R graduated from medical school. He never forgot that no parent was present to watch him receive his M.D. at graduation.

The malpractice lawsuit with which Dr. R was faced was unwarranted and frivolous, but the prospect of a trial terrified him. Once again, he questioned his capacity, even though his own intellectual assessment of his actions in the case and the opinion of many others whom he respected confirmed every decision he had made.

The second session upon Dr. R's return to psychotherapy followed an arduous deposition, during which time the plaintiff's lawyer had pummeled Dr. R with enraging but horrifying accusations. Despite the ordeal, Dr. R spent most of the psychotherapy session talking about his son; he spoke emotionally about the pride he felt about his son's impressive athletic accomplishments. In great detail and with a somewhat driven quality, Dr. R described a recent football game in which his son had made the winning play. Toward the end of the session, Dr. R shared a dream.

> He was the quarterback of his high school football team. He threw a long pass, winning the game; the crowd roared, and he stood on the field in the bright sun, receiving the adulation of the crowd.

Had the dream ended at this point, one might call the dream only a self-state dream. However, Dr. R's dream continues.

> As he stood on the field, eyes roaming through the crowd, he saw his father, alive again and young, walking toward him with arms outstretched. Dr. R found himself running toward his father, but every time he thought that surely he must have reached him, the image of his father disappeared as though it had never been there at all. Dr. R awoke crying.

The therapist commented that Dr. R had ample reason to feel proud of his son, as well as ample reason to feel proud of himself and his own many outstanding achievements. How difficult it must be to remind himself of all that he was and all that he had done, in the face of the vicious lawsuit with which he was engaged. The therapist referred to the dream. Perhaps in the dream, Dr. R was describing how desperately alone he had felt in the past, and how desperately alone he felt now (description of a "self-state" in a self-state dream). If only Dr. R could call up an image of a loving father (internal object representation, which replaces in development a prior self-object function) who had stood by him in the past and would stand by him again now. He needed so badly to be able to find a way to believe in himself in order to cope with the lawsuit (find a way into a "self-state" in which he could believe in himself). The level of character assassination that was occurring in the case was exacerbating a recurrent thought with which Dr. R already lived: he should never have been born anyway, therefore his life was about trying to prove again and again that he was valuable enough to deserve to exist. Dr. R had always been afraid that it would be only a matter of time before he would be discovered to be worthless and would then be destroyed; had that time now come with the arrival of the lawsuit?

This good man's self-worth was shaken by attacks upon his competence. The therapist was able to provide a self–object function for Dr. R; the therapist reminded Dr. R of "the man that he was" and explained the way in which his current situation had served to destabilize the structure of his "self." However, it should be noted that although the therapist was present in the transference and in the dream, the therapist's simple presence ("being there") was probably more important than the "word" interpretations. The therapist as "listener" and "mirror" allowed this patient to find his voice. Dr. R pulled himself back together over a brief number of psychotherapy hours and defended himself brilliantly during a meeting with the judge who was to preside over his lawsuit. The suit was summarily dismissed. Dr. R remained in psychotherapy for another year, during which time he developed a significant capacity to recognize on his own, his very real capacities and worth.

As described in the case of Dr. R, in this dream model, the purpose of listening to a dream or to the content of a psychotherapy hour is to discover and delineate the relationship between the "self" and the "object" (another person or people). Therefore, the dream or the therapy hour describes the dreamer's perception of a relationship to someone; that person may be a parent, significant other, authority figure, or any other figure from past or present, including the therapist.

The self-and-object-relations model of understanding the dream, although overlapping with other dream models (as described above with Dr. R's dream) places particular importance on internal object relationships and the way in which internal object images impact the view of the self (Stolorow 1978). While wish fulfillment may be explicit or implicit in a self/object dream (as it is in Dr. R's dream), the emphasis is on the relationship between self and object. Recall that a therapist can never really know about a patient's objects, can only "approximate" this knowledge, because the patient's perception of objects is always "approximate."

A dream with a self-and-object paradigm may simply reconfirm that which the patient already knows, or it may convey a different relationship than that which is consciously experienced by the patient. The motivation to avoid the examination and understanding of the relationship with primary objects and later "transference manifestations" of the relationship with primary objects has to do with the need to minimize depressive affect, or more specifically, to avoid the painful task of mourning. The most magnificent example of the self/object paradigm is offered by Shakespeare in his rendition of Hamlet;

Hamlet is a character who embodies the tension between being driven to see the truth about one's important objects and the inherent pain in doing so.

Viewed from a self/object perspective, Dr. R's dream is about an "object relationship" and its impact upon Dr. R's "view of himself." A different relationship with his father in the past might have sustained Dr. R in his present circumstances. He needed a father who would come to stand beside him, irrespective of whether he was in the midst of victory or in fear of defeat. A father such as this would have translated into an internal object relationship that Dr. R could have counted upon in periods of great challenge, such as the situation of the lawsuit, at which time Dr. R felt that he was fighting for his life (his belief in himself).

In the dream, Dr. R is astonished to see his father again, only to cruelly lose him once more as his father literally fades away. Ironically, the relationship that Dr. R actually had with his father—that is, that his father wasn't interested in him nor was ever really there for him—occurs within the very substance of the dream. Dr. R "wakes crying," "driven to see the truth" and assume the "painful task of mourning."

THE CASE OF MR. T

Mr. T thought of himself as self-reliant and independent; in contrast, he viewed his wife as needy and dependent on him. To his distress, Mr. T dreamed several times that his wife had left him; each time he woke panic stricken. Later in his therapy, Mr. T dreamed of his wife nursing him.

Both of Mr. T's dreams vividly depict a different posture than he was consciously able to acknowledge to himself. Early in his treatment, his dependent strivings were rejected and projected onto his wife, but in his dreams Mr. T's dependent strivings and primitive desire to be nurtured (nursing) are represented. By attending to the self/object paradigm in the dream, the therapist was able to help Mr. T appreciate what he really felt inside himself.

Every therapist has experienced those times when a patient seems to talk exclusively about other people, avoiding material that has to do with the self. At first glance, the flow of talk about anyone and anything other than the self may seem like a "garden-variety" resistance, an avoidance of feelings that the patient may be experiencing or a way to skirt something that is embarrassing or upsetting to discuss. If however, a self/object paradigm is employed, the therapist may discover that an interpersonal drama or scenario is actually being described, except that the relationship to the self is omitted. Patients often speak of the latest movie that has been released or an important or unimportant news item; often a more personal identification with the story is hidden behind the seemingly unimportant "small talk." A self/object paradigm emphasizes that all human scenarios and interactions of which the patient speaks reveal something about the inner world of the patient, and experiences with and expectations of other human beings.

Communication Dream

The "communication" dream is directed toward the therapist or some other person with whom the dream will be shared; it is intended as a communiqué (Kanzer 1955). This dream model emphasizes the unique middle ground between acknowledging something fully and denying it, in which the dream touches the edge of the patient's ability or willingness to acknowledge something. The idea of a dream as a device of communication is an ancient notion, dating back to biblical times. Dreams have a unique capacity to convey information to the listener. People who have a dream about another person often feel a compulsion to share the dream with the person who appears in the dream. Dream content can be symbolically rich and make a direct statement, but at the same time the dreamer can minimize or disavow the dream as "just a dream." This "in-between" feature allows the dreamer to not only access but also share something that would otherwise be difficult.

Communication dreams play a role that is similar to but distinct from other forms of unconscious communication, such as free associations and parapraxis (Freudian slip). A parapraxis is experienced as a sudden and often embarrassing phenomenon, occurring with no conscious control. Because of this, Kohut (1970) has suggested great caution in interpreting this kind of phenomenon. With a dream, however, the dreamer decides to report the dream, thus acknowledging some willingness to recognize its hidden meaning. Additionally, the abstract and symbolic qualities of a dream permit dream content to be interpreted in multiple ways, including minimizing or denying ownership of the message in the dream.

> Josephine dreamed that she was sitting in her therapist's chair. In the context of exploring this dream, Josephine was able to tell her therapist that she felt he had not been helpful lately. In fact, she had recently been contemplating that she might be better off on her own.

The dream was a shorthand way for Josephine to express to her therapist that she did not feel he had been in tune with her in the recent time period. Feeling alone in the room with him (her therapist) only exacerbated her chronic feeling of aloneness, and that was intolerable to her. This same patient had earlier dreamed that she was being held by one of Harlow's "wire monkeys." The dream served to communicate to the therapist a significant shift in the transference paradigm. Prior to the dream, the therapist had been able to coast somewhat in the context of a predominantly positive ("idealizing") transference. With this dream, the therapist became aware that he had been lulled (in the context of the positive transference) into forgetting that Josephine was a person who had been raised by foster parents who were as cold and cruel as Harlow's wire monkeys. Consequently, Josephine was acutely sensitive to any relaxation of his attentiveness to her. The therapist reminded himself about this situation and redoubled his efforts to "locate" (that is, to be "present in the room with" or aware of) this fragile patient.

Sometimes the dream serves as a communication, not to the therapist necessarily, but to another person outside of the therapy. Although Clair was in treatment at the time of the dream described below and the dream is clearly communicative, the message was already known to the therapist and to Clair herself. The dream, therefore, primarily served to communicate with someone in Clair's outside life.

> In the context of a helpful treatment in which she was increasingly able to express her point of view and assert herself when necessary, Clair dreamed of telling her sister-in-law to "watch her step." As she reported this dream, Clair spoke again of her feeling that her sister-in-law was manipulative, intrusive, and a troublemaker; and yet she often felt intimidated and wary of this sister-in-law. Clair said that she had felt a strong compulsion to share this dream with her sister-in-law, and in fact had already done so. Thus, the dream served as a vehicle, effective but indirect and less threatening, informing the sister-in-law that she was "on notice."

Sometimes a dream is so complex or perhaps so simple that it becomes difficult to decide which model might best deconstruct what the dreamer wanted to say. Sophia's dream (to follow), in its very simplicity and although primarily a dream of communication, is also about material that is consistent with each of the other dream models described.

> Sophia dreamed that she was flying in a commercial aircraft over the ocean when the pilot suddenly announced that the plane's en-

gines had failed and the craft was going down. A somewhat older woman with long red hair was seated next to Sophia. The two woman clasped hands as the plane careened toward the ocean. Sophia was terrified.

Sophia was six weeks postpartum with her second child. She had had a serious postpartum depression after the birth of her first child. After a tortuous course, Sophia finally met her current therapist, who made the diagnosis of her postpartum depression and treated her appropriately. Part of the diagnosis included a carefully collected history. As she put together this history, Sophia recognized that her own mother's suicide, of which she had long been aware and had occurred when Sophia was ten years old, had actually occurred after the birth of Sophia's brother. Thus, Sophia's mother had killed herself in the context of a postpartum depression.

Although Sophia recovered quite well with a combination of medication and psychotherapy, the treatment was delayed for a long enough period of time (the time involved before she met her current therapist) for Sophia to have been quite traumatized by the anguish and debilitation that accompanied her depression. Consequently, Sophia was afraid to chance another pregnancy, even though she and her husband very much wanted another child. Eventually, arranging with her therapist that all involved would closely monitor the vulnerable postpartum period, Sophia decided to get pregnant again.

In the dream, Sophia is "going down" ("down" in the plane, "down" into the depression), but not alone. She is with another woman, and the two are holding hands as they plunge to their death. The dream was a communication to the therapist about Sophia's dawning awareness that she was beginning the slide into that all-too-familiar depression. A more deeply hidden reminder in the dream and further communication to the therapist is present as well: one of Sophia's greatest fears had always been that she would someday end up like her mother, and in that state, abandon her children as her mother had abandoned her. Sophia's mother had had long red hair.

Mixing Dream Models

Dreams often fit more that one model, as do some of the dreams described above. When making an interpretation to a patient, the most important reason to choose one model over another model is that the model chosen is useful. No dream interpretation is ever valuable to a patient if it cannot be made use of by the patient in the service of further clarification or understanding.

Sophia's dream actually fits the entire spectrum of dream models described, which is an unusual occurrence. The communication aspect was by far the most basic or "fundamental" function specifically of Sophia's dream, and therefore the communication dream model became the focus of the therapist's interpretation to her. Sophia needed to notify the therapist and herself, that is, to provide a signal that she was beginning to experience the familiar symptoms of depression. However, she wanted to ignore the warning signs. She had so hoped that she would be "home free" with this second pregnancy, that to face her awareness that it was not to be so felt unbearable; Sophia repressed her awareness of her mood state, and the thoughts appeared instead in the communication aspect of the dream.

For the sake of clarification and understanding for the reader, Sophia's dream fits other dream models as well:

1. Sophia's dream is a self-state dream, because it depicts Sophia's awareness of her depressed state.
2. The dream is a self/object dream because in the dream appears: (a) Sophia's relationship with her mother and (b) the fear that had lived inside Sophia ever since her mother's death, that she was like her mother (identification with an internalized object) and would therefore someday succumb to her mother's fate.
3. The trauma element in the dream is obvious, as Sophia relives the memory of the awfulness of her prior descent into depression, in the context of her recognition that it was happening to her again.
4. The wish-fulfillment aspect of the dream is present, but to grasp this feature of the dream requires a context: Sophia remembered her mother. She was old enough by the time she lost her mother to have many conscious memories of the mother (prior to her mother's depression) whom she had loved and to whom she had been close. A cherished wish, that at one time had been conscious but had been repressed until revealed by the regression of Sophia's depression (severe depression tends to open up holes in the repressive barrier), was to be with her mother again. In the dream, as she knows that she is going to die, she is comforted by the recognition that she is reunited with, that is, "sitting next to" her mother again.

The therapist is not infrequently confronted with a dream such as Sophia's. Various ideas come to mind. The opportunity is presented to offer something of meaning, and sometimes only minutes are available to decide which choice to make. When using the different dream models, always of first importance is not necessarily which model most appeals to the thera-pist, but which interpretation the patient is most likely to understand, tol-erate, and be able to assimilate in a helpful way. The dream models serve the purpose of providing an outline with which to begin this task. Additionally, sometimes the most fitting dream model and the meaning of the dream are apparent to the therapist, but the moment is clearly not suitable to share this understanding with the patient. Without proper tact and timing, no matter how clever the interpretation, it will be lost on the patient.

> Mr. Jones was a middle-aged professional man. He complained of chronic unhappiness and a feeling of inner restriction, despite the appearance of being a well-functioning person. Although he had been reasonably successful in his professional life, his accom-plishments were less than his probable potential, due in part to his great difficulties in expressing and asserting himself. He was un-able to acknowledge anything with intense emotional valence, es-pecially if whatever he was experiencing seemed less than re-sponsible and adult. Most difficult of all for him, however, was the acknowledgment of any pain or vulnerability that seemed not in keeping with the strict, religious, stoic male model that was pro-vided by his father.
>
> In the second year of his treatment and in the context of his in-creasing ability to explore the painful losses of his childhood and current life, Mr. Jones reported the following dream:
>
>> He was watching a doctor perform surgery on a little boy. The doctor removed the little boy's two lower ribs and then put them back in. The little boy was quite serene and beautiful, and smiled throughout the procedure. The patient (still within the dream) thought this odd; the boy was given only local anesthesia, certainly inadequate to control the pain.
>
> Mr. Jones was quite affected by this dream, yet during the hour in which it first came up he had little direct association to the dream material. In the session prior to the dream, however, Mr. Jones had spoken of his preoccupied mother and her inability to stretch be-yond her narrowly circumscribed universe in order to appreciate or even notice his victories or the struggles he was having. He had also mentioned that he sometimes felt similarly about his wife, whom he felt did not take into consideration or sometimes even recognize the burdens he felt.
>
> With the above disclosure, a subtle shift seemed to take place in the transference. The idealizing father transference melted away

and was replaced by a strikingly negative mother transference. The biblical reference and the theme of bodily harm (castration) and insensitivity to pain (inadequate pain control) apparent in the manifest content of the dream reflected the shift in the transference. Because of his great difficulty in accepting transference interpretations but in keeping with his increasing ability to acknowledge that he might feel emotional pain, the therapist simply said to Mr. Jones that the smiling boy might be himself. The comment made a profound impression on Mr. Jones and he began to cry softly.

Several weeks later, the dream came up again. This time the therapist suggested to Mr. Jones that he might have begun to experience the therapist as he had his mother. Perhaps he felt that the therapist was a person who made demands upon him (to feel things and express himself) and then failed to fully appreciate the pain that those demands were causing him (the painfulness of revisiting the past). Mr. Jones was startled but nodded with understanding.

The first interpretation located the figure of the boy within Mr. Jones, but made no direct interpretation about the self-state aspect of the dream. The second interpretation directly referred to the self/object aspect of the dream, the relationship between Mr. Jones's mother and the therapist as transference object and the relationship between Mr. Jones and his mother (and with the therapist again as transference object) that involved pain.

The Course of Dreams

Dreams ebb and flow in the course of life as well as in psychotherapy. At times a person dreams or seems to remember dreams more frequently; this ebb and flow of dream material can be significant. Dreams frequently increase at times of internal (emotional) unrest, becoming less frequent again during periods of psychological quiescence. Sometimes, however, the decrease in dreaming reflects not quiescence, but increased "resistance." Great variance can exist in the frequency of remembered dreams between individuals. Ella Freeman Sharp (1937) noted that people who tended to dream little before psychotherapy, dreamed more after therapy. Those who dreamed profusely before psychotherapy tended to dream less after therapy. Sharp also noted that over the course of therapy repetitive dreams became less common, nightmares decreased, and dreams become more gratifying and more succinct as "working through" (in the treatment) proceeded. Dreams that have a recurrent theme or dreams that become repetitive during the course of a treatment are particularly important to disentangle. A pattern in dreams that involves something "recurrent" or "repetitive" marks the dream theme as particularly important.

Dream Symbols

For better or for worse, dreams tend to be labeled or categorized on the basis of broad symbols. Provided a therapist doesn't become carried away with enthusiasm about predictable symbolism, dreams are fun to speculate about and speculation assists in the expansion of imagination about unconscious symbolism. However, categorizing a dream on the basis of a broad generalization about a symbol, and then telling the patient about that categorization, can be moderately to more than moderately unwise. The interpretation of an individual's dream, based on a formula that is not necessarily applicable to the patient in question, can be experienced by the patient at best as nonempathic, and at worst as depersonalizing, humiliating, and demeaning.

> *Dreams of travel and journeys* are common in the early phase of a treatment, and usually represent an unconscious commentary about the recognition that psychotherapy is an "evolution," that is something that unfolds (a "journey"). These dreams may convey either hopes or fears, and may presage transference themes to come.
>
>> A woman patient with a history of alcohol abuse and difficulty controlling her emotions dreamed of being the driver of a large sixteen-wheel truck when the brakes failed. This dream reflected this new patient's burgeoning awareness, as she began to reveal herself in psychotherapy, about the "power" of her feelings (the large truck) and her recognition that she was dangerously out of control.
>
> *Dreams involving eating, drinking, and food* may be more common in dependent, orally fixated people who are inclined toward addictions; however, they can also be found in people with other types of conflicts or difficulties. Nevertheless, dreams that refer to feeding may be about a primary need for maternal nurturance. These dreams often have a self-soothing quality.
>
> *Dreams of amusement parks, carnivals, or playgrounds* may represent forbidden desires, abandonment of restrictions ("letting go"), or sexual desires.

Dreams of conquest or sporting achievements may represent exhibitionistic desires, or more commonly may represent an attempt to reverse doubt about physical capacity or reverse concern about bodily intactness.

Dreams of rediscovery (i.e., archeological digs, old suitcases, or old things) frequently refer to repressed material or regressive memories within the patient.

Dreams of bathrooms and exposure may reflect concerns about bodily integrity/intactness and the comparison of body parts (penis, genitals, breast, etc.). These dreams may also reflect concerns about loss of control of bodily functions and being ashamed.

Dreams of nakedness may reflect desires to exhibit oneself sexually without shame or guilt.

Dreams of flying were classically thought to reflect fantasies about erection and sexual excitement (Freud 1900). However, flying dreams may also have other meanings. Flying may symbolize a desire to escape an uncomfortable situation, or to feel independent and free. Alternatively, flying may be an expression of grandiosity; flying would then represent the ability to challenge gravity or escape being bound on earth.

Dreams of staircases and movement classically refer to sexual intercourse.

Phallic objects, such as cigars, swords, guns, and snakes, understandably often refer to a penis.

Mountains may symbolize breasts.

Purses and boxes are often representative of women and their "vagina"-like spaces.

Home and house may be symbolic of the "self" (the person of the dreamer).

Examination dreams are common dreams. These dreams typically depict a concern about being ill prepared for an upcoming exam or failing an exam, except that the exam in question was previously taken and passed! Freud (1900) thought that the examination dream depicted a wish fulfillment: even though the dream conveys anxiety, at the same time it insinuates that the anxiety and concern is unnecessary (because the exam was previously taken and surmounted). Others have suggested that examination dreams have something to do with a person's awareness of having pushed passed the limit (having gone too far), so that failure is a real possibility.

Dreams of teeth and loosing teeth often reflect conflict around the expression of hostility and concerns about bodily integrity; that is, hostile wishes will be punished with an intensity commensurate with the imagined (hostile) crime ("castration fears").

Dreams of kings, queens, big people, and giants often represent the grown-up, "big and powerful" figures of childhood.

Dreams of judges, policemen, and prison guards are often representative of the conscience (superego). The authority figure (judge, policeman, prison guard) is that representative of what one should or shouldn't do.

What Does One Do with Dreams?

What one does with a dream depends on the position of the treatment. Is the patient already sophisticated about psychoanalytic psychotherapy and the use of dreams, or not? Is it early or late in the treatment? Has the patient been able to use dream material before? Early in a treatment, a therapist must be cautious about the use of dream material; emotionally sensitive elements in a patient's dream can be frightening and potentially overwhelming. At the risk of being repetitive, the therapist must always keep in mind that a dream is only useful if it's useful!

It may be worthwhile to educate patients about the value of dreams, especially with respect to the importance of the "communication to the self" aspect of the dreamwork. Opportunities for the therapist to introduce the value of dreamwork to a patient will arise, such as: marking the potential utility of dreams early in treatment, observing dreams when they arise, listening closely to a patient's dreams when reported, and offering tactful feedback as early as possible.

Exploring Dreams

In order to figure out which dream model might best help to understand a patient's dream, actually in order to understand a dream at all, a certain amount of exploration of the dream must be done. It is helpful in the service of this goal to have ideas about what information might be useful.

1. What was the patient talking about immediately prior to reporting the dream? Whatever made the patient think of the dream is probably connected to the manifest or latent content of the dream (Freud's rule of "psychic determinism"; see chapter 3, "Formulation").
2. What came up in the previous session, and was an interpretation offered about a particular theme? Is that theme carried through into the reported dream, helping to refute or confirm that interpretation?

3. What has the patient been talking about recently? What seems to be the most bothersome issue or issues? Is any of this visible in the current dream?

4. What does the patient report after the dream? Does the patient have thoughts or particular associations to the dream? Some patients will have spontaneous reactions or associations to or even hypotheses about a dream. Other patients may be uncomfortable with the content of a dream, or simply not have any idea how to start thinking about a dream. As a technique, it is generally best to listen to the direction of the patient's own associations or observations first, before asking specific questions or offering thoughts. Frequently, only at the end of the hour or even at some later date, does it become clear that certain associations or ideas are meaningfully related to the dream content.

5. How has the patient been reacting to the therapist in the recent past? Is an issue within the transference visible in the dream, or is an evolving transference concealed within the dream (as it was in Mr. Jones's dream)?

In addition to the general ideas offered above, specific guidelines about avenues to pursue have been suggested (Freud 1900; Sharp 1937).

1. Most out-of-place element: Freud suggested that it is useful to focus on the dream element that seems most out of place or least congruent with the dream narrative. This element is usually something that strikes the patient and/or the therapist as strange: an ostensibly insignificant person from the past, a color, strange scene or figure, etc.

2. Predominant affect: What is the predominant affect of the dream; that is, how did the dreamer feel within the dream?

3. Clear sense of place: When there is a clear sense of place or circumstance, the therapist may ask if the dream image reminds the patient of a familiar place. A vivid sense of place, especially when combined with intense affect, may suggest the presence of an old trauma (Pulver 1987).

Screen Memories

Freud's (1899) concept of the "screen memory" offers another vitally important addition to the understanding of and way of listening to a patient's (past) memories. Freud observed that people seemed to have specific memories, which led him to ask a crucial and brilliant question. Of all the potential memories of childhood that one could possibly remember, why is it that certain memories are recalled (often with great vividness) and others are forgotten? This question led Freud to investigate the character and meaning of childhood memories. The retention of some memories seems logical and understandable. For example, no one would have difficulty understanding why a child who grew up in Los Angeles would recall a memorable earthquake. Other memories, however, make less sense, either because they seem so unimportant (as to be of no value to remember) or because the event that is recalled in the memory seems improbable or impossible (even though the person who recalled the event insists that what is recalled really happened).

Freud described a specific type of memory that he labeled a "screen memory." Screen memories frequently have a particularly vivid quality; the vividness is often manifested in clear visual images. Obvious distortions or a lack of logic characterize some screen memories; others simply appear trivial or inconsequential. Freud suggested that examination of the patient's associations to a screen memory eventually allows the significance of the memory to become clear. Freud postulated that these seemingly trivial memories served a "screen function"; that is, the emotionally significant material is displaced onto or hidden behind a related but less significant aspect of the recalled scene or event. Through the defense mechanisms of repression and displacement, one set of memories is remembered while another is forgotten (selected features of the circumstance are retained while much is lost to memory). Thinking about memories in terms of their "screen function" is clinically useful; it requires the therapist, once again, to listen to the patient's material and consider the story in terms of "symbolic meaning." Visual imagery and symbolism in screen memories tell a story, similar to the adage "a picture tells a thousand words." The story, however, may not be obvious.

Alternatively, sometimes the story in a memory may be obvious, and the memory may be obviously painful. The screen function, however, is that what is hidden behind the obvious and obviously painful memory is an even more painful and overwhelming event or events.

> During a treatment of several years' duration, Sam repeatedly recalled a memory from childhood. He was four years old and he and his father took the beloved family dog to the veterinarian. The dog was old and very ill, and the plan was to put the dog to sleep.

Sam waited in the car while his father took the dog inside. Sam recalled with crystal clarity the exceedingly warm weather of the day, the model of the car—a Studebaker—and the visual image of the scene outside of the veterinarian's office. A first pass would locate the reason for the memory in the loss of the dog, one of the inevitable traumas of childhood. However, in the context of therapy this memory came up again and again. With each new reappearance, other memories of and feelings about this time in Sam's life also appeared. Gradually it became clear that during this same period in which the dog had been put to sleep, Sam's life had also changed in many significant and traumatic ways. His mother gave birth to his younger brother, the family moved to a distant city, and Sam's father developed an illness from which he (the father) never really recovered and which became a grave and enduring burden for the family until the father's death many years later.

In the context of Sam's therapy, many memories and their associated feelings of loss, sadness, and anger arose, together with a powerful sense on Sam's part that life is unsafe and people are unreliable. The memory of losing the dog functioned as the screen behind which were hidden greater losses and more difficult life circumstances. Although the memory of losing the beloved dog was in and of itself painful, it was less painful and difficult to integrate than the other calamities in the child's life.

Many screen memories have illogical components; sometimes, however, the improbability or impossibility of the situation is also recognized by the individual who has the memory, although experientially this individual will report that the memory feels "as real" as if it had happened.

Lars grew up in Scandinavia. He vividly recalled that when he was two-and-a-half years old, his mother accidentally locked him out of the house without a coat for several hours, during the height of a severe midwinter snowstorm. Whenever Lars would recall this memory, and he often did, he would note the impossibility of this scenario. Of course, had this event really occurred, he would "not be alive today to tell tall tales." Nevertheless the memory felt uncannily real to Lars.

As he began to reexamine and relive his early childhood experiences, gradually the memory began to make more sense to Lars. He realized that the screen memory seemed to represent the way in which he experienced his mother. Although his mother had been at least superficially responsive to his physical needs (reversed in the screen memory; the mother left Lars out in the cold),

Lars recalled and was now able consciously to integrate his awareness that she was otherwise icy, aloof, and emotionally rejecting
(his mother left Lars "out in the icy cold").

Irrespective of whether memories are defined as "screen memories" or
not, certain select memories tend to appear again and again in the course of
the psychological investigation of a person's mind. Pine offers another way
of viewing the same phenomenon with his concept of "psychologically significant moments" (Pine 1988, 1989). Pine postulated that the recollection
and organization of "nodal" memories provides a psychological purpose
and serves "multiple functions" (a concept borrowed from Waelder). Nodal
memories may not be screen memories in the strict sense, but serve the
master of "multiple function" by becoming a way of acknowledging reality,
serving the purpose of defense, expressing a drive, providing a means of repeating an object relationship, and becoming a means to maintain self-
esteem. These multiple functions are not necessarily immediately apparent.
As a memory continues to appear and is reexamined in the context of other
feelings, associations, and experiences in the transference, underlying meanings have the opportunity to crystallize. With clarification of the underlying meanings of the memory, the fascinating process whereby memory dis-
torts and accepts logical incongruities in order to record and at the same
time protect against pain, becomes apparent. The patient's feeling of conviction regarding the reality of the memory may consequently diminish, as
the past is sorted out in the present.

Listening

The models presented above for the understanding of the dream and its
related associations condense points of view, reflecting contributions from
different theoretical schools of thought. The task for the therapist in listening, whether presented with a dream, associations in an hour, or a screen
memory, is to receive the patient's communications with an open mind or
"evenly suspended attention" (Freud 1912) while simultaneously developing
and then utilizing a conceptual model within which the patient's story can
be understood. The dream models presented provide a schema for the therapist to look not only at dreams but also at the content of each clinical hour.
The models encourage the therapist to step back or "decenter" from concern with reality alone, in order to wonder about underlying and more enduring emotional currents. This is not to diminish the importance of reality;
it is only to say that the content of a patient's associations can be thought of

not just as factual information, but also as a dream, a story, or collection of thoughts tied together by an underlying theme.

The therapist's understanding of the patient, and the patient's understanding of him- or herself is always evolving. A patient's understanding of the internal world of the self is never complete (how uninteresting that would be!), ideally continuing to grow throughout life. Psychotherapy fosters and expedites the process of opening the patient up to the curiosity of the mind and its workings. Hopefully, however, what is understood by the patient at the conclusion of therapy will still undergo many revisions long after termination and without the therapist, as the patient continues to listen, ask questions, and answer them.

REFERENCES AND READINGS

Blum, H. P. (1983). Sadomasochism in the psychoanalytic process, within and beyond the pleasure principle: discussion. *Journal of the American Psychoanalytic Association* 39: 431–50.

Bradlow, P. A., and S. J. Coen. (1975). The analyst undisguised in the initial dream in psychoanalysis. *International Journal of Psycho-Analysis* 56: 415–25.

De Saussure, J. (1982). Dreams and dreaming in relation to trauma in childhood. *International Journal of Psycho-Analysis* 63: 167–75.

Dowling, S. (1982). Dreams and dreaming in relation to trauma in childhood. *International Journal of Psycho-Analysis* 63: 157–66.

Freud, S. (1899). Screen memories. *Standard Edition* 3: 299–322. London: Hogarth Press, 1962.

———. (1900). The interpretation of dreams. *Standard Edition* 5: 6. London: Hogarth Press, 1953.

———. (1911). The handling of dream interpretation in psycho-analysis. *Standard Edition* 12: 89–96. London: Hogarth Press, 1958.

———. (1912). Recommendations to physicians practicing psychoanalysis. *Standard Edition* 12: 109–20. London: Hogarth Press, 1958.

———. (1920). Beyond the pleasure principle. *Standard Edition* 18: 1–64. London: Hogarth Press, 1955.

Kanzer, M. (1955). The communicative function of dreams. *International Journal of Psycho-Analysis* 36: 260–66.

Kohut, H. (1970). Narcissism as a resistance and as a driving force in psychoanalysis. In *The Search for the Self*, vol. 2, ed. P. H. Ornstein. New York: International Universities Press.

———. (1971). *The Analysis of the Self.* New York: International Universities Press.

———. (1977). *The Restoration of the Self.* New York: International Universities Press.

Lowenstein, R. M. (1961). Contribution to the study of the manifest dream. *Psychoanalytic Quarterly* 30: 464–66.

Pine, Fred (1988). The four psychologies of psychoanalysis and their place in clinical work. *Journal of the American Psychoanalytic Association* 36: 571–96.

———. (1989). Motivation, personality organization, and the four psychologies of psychoanalysis. *Journal of the American Psychoanalytic Association* 37: 31–64.

Pulver S. E. (1987). The manifest dream in psychoanalysis: a clarification. *Journal of the American Psychoanalytic Association* 35: 99–118.

Rosenbaum, M. (1965). Dreams in which the analyst appears undisguised—a clinical and statistical study. *International Journal of Psycho-Analysis* 46: 429–37.

Saul, L. J. (1966). Embarrassment dreams of nakedness. *International Journal of Psycho-Analysis* 47: 552–58.

Saul, L. J., and G. C. Curtis. (1967). Dream form and strength of impulse in dreams of falling and other dreams of descent. *International Journal of Psycho-Analysis* 48: 281–87.

Sharp, E. F. (1937). *Dream Analysis, A Practical Handbook for Psycho-Analysts*. New York: Brunner/Mazel.

Spanjaard, J. (1989). The manifest dream content and its significance for the interpretation of dreams. *International Journal of Psycho-Analysis* 50: 221–35.

Stolorow, R. (1978). A brief contribution to therapeutic technique. *International Journal of Psycho-Analysis* 59: 473–75.

Stolorow, R, B. Brandchaft, and G. Atwood. (1987). *Psychoanalytic Treatment: An Intersubjective Approach*. Hillsdale, NJ: Analytic Press.

Walder, R. (1936). The principle of multiple function—observation on overdetermination. *Psychoanalytic Quarterly* 5: 45–62.

Wolf, N., M. Gales, E. Shane, and M. Shane. (2000). Mirror neurons, procedural learning and the positive new experience: a developmental systems self-psychology approach. *Journal of American Academy of Psychoanalysis* 28: 409–30.

Yarmajian, R. V. (1964). First dreams directly representing the analyst. *Psychoanalytic Quarterly* 33: 526–51.

5

RESISTANCE AND DEFENSE

R esistance and defense are concepts that go hand in hand. Resistance is any force that interferes with the flow of material in psychotherapy and therefore hinders the assimilation of insight. The mechanisms of defense are the most obvious means by which resistance is enacted.

Resistance is a very old notion in psychoanalysis, dating back to Freud's early attempts to reach the unconscious of his patients through the use of hypnosis. Freud observed that some individuals were more difficult to hypnotize than others; these individuals were "resistant." Over time, the concept of resistance was expanded to describe those forces that keep (unconscious) thoughts, wishes, and impulses out of conscious awareness. Freud originally postulated five broad motivations that fuel resistance: repression, transference, repetition compulsion, gain from illness, and the superego (delineated below). As psychoanalytic thought evolved, together with a growing appreciation of how difficult it is to change a person's psychology, the concept of resistance evolved. What is being resisted, and what does the resisting accomplish? With the development of psychoanalytic theory, resistance was discovered to be a much more complex psychological phenomenon than was initially appreciated, and the utility of understanding behavior as a simple resistance or a simple defense diminished. Several shifts occurred.

The emphasis changed from the recovery of memories per se to a greater focus on understanding and interpreting transference. Transference became a way to understand past experience, and elicit memory as well as the associated feelings. Transference was viewed as a substantial resistance, but also as a means to gain further understanding of the patient. Eventually, the analysis of transference became the most prominent method through which past memories could be accessed and change could be furthered.

Another major shift that led to an expansion of analytic thought involved the development of the concept of "character." Within psychoanalysis, the concept of character arose as a way of explaining and understanding the resistance that arises from a person's usual and enduring qualities and traits, and the maladaptive patterns that are consequent to both. Character is a composite of the quality of temperament, customary defenses, method of conflict resolution, and manner of expressing wishes, desires, or needs that coalesce into an established psychological constellation and a habitual manner of relating to or interacting with the world.

Early psychoanalysts, such as Wilhelm Reich (1931a, 1931b) and Karl Abraham (1923, 1925), theorized that character is a powerful force that impedes the identification of affects, the retrieval of memories, the assimilation of insight, and the motivation to change. Therefore, the understanding of "character" (as defined above) becomes a vitally important factor to assess in any psychotherapy that hopes to effect meaningful change. As the field of psychoanalysis has evolved, ideas about transference, resistance, and the role of character have become increasingly complex. Nevertheless, the awareness of the presence of resistance and the identification of at least some of the patient's primary defenses allows the therapist to appreciate and avoid a potentially difficult predicament. Resistance can "polarize" (as in "polarity," or the having or showing of two contrary tendencies) a patient and a therapist, resulting in a frustrating and antagonistic struggle that eventually is called a "stalemate," and in which the patient is called "resistant" (which is not a compliment).

Ultimately, the *resistance to accepting an interpretation* may be more significant than the issue being resisted, which may point once again to an issue of character (the patient's habitual manner of interacting with or relating to the world, as above). A cautionary note, however, is that an interpretation can be resisted because the therapist is insistent about an interpretation that is simply incorrect; in this situation, the problem is located in the therapist's lack of empathy, countertransference, or narcissistic response to (feeling injured because of) an inability to make sense of the material.

FORCES THAT DRIVE RESISTANCE

Freud (1901, 1912, 1914) thought that resistance, from a theoretical standpoint, sprang from five broad forces (A. Freud 1938); in other words, Freud was trying to figure out what fuels resistance. This is an important issue that therapists think about all the time, whenever certain questions arise. Why is the patient silent? Why are some topics difficult for the patient to talk about, or sometimes even to think about? Most therapists probably do not think in terms of Freud's broad categories, but instead may wonder what came up in the therapeutic interaction, what is coming to the surface in the patient's mind, what feeling is being engendered that causes the patient to be silent or renders some issues difficult to share?

REPRESSION

In a broad sense, people tend to "forget" whatever is disliked, or is painful, or is the cause of conflict. Freud was fascinated with the workings of memory: what is remembered and what is forgotten. From a clinical standpoint, what is observed is that memory is "selective," and that what is recalled or what is buried probably has psychological relevance. Forgetting frequently tends to be a way of managing pain; for example, an everyday comment, a comment that even women who have had children endorse, is that women "don't remember the pain of childbirth." Another example is that of the patient in therapy, who reports recalling nothing of the previous session. This may be due to the unremarkable quality of the session, but more likely the forgetting reflects a reaction to the material discussed and feelings aroused. The understanding of what might be omitted (forgotten or missing) from the patient's associations is as important as what is included or reported.

Freud (1908) suggested that different neurotic character types have different forms of repression. The "hysteric" represses globally; nothing of a disturbing event is remembered, not the traumatic experience, the reaction, or the associated affect. The "obsessive" remembers the events from the past, but the associated affects (shame, pain, etc.) are forgotten; with the defensive removal of affects, the psychological meaning and significance of the memory is denied.

Freud's use of the term repression is confusing because he described repression as a broad, essentially neurologically based motive for psychological functioning; only later was repression used to mean a more specific defensive operation. While many therapists might question the usefulness of Freud's ideas about repression, it is now well known (as Freud correctly assumed) that most of the brain's activity is unconscious activity, most of which can never achieve conscious significance. Alluded to in the conceptualization of "implicit" memory as distinct from "declarative" memory (Tuch 1999), innumerable automatic, visceral reactions are involved in certain types of memory.

In order to focus on and deal with the requirements of everyday reality in a civilized society, people necessarily "filter" out ("repress") thoughts all the time. The inability to repress is demonstrated most graphically in the individual with obsessive-compulsive disorder, who is unable to filter out thoughts that often have symbolic content and reflect unwanted motivations or desires. The obsessive is plagued by thoughts and emotions that otherwise would be repressed, and so must make use of a less efficient way to undo and contain impulses and thoughts; of course, this refers to conscious thought or "obsessions," or behaviors that allow an impulse to leak through ("compulsions") (Thompson, Baxter, and Schwartz 1992; Kissin 1986). Therefore, Freud's global notion of repression is essentially a biologically based, protective as well as defensive mechanism.

TRANSFERENCE AS A RESISTANCE

"Transference as a resistance" refers to the idea that the repetition of stereotyped patterns in behavior, particularly in relationships with others, is a substitute for and allows the avoidance of remembering or feeling. An example of this would be the person who finds situations in which a chronic potential for deprivation exists, and the constant potential for abandonment is likely. These interactions offer the possibility at least in fantasy, of reexperiencing and reworking old painful experiences so that the past is changed in the present; simultaneously, having to think about the primary past painful experiences and their consequences is avoided. To paraphrase Freud (1914), "we repeat until we remember." Freud (1912) viewed transference as the most powerful kind of resistance.

An example of transference that serves as a resistance, is illustrated in Sally's story:

> Sally married a man who was "just like my father," "verbally abusive and emotionally unavailable." Sally felt chronically deprived, and wondered occasionally how she could have ended up in this situation. The choice of this seemingly unattractive husband served Sally's purposes, however. Sally was able to remain continuously angry and punish her husband. By fending off memory, she was able to avoid the more profound sadness and mourning regarding the absence of a kindhearted or accessible father; however, restitution for the deprivation she felt was no longer possible in her adult life because the past cannot be changed. In the process of making use of "transference as a resistance," Sally lost sight of her opportu-

nity and sabotaged the possibility of improving the present-day situation with her husband.

Merton Gill (1979, 1982) has delineated two different types of resistances that relate to the transference: (a) "resistance to the awareness of the transference" and (b) transference as a resistance in its own right, or "resistance to resolution of the transference" (see chapter 6, "Transference").

In resistance to awareness of the transference, the patient is unable to acknowledge the presence of feelings and reactions about the therapist; therefore the patient is unable to make use of these feelings in the service of understanding and consequent change.

> Bonnie sought psychotherapy because she felt "emotionally removed" from her husband, and perceived herself to be distant from her children. She had no idea why she felt so distant, but recognized that she was missing an important aspect of human experience, and those close to her were missing an aspect of a human experience with her.
>
> Outwardly, Bonnie was very independent and prided herself on her capacity to be businesslike, unsentimental, and efficient. She minimized any feelings of connection with or dependency upon others. Paradoxically, just prior to the first separation from her therapist, a consequence of a holiday break, Bonnie suddenly decided to quit treatment, leave her husband and family, and move to another city. After some discussion in her treatment, Bonnie somewhat reluctantly decided to postpone her decision. However, when the therapist suggested to Bonnie that her sudden decision to leave everything might in some way have been precipitated by feelings about the impending separation from the therapist, Bonnie scoffed with scorn and disbelief.
>
> This dramatic scenario occurred three subsequent times in the first two years of Bonnie's treatment. Each time, the precipitous decision to leave her life occurred around a separation between Bonnie and her therapist. Eventually, even Bonnie found it impossible to deny the possibility that a link existed between the breaks in therapy and the impulsive decision to leave everyone.
>
> Bonnie's childhood was impoverished. Born to an out-of-wedlock teenage mother, Bonnie was given up for adoption at birth. She lived in a series of foster homes for the first three years of her life, but was eventually adopted by a kindly, childless, and much older couple. When Bonnie was sixteen years old, her adoptive mother died. Her heartbroken adoptive father died within a year of her adoptive mother's death. Bonnie lived with her nearby maternal

aunt until she could finish high school, and then went away to college. She never returned to the town in which she had lived with her adoptive family and her aunt.

Bonnie had a profound resistance to the acknowledgment of any deep attachment to anyone. It was the only protection that she had been able to count on that allowed her to survive the yawning deprivation and losses of her childhood, and continue to grow up.

At least initially, Bonnie evidenced "resistance to the awareness of the transference."

The second type of transference resistance, in which transference provides the resistance, or "resistance to resolution of the transference," is a more difficult concept. In this type of resistance, the transference may be acknowledged: that is, that feelings exist and are experienced toward the therapist. That the transference is determined in factors from the past, however, is denied. Therefore, transference wishes are clung to all the same in the hopes of achieving restitution for past losses.

Bonnie came to understand that her desperate wish to leave all with whom she was intertwined whenever a break from her therapist occurred had to do with a wish to be "the one who leaves" rather than to be the passive recipient, that is, to be "the one who is left." She could not accept, however, that a connection existed between her wish to master the trauma of being left and her wish to leave her therapist more dramatically than he could ever leave her. Additionally, Bonnie could not integrate that all of this had something to do with the deep pain and suffering associated with the multiple and excruciating losses of the past. Even when Bonnie did come to understand all of the foregoing, her wish to achieve restitution for all that she had been subjected to and had had to withstand alone got the better of her. Bonnie's wish to punish, retaliate, seek revenge, vindicate herself, etc., functioned to stand in contrast to and protect her against the recognition of the extreme emotional poverty of her childhood. That is, the transference served as a formidable resistance (resistance to resolution of the transference) against the recognition and experience of unbearable memory, and the possibility of subsequent "working through."

To the therapist a transference is a transference; once visible, the "misrepresentation" of or "buckle" in reality that sits at the essence of the transference concept is something to be interpreted, understood by the patient, and then "worked through" (see chapter 9, "Working Through"). For the patient, however, the transference experience is so much a part of a habitual mode of perceiving others that it seems natural, reliable, and unquestionable.

This "vision" or "perception" of others constricts or "stereotypes" the patient's experience of other people; unfortunately, "other people" includes the therapist, thus making it impossible for the patient to see or experience the therapist in ways that differ from transference-based expectations. As long as transference-based expectations and behaviors are repeated, a compromise is effected: the individual is confined to past maladaptive paradigms, even if also spared repressed feelings, wishes, and memories. The concept that transference serves as a resistance may seem vague at times, but fundamentally means that the individual, the patient, by virtue of some transference reaction or pattern, is prevented from seeing or experiencing other human potential. The converse of transference repetition is to have a new, unique emotional experience, which, even if positive, often highlights past experiences that may have been painful; this concept is depicted brutally in the story of "Bonnie."

Gain from Illness

Gain from illness encompasses the closely related "primary gain" and "secondary gain." Primary gain either resolves a conflict or achieves something directly from the resolution of a fundamental conflict. Secondary gain is whatever reward follows from the primary gain, and perpetuates the resistance once it has begun.

"Vinnie" was a "pseudo-imbecilic" adolescent boy; a student who performed at a paltry fraction of his incredible intellectual potential. He provides an example of gain from illness:

> Vinnie's father was a "brilliant" and self-absorbed man, prideful of his intellectual prowess, but was also "brittle" (fragile, easily shattered) and therefore narcissistically vulnerable with respect to any confrontation that challenged his reign in the kingdom of the intellect.
>
> Vinnie behaved like a "dunce" (pseudo-imbecile), a symptom that served the principle of "multiple function" (a symptom can serve multiple functions simultaneously) and the purposes of "primary" and "secondary" gain. His poor academic performance distressed his parents, prevented any direct intellectual competition with his father, and served the purpose of the disavowal of any wish to identify with his father ("disidentification").

Vinnie's symptom (pseudo-imbecility) avoided the dreaded consequences of competition with his father (oedipal defeat was preferable to an oedipal victory and its attendant consequences) while punishing his father at the same time. Vinnie's symptom avoided identification with a father he hated, while at the same time protected a father he loved. Vinnie sensed that any challenge to his father's intellectual superiority was unbearable to his father, even if that challenge came from his father's own flesh and blood—that is, his son. All of the foregoing served the purposes of primary gain.

The secondary gain from Vinnie's symptom resulted from the attention he received from his family and others for being a failure in school, and whatever pleasure eventuated from having an excuse to escape the "work of life" (in this case, to go to school and to perform in that capacity).

The child who develops a "tummyache" just before it's time to leave for school in the morning is another example of gain from illness: On the surface the secondary gain is apparent; illness allows the child to stay home and skip a day of school. However, a primary gain is usually existent as well.

Abby, five years old and a force to reckon with, would often "pitch a fit" with her mother, at night, around some aspect of the routine of going to bed. Defiant and obstinate, Abby would push the limits until her mother would finally explode. Abby's father would then intervene, and Abby would go sweetly off to bed at his request. The morning after these events, Abby would have a "tummyache" and become panicky about going to school.

Abby was a typical five-year-old "oedipal" little girl. Taunting toward and insubordinate with her mother, seductive with her father, Abby would act out the wish to dispose of her mother (render her useless; unable to put her to bed) and engage her father for herself (Daddy would come to the rescue because Mommy couldn't put her to bed). Abby also loved her mother, however. Therefore, the morning after these events, Abby would be remorseful and fearful that her hostile and angry thoughts had damaged her mother. Thus, she couldn't let her mother out of her sight by going off to school (primary gain).

Repetition Compulsion

Freud believed in the existence of a biologic, "hard-wired" propensity to repeat behavior; additionally, he believed that once this propensity is set in motion with a particular behavior, it becomes a force that is resistant to change. Freud later expanded his ideas, viewing repetition as the visible derivative of an internal attempt to overcome an old trauma.

Most repetitions are probably linked to and are the consequence of past experiences. These repetitions become recurring because they are an attempt to provide a solution to or are reflective of a compromise that addresses the individual's needs and at the same time meets the demands of the environment. Beyond the expression of innate (hard-wired) propensities to repeat and/or the residua of early trauma, repetitions endure because they serve a function or subserve the principle of "multiple function." For example, repetitions might allow for certain critical relationships to be preserved, or somehow preserve self-esteem, or further coping with the demands of reality, or serve to act in accordance with the requirements of the conscience or superego (Walder 1936; Pine 1989).

Superego

The superego or conscience functions as a judge, scrutinizing thoughts, wishes, desires, actions, and deeds. Classical psychoanalysis views the impulses that are derivatives of the libidinal and aggressive drives to be the thoughts/wishes/desires/actions/deeds most likely to be monitored, judged, and considered unacceptable by the superego. Less orthodox analysts also emphasize thoughts, needs, and impulses that are (were) not acceptable to family and culture as also subject to superego prohibitions. "I shouldn't be weak" or " I shouldn't want what I don't need" would be examples.

In any given therapy hour, a thought, wish, desire, action, or deed may be perceived by the patient to be prohibited. The resistance is created because in having the "unacceptable" thought, etc., a cascade is initiated in which the patient projects the patient's own internal judgment onto the therapist, and then expects the therapist to make a judgment in accordance with the patient's own superego. The projection of the superego onto the therapist is the most common defense.

> Rachael, a young woman who had previously expressed predominantly positive feeling for her father, reported an interesting, recent encounter. She was listening to her father play the piano during a party. A man approached Rachael and her sister, also at the party. Not knowing of the sister's relationship to the pianist, the man began to criticize the pianist's technique. Rachael's sister quickly responded, defending her father. The patient stood quietly,

saying nothing. Afterwards, Rachael felt badly and remembered the following incident:

> On her first day of the fourth grade at a new school, Rachael's father accompanied her to school. She recalled arriving at her new classroom, and all the other children were staring at her father, who had an obvious physical defect. She remembered feeling humiliated by and ashamed of her father.

Rachael went on to say that, even thinking about the memory, made her feel that she was "bad," and that her therapist must think that too.

For this young woman, the act of not defending her father reflected her ambivalence about him. Rachael's unconscious criticisms and misgivings about her father were echoed by the stranger's criticism that she did not contradict and the process of psychotherapy provided a place in which these feeling (badness and guilt) could be experienced, and with time, examined.

Had the sense of "badness" not been recognized in a context of safety, the expression and examination of Rachael's many thoughts about her father, some of which were critical, would probably not have occurred.

DEFENSES

The model of the "defenses" is probably the most testable and researched concept in dynamic psychotherapy. From the perspective of structural theory (Freud 1923; A. Freud 1938), defenses are part of the ego. From the perspective of psychometrics, defenses can be measured with tools such as the MMPI and Bellak scales, as well as other testing scales (Bellak, Hurvich, and Dediman 1973; Haan 1969; Vaillant, Bond, and Vaillant 1986; Vaillant 1977, 1992). Vaillant, in particular, has completed many studies that examine the defenses, especially the relationship between correlates such as long-term health, productivity, etc., and levels of defensive functioning. This research focuses on the adaptive and predictive value of various defenses.

Defenses are often divided into three graduated levels: primitive defenses, middle-level or neurotic defenses, and more advanced or mature defenses. Primitive defenses include splitting, dissociation, primitive denial, projective identification, and primitive projection. Middle-level or neurotic defenses include denial, hypomanic denial, somatization, projection, reaction formation, repression, undoing, intellectualization, compartmentalization of affect, and identification with the aggressor. Higher-level defenses include suppression, sublimation, humor, and altruism.

Freud thought of anxiety as a "signal" affect, that is, an affect that activates the defenses. The defenses then serve to protect the person in question against potential danger. Anxiety is, therefore, part of a potentially adaptive reflex. Anxiety and fear are closely related, often indistinguishable in practice. Nevertheless, strictly speaking, fear is related to the awareness of real danger, whereas anxiety is related to the perception or experiencing of internal distress. Signal anxiety is comparable to fear in that each tends to stir a person to action. When the enemy troops are cresting the ridge, a responsive action is required, whether it be to flee, ready weapons, raise the white flag, etc. When a person is experiencing intense anxiety that has arisen without a clear precipitant (with fear, a clear precipitant should be visible in the external world), a responsive action is usually the consequence, whether that action is to pace, pop a Valium, run to the emergency room, call a therapist, or employ one of the "mechanisms of defense" to cope with the rising anxiety.

Freud's theory of signal anxiety emphasizes the power of unacceptable impulses and the conflicts that are related to these forces and serve to invoke the defenses. Later authors have emphasized other potent activators of signal anxiety: the threat to self-esteem (Kohut 1971, 1977), the threat to one's sense of psychic cohesion (Kohut 1977), or the threat to the ability to rely upon an experience of reasonable ego control (Sandler and Joffe 1965; Pine 1989).

Why Is the Recognition of Defenses Important?

The activation of a defense is a marker that something of significance is going on beneath the surface of the seemingly calm ocean. An example would be the not uncommon experience of being at a social function and talking to a stranger; suddenly it becomes apparent that something has gone awry. The other person has stiffened, become quiet, and the jaw seems tighter than it was before; the other person has become "defensive."

The therapist recognizes the activation of the "defenses" as a marker for what is bothersome, difficult, and at the same time important; only psychologically significant issues activate defenses. The therapist's familiarity with and knowledge of the patient's dynamics and defensive styles is an invaluable guide in the service of choosing the most tactful and effective delivery of any interpretation.

Al was a twenty-nine-year-old man who had come to psychotherapy complaining of relationship difficulties with women. He was
anxious, narcissistic, "macho," and had a history of episodic, excessive use of alcohol, which seemed relatively in abeyance at the
time he came to treatment.

After what appeared on the surface to have been a relatively un-
eventful therapy session, Al uncharacteristically missed his next
hour and didn't call to explain his failure to attend. At the next session that he did attend, Al reported having felt despairing and "out
of control" in the interim between sessions. He had gone on a prolonged drinking binge; it was this that had been responsible for his
having missed the hour.

The therapist thought back. What had happened in the original
hour that might have been responsible for Al's acute distress? The
therapist had offered a clarification about Al's associations in the
hour. Al had spoken about his parents' chronic heavy use of alcohol, the rationalizations about their excessive use, his perception
that both his mother and father were dependent upon alcohol. The
therapist simply clarified what had seemed quite obvious; he
agreed that both of Al's parents seemed to have had a serious problem with alcohol.

The significance of the insight (clarification) and the magnitude
of its psychological meaning to Al were only apparent retrospectively, by observing the patient's intense reaction after the hour.

The direct acknowledgment by Al's therapist about the parents' alcoholism, and Al's consequent inescapable recognition of the truthfulness of
his therapist's words, must have been overwhelming to Al. The disturbing
painfulness of the insight resulted in "acting out" and "denial" (defenses),
manifested in the form of a regressive flight into an alcoholic binge. Al's behavior represented another defense as well. The episode of prolonged binge
drinking was an "identification" with the alcoholic parents (the identification is the defense), and served the purpose of avoiding the despair attendant to the recognition of who his parents really were. That is, Al took his
parents "inside his mind"; he became like them in order to preserve or hold
on to them. Colloquially, his attitude (character defense) was like the aphorism "if you can't beat them, join them."

Al's therapist felt retrospectively that he had inadequately estimated the
tenacity with which Al would hold on to his denial about his parents' alcoholism, and had not fully appreciated the consequent defensive identification with the parents' drinking. However, Al's superficial "macho" stance
and the marked narcissistic features had been distracting and difficult to

manage, deflecting Al's therapist from the recognition of the fragile and frightened man that lay just beneath the surface.

Classification of the Defenses

Defenses are evaluated on the basis of their ability or inability to fulfill a protective function, their adaptive capacity, and the energy required to maintain the defense. Defenses are not rated on the basis of whether they are "good" or "bad" defenses. The level of defense assists in identification of the level of functioning of the patient. On a psychological spectrum, how primitive to mature is the patient's psychological functioning? Generally speaking, primitive defenses are more likely to occur in patients with psychologically primitive psychodynamics; mature defenses are seen in the person who is farther along on the developmental spectrum. Defenses, as noted above, are categorized typically as primitive defenses, neurotic defenses, and mature defenses.

PRIMITIVE DEFENSES

The most primitive defenses are splitting, projective identification, and extreme degrees of denial and projection. Individuals who cope through the use of primitive defenses pay the price of a compromise in the ability to perceive reality; consequently judgment and the ability to adapt to the demands of the world are impaired. With the capacity to utilize resources and maintain relationships short-circuited, the ability to obtain reasonable gratification from life is strained. More primitive defenses also require more energy to maintain, depriving the individual of internal resources that ideally could be used in other ways.

Splitting   "Splitting" refers to the lack of integration of internal self and object representations, which results in the lack of integration of external object relations and a lack of integration in the concept of the "self." People (objects) are viewed in a "black-and-white" fashion, divided into camps of opposing qualities (absolute bad and absolute good). Splitting interferes with, moreover is diagnostic of, the failure or lack of libidinal object constancy.

Splitting as a primary defense is perhaps most evident in the person whom we might diagnostically refer to as having a "borderline personality disorder." As a patient, this person typically views the therapist in an "all-or-nothing" fashion, ignoring or failing to notice altogether pieces of reality that contradict an absolute and rigid perception. A primitive patient who possesses the dynamic of splitting may believe the therapist to be a wonderful and kind human being. Any disappointment in the therapist can become magnified and perceived as unforgivable, however, resulting in a switch to an opposing perception in which the therapist now possesses only negative qualities in the place of the former positive qualities. The inability to simultaneously integrate alternative perceptions of the therapist or other people sets the stage for a chaotic life situation and a challenging therapeutic process.

> Following each lonely weekend, Cammy would invariably feel humiliated on Monday when she returned to see the male therapist whom she saw several times a week. Cammy would spend the weekends feeling disadvantaged and longing for companionship, including the "companionship" of her therapist. During these times she would imagine that her therapist missed her, too, alternating with a belief that he never thought of her. She would imagine that her therapist was silently longing for her, alternating with a belief that he was contemptuous of her because she was so "needy." Occasionally, Cammy would have the thought that her therapist saw her as a "loser" because she was not more "put together," because she could not "make it" in a relationship, because she had nothing exciting to report about her weekends. This thought was quickly overridden by the thought that her therapist found her fascinating and enticing, and was secretly imagining what it would be like to have sex with her.
>
> The anticipation of the therapist's contempt was a projection of Cammy's own self-contempt; however, her self-contempt alternated with an inflated image of herself as an irresistible "siren," about whom her therapist was secretly fantasizing. The therapist would try to clarify these alternating images that Cammy had about herself, and attempt to explore the painful feelings that Cammy was reporting. Cammy, however, would then become enraged. She would accuse the therapist of being spiteful and money-grubbing, enjoying the "ego stroking" that he was getting from her. He (the therapist) needed stroking, he had nothing to offer, and she had it all! Cammy was only coming to therapy because she was wealthy and generous; she knew that her therapist "needed a patient."

Projective identification   Projective identification, a term introduced by Melanie Klein (1950), is a mechanism in which the subject inserts a part of the self (in whole or in part) into the object, in order to harm, possess, or control the object. Primitive projective identification therefore denies the psychic reality of the object, because a part of the self is deposited in the object. In order to occur, this mechanism requires a lack of differentiation of self and object on the part of the person using projective identification.

Projective identification keeps an unwanted affect outside of the self, by "projecting" that affect (feeling) into another person; consequently, this defense is dependent upon another person into whom that affect can be inserted. Authors such as Klein (1946), Bion (1955), and Malin and Grotstein (1966; Grotstein 1994) have suggested that projective identification is therefore a primitive, nonverbal form of communication. Other theorists have emphasized that the therapist's vulnerability to the primitive feeling that is being projected by the patient is an essential ingredient for projective identification to be effective, that is, to take hold of the therapist. If the therapist were not vulnerable to the particular feeling that was being projected, that feeling would not likely "get under the therapist's skin."

> Kimberly was a red-haired and fair-skinned young woman who was subject to severe anxiety and panic attacks. Although Kimberly was engaged to be married, she was an incorrigible flirt, and would often sleep with the men whom she had enticed. It was usually after she had "seduced a man" that Kimberly would have a panic attack. However, Kimberly's panic attacks were usually initiated not with a guilty recitation of her infidelity to her therapist, but instead by a preoccupation with her skin and a conviction that a new freckle on her skin was a deadly melanoma, which would ultimately be the cause of her death.
>
> On the occasion of one particular panic attack (following a rendezvous with a man), Kimberly spent the hour in a hysterical state, obsessing about a "dark spot" on her upper thigh. The therapist attempted to engage Kimberly in reflection about the connection between her frantic state and her guilty feelings about "cheating" on her boyfriend. It was to no avail.
>
> By the time Kimberly left at the end of the hour, the therapist found himself wanting to call a dermatologist immediately and have a "skin check."

With projective identification, the power and the disturbing quality of the patient's internal experience is conveyed unmistakably to the therapist; the therapist has the opportunity to feel what the patient actually feels. This is not unlike the nonverbal communication that exists between a mother and her small child. A small child's panic or rage (primitive emotion) is communicated to the mother by projective identification; the mother then begins to oscillate with and experience the child's panic or rage. In practice, projective identification and the potential subsequent discomfort of the therapist will be more or less intense and powerful, depending upon the therapist's ability to recognize the process and to be comfortable with primitive impulses and feelings.

For example Valerie was referred by one therapist, "Dr. A," for a consultation with another therapist, Dr. B, in order to provide consultation about the seemingly stalemated treatment with Dr. A and to provide treatment suggestions. At first, Valerie did not want to speak with Dr. B at all. When she finally did speak, Valerie attacked Dr. B with her words:

> *"How could anyone want to talk with a person who dresses like you? How could anyone even imagine talking with you, who has such poor taste, those striped pants, and tie that pretends to look expensive. You are a caricature. Most psychiatrists are caricatures and fools."*

The therapist replied,

> *"I would assume that it must be very difficult for you to have to come and tell your story to someone else, especially since I imagine this wasn't really your idea, or your choice."*

Valerie quickly responded, her tone dripping with mockery and sarcasm:

> *"That's a psychiatrist's comment if I ever heard one. Can I help it if I can't talk to someone who looks as silly as you?"*

The therapist initially felt hurt, irritated, and defensive, but then had a thought: he didn't dress that badly, and even if he did, clothes and external appearances were not that important to him. Why then had this patient "gotten to him"? Why had she caused him to feel hurt? Valerie must have wanted him to feel badly; was trying to make him feel worthless. What could be her motivation?

In this moment, the explanation came to Dr. B. Valerie must have had a lot of feelings about Dr. A's decision to send her to another therapist. Perhaps she felt hurt and afraid, small and powerless, the very feelings that Valerie had been trying to induce in Dr. B.

Dr. B said,

"How did you understand Dr. A's decision to refer you to me?"

Valerie gathered herself up and Dr. B braced himself for another scathing round of words, but the words didn't come. Valerie turned her face slightly and Dr. B could see that she was crying. He spoke again,

"I didn't mean to upset you. I'm sorry."

The tears flowed more freely now, and between the sobs, Valerie whispered,

"He must want to get rid of me, and he's all that I have. Where will I go without him? I'll be nowhere without him."

This example of projective identification exemplifies the use of this defense as a mode of communication. Valerie injects the feelings that she has inside herself into Dr. B. Thus, for a moment, Dr. B is able to feel what Valerie feels. The projective identification doesn't last, however, because Dr. B is not really susceptible to the feelings that Valerie attempts to put into him. Dr. B is secure and aware of himself. He recognizes that the attack that Valerie leveled at him is simply an attempt to tell him something. Consequently, after a moment's reflection and self-analysis, Dr. B is able to readjust himself and figure out what Valerie is trying to communicate. This is in contrast to the example above with Kimberly's therapist.

Kimberly's therapist was susceptible to the primitive panic that Kimberly injected into him. Of course, Kimberly's primitive anxiety had more to do with her dim awareness of the dangerous destructiveness of her own behavior than with a realistic fear of a deadly melanoma. However, the form in which the panic was packaged—that is, the fear of a skin cancer with a terminal prognosis—was an anxiety with which, for whatever reason that had to do with his own history, Kimberly's therapist could identify.

Projection Simple "projection" (that is, without the identification) is a related but distinctly different defense from projective identification. When projection is at work, although arising from within the self (subject), an impulse, emotion, thought, or perception is experienced as though it belongs to someone else (the object). This happens quickly and with much less effort than projective identification. Additionally, unlike with projective identification, the person (the object) onto whom the impulse, emotion, thought, or perception is projected is not susceptible to assuming ownership, because the thing that is projected does not have the required primitive, common denominator (like the fear of having a terminal disease) that is required for the "object" to be ensnared.

The defense of projection is ubiquitous, perhaps because it is a defense that has its inception early in childhood. A common protective device of children is to blame the sibling, or the dog, or the imaginary friend, one or all of whom were surely responsible for eating all the cookies in the cookie jar or drawing with crayons on the wall. Projection can grow to be a predominant defense in a person's character, or it can recede and make only brief appearances with minor effects.

Projection can be of a primitive quality, recognizable because a large amount of obviously distorted feeling or an obviously distorted perspective is projected. This is distinct from projective identification, because with projection, that which is projected is recognizable as inapplicable or unbelievable. Primitive projection can have a paranoid quality; if paranoid thoughts persist, a paranoid character structure and even a paranoid psychotic thought disorder is suggested. Individuals who utilize primitive projection typically utilize other primitive defenses as well.

On the other hand, people who use projection only during discrete periods, or when the projection is present it is of a less primitive quality, often utilize other middle-level defenses. Projection of a less primitive and less disruptive quality is surmountable with help and the time to integrate feelings and thought. The following example is illustrative:

> From the very first few hours that Melissa spent with her new male therapist, she seemed to be struggling with a rapidly evolving erotic transference. On one occasion during this period, the therapist happened to shift his position and cross his legs. Melissa quickly noted the change in posture, and accused the therapist of trying to be seductive. The therapist was baffled. He considered the possibility that Melissa's thought might reflect a countertransference propensity of which he was unaware, that he was unwittingly responding to Melissa's veiled overtures. He decided, however, that this was not the case. He was also quite certain the gesture of crossing his legs was not a part of what he considered the repertoire of his own seductiveness or sexuality. He was simply uncomfortable in his position, and therefore crossed his legs (the therapist did not assume ownership of Melissa's projection of her own sexual feelings).
>
> As Melissa's initial anxiety about coming to treatment subsided, the erotic quality of the transference became less apparent and the concern about the therapist's provocativeness disappeared. Melissa's defenses then appeared to be predominantly neurotic in quality, and she went on to have a positive psychotherapy experience.

Projection and displacement   The defenses of "projection" and "displacement" often occur together, as exemplified in the way that Freud conceptualized a phobia through the vehicle of the case of "Little Hans" (Freud, 1909). Little Hans, the son of a colleague, developed a phobia about horses; the phobia took the form of a fear that a horse would bite him. During the time that Little Hans lived at the turn of the century, horses were the major means of transportation and therefore ever present. The phobia developed at the height of Little Hans's "oedipal phase," a time during which Little Hans was struggling with the conflict between his desire to have his mother all to himself (necessitating moving his father out of the way), and his love for his father and need to maintain a relationship with him.

Freud hypothesized the following:

1. Little Hans projected his anger and competitive feelings onto his father; that is, Hans assumed that if he felt hostility, competitive feelings toward his father, or a wish to get rid of his father, then his father must in turn have exactly the same feelings toward him.
2. A compromise was then effected that allowed Little Hans to maintain a relationship with his father. He displaced the hostility that he felt toward his father onto horses; by then avoiding horses, the fear of retaliation by his father (Little Hans wanted to get rid of his father; his father would therefore want to get rid of Little Hans) could be avoided by simply avoiding horses instead.

Toby was four years old when she developed her balloon phobia. The fear of balloons became evident shortly after the birth of her second brother. The phobia imposed a substantial limitation in Toby's young life, because she was unable to attend any event in which a chance existed that balloons would be present.

Toby's mother had often commented (perhaps bragged) that the little girl had been such a wonderful older sister, evidencing no resentment whatsoever toward her younger brother, and now, even younger brother. Toby's mother was always quick to add that Toby was so much like herself; she had always had a close relationship with her own siblings growing up; "there was never any anger or jealousy at all."

Freud's model would explain Toby's phobia as follows:

1. Toby was jealous of her siblings and angry at her mother for introducing competition into her little world.

2. Toby imagined that her mother must be as angry at her as she was at her mother; therefore her mother would want to get rid of Toby as the little girl had wanted to get rid of her siblings.

3. The little girl then projected her anger at her mother and her siblings (for having siblings and for being siblings, respectively) onto balloons. By then avoiding balloons, she could avoid the symbolic wish to pop her mother's (pregnant) abdomen. Perhaps by popping the "balloon," Toby could prevent any other forms of competition from arriving on the scene.

MIDDLE-LEVEL OR "NEUROTIC" DEFENSES

Denial   "Denial" is a defense that operates by putting out of awareness a painful feeling or something that is or could be perceived through the senses. Thus, an internal or external problem is avoided through a failure to perceive the existence of certain "data." The classic example of denial belongs to the alcoholic who refuses to "allow in" the awareness of a drinking problem, even though everyone around him or her is aware that the person drinks too much.

Denial can be a transient adaptive defensive reaction to an overwhelming and specific situation, which is too difficult to manage at the time. Denial can be more extensive, becoming a pervasive aspect of a person's character. To some degree, denial is universal, and at times some degree of denial is useful. For example, denial serves an adaptive coping function in situations in which a person would be overwhelmed unless information were either processed in a graduated fashion or not accepted at all. Some degree of denial is part of the normal process of grief when a person is informed of the death or terminal illness of a loved one. Some degree of denial is part of the normal process of grief when a person is presented with a diagnosis of a terminal illness.

Denial is a ubiquitous defense: it can be applied in most or all situations, and it is rarely influenced by education or social class. Even a cardiologist, in the face of crushing chest pain, may deny the possibility of a cardiac etiology. Running up a flight of stairs in the hospital to visit the next patient the cardiologist attempts to deny that the pain is significant.

Naïveté   To be naive, is to be "foolishly simple ... childlike ... or unsophisticated" (*Webster's Twentieth-Century Dictionary*). "Psychological naïveté" is a more complicated phenomenon, which serves as a defense, and is closely related to denial. Psychological naïveté has a life of its own, persisting in a person who should not be naive, because sufficient intelligence, experience, and education are present (so that the person should not be naive).

Naïveté, or the state of being naive, can in some individuals exist as a character trait of long standing. The major component of naïveté is denial. The adage "hear no evil, see no evil, speak no evil" conveys the idea most aptly. With naïveté, the individual who is naive denies the presence of perceptions or knowledge that would be uncomfortable or disturbing. The perceptions or knowledge are usually in an arena that if acknowledged, would "upset the apple cart." An inner filter removes the noxious perception or knowledge; a revised, idealistic, and unrealistic view takes its place.

> Mrs. Q married a man who had rarely touched her before the two were married. Mrs. Q was unusually beautiful, and her husband seemed to enjoy her company and be proud to present her to friends and bring her to work-related events. During the occasion of a work-related party, Mrs. Q's husband would hold Mrs. Q's hand, reach over to touch her, dance with her cheek-to-cheek. However, when the pair was alone, none of the just described intimacies occurred, and in fact, the marriage was never consummated. Eventually Mrs. Q discovered that her husband had a long-time male lover on the side.
>
> Mrs. Q had been a professional dancer until marrying Mr. Q. She had been exposed to homosexuality throughout her career. Despite her intelligence, experience, and education in the "real" world of people with different sexual preferences, despite the fact that her husband had never touched her in a sexual way, Mrs. Q never contemplated that Mr. Q might have a preference for men instead of women.

Mrs. Q demonstrates "psychological naïveté," a defense that is closely related to denial. Mrs. Q, a very beautiful and appealing woman, should have been able to come to the conclusion that her husband did not have a preference for women.

Hypomanic denial   Hypomanic denial is a form of denial that is characterized by activity. In other words, hypomanic denial makes its appearance in the form of a state of busyness, which replaces the experiencing of a feeling, perception, or the impact of a situation. Most people can identify moments of being "very busy," subsequently wondering, "What was going on?"

Hypomanic denial is perhaps akin to the old saying, "Idle hands make for the devil's work shop" (Isaac Watts). It is probably not uncommon to hear very busy professional people comment that the only thing worse than working too hard is not working at all. Even in the event that finances are secure, some people find the activity of working preferable to the activity of thinking, especially if thinking becomes about that which is worrisome or disturbing. For some constantly busy individuals, activity or hypomanic denial may become a character trait.

> Mr. B was a successful businessman. His success was the product of hard work, tenacity, and innate business intelligence. He longed for the time when he would be sufficiently financially secure to retire, and then be able to spend leisure time with his long-time and beloved wife.
>
> Around the time that Mr. B was close to achieving his goal, his wife decided to go away for a "women's weekend" with several close friends. Several days into his wife's trip, Mr. B received a call from the local sheriff's department in the town to which his wife had gone. She and her friends had been killed in a head-on collision with a drunk teenager, who had lost control of the car and crossed the center divider.
>
> Mr. B went to work the day after he received the news, and worked long hours. He went to work and worked long hours the day after that, and the day after that, and the day after that, punctuated only by the time taken to make funeral arrangements and the time period of the actual funeral. Then Mr. B went back to work and worked long hours the day after that, and the day after that, and the day after that . . .

Mr. B could not manage the news about his beloved wife; he could not manage the reality of her death. He made use immediately of the defense of hypomanic denial to avoid the reality of her death. He made use chronically of the defense of hypomanic denial, in order to avoid the incalculable pain of his grieving.

Somatization   Somatization, comes from the Greek *soma*, "a dead body" or "the body as opposed to the spirit" (*Webster's Twentieth-Century Dictionary*). To somatize means to express a psychological feeling or thought through the venue of the body, or by means of a bodily sensation or concern. A woman who had just received news that a close friend had finally died of a long-standing illness said, "I don't know what is wrong with me. I feel sick to my stomach and my head is pounding." Children who don't want to go to school often develop "tummyaches." Somatization usually has elements of primary and secondary gain.

The "choice" of somatization as a defense usually has cultural determinants, and is or can be further influenced by environmental modeling. A family who communicates distress through "succumbing" to frequent physical complaints and illnesses, rather than being in contact with and therefore expressing uncomfortable or distressing feelings directly, produces a "culture medium" for the "infection" of somatization. This situation is particularly prevalent in cultures in which the expression of sexual or aggressive feelings, particularly by women, is forbidden. Additionally, even across varying cultural and social groups, the expression of "neediness" or demonstration of (emotional) dependency is eschewed in certain families, except within the context of a physical illness. Somatization may also emerge in the context of real medical illness; this is particularly true with children, or with people who are not able to access feeling states. The medical illness lays down a pathway in the mind that is returned to in the context of subsequent stressful events, especially if the stressful event is reminiscent or evokes images of the previous illness. The defense of somatization usually has a complex origin, may be unalterably ingrained, and may be difficult to manage or to change.

Conversion   Webster's Dictionary defines conversion as "a turning or change from one state to another." "Conversion" as a phenomenon and a defense is defined as follows: A "symbolic representation of psychical conflict in terms of motor or sensory manifestations . . . the symbolization is the means by which repressed instinctual tendencies gain external expression" (Hinsie and Campbell 1970). The defense of conversion is infrequently encountered or identified in present-day North American and European cultures. Conversion is, however, commonly encountered among some Middle Eastern and Latin American cultures. Conversion was a relatively common phenomenon in Freud's time.

Freud's theory of conversion was that an impulse or forbidden wish was discharged through the route of a somatic symptom. Furthermore, he hypothesized that since both the forbidden impulse and the accompanying prohibition were (somatically) discharged simultaneously, the symptom could occur without any conscience awareness of its origin. A classic, but admittedly overly simplistic and perhaps apocryphal, example is the person who is tempted to masturbate but feels conflicted and guilty about doing so. Thus, after some initial stimulation and rise in sexual tension, the person's arm becomes paralyzed. The theoretical explanation from Freud's perspective is that the arm that otherwise would have been used to masturbate becomes unusable; this "symptom" then somatically expresses "the forbidden impulse" (the desire to masturbate and become sexually excited) and the "accompanying prohibition" (the impulse is forbidden, and so the arm is prohibited from carrying out the impulse to masturbate).

Emotionality   "Emotionality" is the "quality or condition of being emotional" (*Webster's Twentieth-Century Dictionary*). When emotionality is used as a defense, the adage "light one fire so another will not be seen" applies. An often exaggerated and visible emotional state masks another underlying and more overwhelming internal state. A common example of emotionality at work is with the person who is seriously medically ill, and is loudly demanding and angry in order to mask a more significant emotional state of fear, helplessness, and hopelessness.

Regression   Regression means to move backward, or to go in reverse. "Regression" as a defense means to return to an earlier developmental stage, in which a less advanced means of adaptation or method of managing or coping existed. If the therapist is unfamiliar with the patient, regression may be a more difficult defense to recognize or evaluate than some of the other defenses. This is because the recognition of a regression is dependent upon foreknowledge of the patient's highest (most mature) level of adaptation. Most people, even "psychologically healthy" or mature people, will "regress" in the face of certain characteristic situations. These situations include fatigue or overwork, stress or the worry about a threatening external situation, illness, and the state of loss or mourning.

What are the markers for a state of regression?

1. Regression is recognizable when the regressed state clearly contains a significant element or elements of a prior developmental stage or stages. Overeating, drinking, or use of drugs (the "incorporation" of substances for the purpose of self-soothing) is reminiscent of the wish for an "oral" form of comfort or gratification.
2. Regression may be visible because a loss of the usual repertoire of ego functions is evident. Regression would be suggested with a loss of judgment or the ability to plan ahead and/or foresee the consequences of one's actions, a loss of the ability to be self-protective or self-preservative, a loss of the ability to assess reality (reality testing), and a loss of the ability to relate to people in a successful manner (object relations).
3. Regression may be visible because of a loss of the ethical and moral boundaries that usually characterize a given person.

An example of the use of regression as a defense follows:

Brady was angry and upset with his girlfriend, who had refused to have sex with him on a particular night. He described this and the series of events that followed to his therapist. As Brady drove away from his girlfriend's house, his initial intense anger soon gave way to a sense of despair. This sense of despair took the form of an irresistible desire to have a cigarette: smoking was a habit that he had recently given up. He then obsessed about chewing gum, switched to thinking about getting something to eat, turned back again to thinking about cigarettes, and eventually succumbed to his desire for a cigarette. Brady stopped at a gas station and bought a pack.

Brady's sexual frustration and feelings of rejection and belittlement following his girlfriend's physical rejection of him led to a regression to oral forms of comfort. Of course, it is possible that this episode demonstrated not a temporary regression in the face of a narcissistic injury (that his girlfriend did not want to have sex with him), but an index of Brady's developmental maturity. The urgent need for sex (enough so that the frustration of his urgent need eventuated in the above response) could be a need of the oral variety as well. This is the reason that a foreknowledge of the patient is useful and necessary in order to differentiate regression (as a defense) from a prior developmental fixation.

Marianne was a very independent woman. Although her boyfriend Chris was quite smitten and certainly devoted to her, Chris often wished that Marianne would sacrifice some of her need to be independent in order to be more available and affectionate with him.

Marianne developed an acute pyelonephritis (kidney infection). Chris took her to the emergency room and Marianne was hospitalized for several days. During this period of high fever and terrible discomfort, Marianne was very affectionate. She begged Chris to stay with her at night, implored him to lie in bed and cuddle with her during the day, and reiterated again and again how much she loved him and wanted to marry him.

The antibiotics took effect, Marianne's kidney infection subsided, and she felt again like a human being. The daytime cuddling disappeared, Marianne went back to her former schedule of not wanting to spend every night with Chris (they had separate apartments). She no longer spoke of wanting to marry "sooner rather than later."

Marianne suffered a temporary regression in the context of an acute medical illness, which impaired the usual background rhythm of her ego functions. When her illness remitted, the "needy" and dependent quality that she had displayed during that regressed period disappeared.

Repression   To restate the above explanation of the defense of repression: "in a broad sense, people tend to 'forget' whatever is disliked, is painful, or is the cause of conflict." Thus, with the defense of repression, the individual has literally "forgotten" painful affects and/or memories. The memory of a past trauma or conflict may be "forgotten," or the memory of a past trauma or conflict may be remembered, however the painful feelings that accompanied the memory are "forgotten." In this context, "forgotten" really means that the memory of a feeling state is deleted from the individual's conscious awareness. As with an accidental erasure on a computer screen, the deleted section is not altogether irretrievable all of the time, but a lot of work may be required to retrieve the "deleted passage."

> Glen had had a bad day. He felt irritable, depressed, and pessimistic. The problem was that he could not figure out what would have caused him to feel as he did. Nothing out of the ordinary had happened, and he wasn't tired or ill. While driving home in his car, he reviewed in his mind the events of the day; nothing at all stood out. Glen arrived home and told his wife that he had "had a bad day" and he couldn't figure out why. His wife said, "Perhaps you have 'forgotten.' Today is the tenth anniversary of your father's suicide."

Glen's wife was able to remember the exquisitely painful "passage" that was "deleted" from Glen's mind. The danger of repression is that the sentiment that is "forgotten" will reappear or "come out" in some other form. This occurrence can eventuate in "symptoms," such as Glen's depressed and pessimistic state.

Identification   "Identification" means to take into the self an aspect or aspects of another person. The aspect that is internalized may be a quality, characteristic, gesture, value or belief, goal or aspiration, or an attitude. Identifications are usually unconscious or preconscious; the aspect that is internalized is experienced as though it were a seamless part of the self, a fluid part of the self-representation. Attention must first be called to the identification, and thought is then required in order to figure out from where the quality, characteristic, gesture, value or belief, goal or aspiration, or attitude came.

Dr. Spiro, a psychotherapist, had a patient who had developed a serious medical illness during the treatment. As the patient spoke one day, through tears, of her sense of despair and her belief that she had done something "bad" that had caused this to happen to her, Dr. Spiro found himself quietly saying, "Sometimes, bad things happen to good people." The patient stopped crying and responded, "I can see that that could be the case."

After the hour, Dr. Spiro had an odd feeling. The phrase had just come out of him, as though from nowhere. Then he remembered. Early in the medical part of his training, Dr. Spiro had watched a wonderful family, with whom he had become quite involved, lose a beautiful and brilliant child to leukemia. The situation had torn him apart. One day, as he discussed with his psychoanalyst his incredulity at the cruelty of fate, his analyst had said to him, "Sometimes, bad things happen to good people." Dr. Spiro recalled that at the time his analyst spoke these words, the simple comment had somehow made great sense to him, and been strangely and enduringly comforting.

The above small example of an identification provided a useful addition to Dr. Spiro's repertoire as a therapist and as a person. The phrase that his analyst spoke was more than an empathic comment; the phase was a maxim about life, an evidence of the humanity and wisdom of the analyst, a description of the character of the person who spoke it. It was actually all of this that Dr. Spiro had taken inside himself, identified with, and incorporated into his self-representation.

Identification can also function, however, in a manner that is pathologic. With a pathologic identification, or an identification in the service of defense, the identification serves the purpose of protecting the individual who uses the defense against some underlying anxiety.

Tammy was just like her mother, a beautiful, superficial, and narcissistic woman who made use of Tammy as a companion for the mother's various adult activities. From the time that Tammy was six or seven years old, and in between her mother's marriages or affairs, Tammy accompanied her mother on elaborate adult vacations, went to parties with people three times her age, participated in activities and sports that were not appropriate for a child, and was dressed for all occasions to match her mother's expensive tastes.

Tammy's mother was independently and extremely wealthy. She had been married multiple times (Tammy was a product of

the second marriage), and had had multiple boyfriends in between marriages. Tammy's mother drank too much, "partied" too
hard, and never worked at a job a day in her life. Tammy's mother
was a "socialite." Social standing was her only major aspiration
("ego ideal").

By the time Tammy was fourteen, she was having indiscriminate
sex with boys, getting drunk on a regular basis, and getting failing
grades at her exclusive private school, despite intelligence in the
superior range. Tammy came to treatment when she was sixteen
years old, and then only because it was a condition of her continued attendance at the private school in which she had previously
been a student in relatively good standing.

Tammy's therapist found it impossible to engage Tammy in any
reflection about the destructiveness of her behavior, or the dynamics that might explain it. Tammy was unable to reflect about her
mother and the tie between the two in any way. She became angry and sullen in the face of suggestions or attempts on the part of
her therapist to explore the deep connection and identification that
Tammy had with her mother.

Tammy was desperately afraid of losing her mother, the only parent
that she had ever had much of a relationship with. Tammy's father had had
little to do with her since the divorce when she was three years old, largely
because Tammy's mother had made any relationship between father and
daughter impossible. However, the relationship with her mother was con-
ditional, tenuous, and unreliable. When her mother had a boyfriend or a
husband, she was not very interested in Tammy. When her mother had a
"pressing" social activity (which was most of the time) and she was not
with a boyfriend, Tammy could spend time with her mother if she were
able to blend in with the mother's activity. Tammy became "like" her
mother (identification) in order not to lose her; she joined the world of
the "socialite" (identification) because life in the fast track was better than
life alone.

The person who uses the defense of identification becomes like someone else, and loses the recognition and possibility of experiencing differences in feelings and thought. Tammy had become like her mother, and
there was nothing the therapist or anyone else could do about it. Tammy's
story is an example of a "characterologic" identification. Her identification
was not simply a "moment-to-moment" identification, as a small daughter
might walk around in her mother's shoes. Tammy's identification had become inextricably welded into her character.

Identification with the aggressor Identification with the aggressor is a specific form of identification in which the identification is with the aggressive—that is threatening or frightening aspect—of the object of identification. Identification with the aggressor follows the aphorism, "If you can't beat 'em, join 'em."

> Ben's father was a bully. Huge and frightening, Ben's father was intimidating to everyone, especially to Ben because Ben lived with him. Ben had a paper route. Every weekday, he would wake at 4 A.M. in order to complete his route and ready himself to catch the bus to school at 6 A.M. Every weekend day, Ben would rise at 6 A.M. in order to complete his route before starting the many chores assigned him on his father's working farm. Ben was always exhausted. Every week when Ben collected the pay for his paper route, his father would confiscate his money.
>
> By the time Ben was in eighth grade, he was a bully on the schoolyard. Picking on the smallest and, therefore, most vulnerable boys, Ben would threaten to beat up the boys if they failed to turn over all of their lunch money to Ben. Ben collected on a weekly basis, and carefully counted every penny to make sure that he hadn't been cheated.

An example of "identification with the aggressor" in a psychotherapy process appears in the following example:

> A patient had a severely critical mother who was quite preoccupied with the evils of sexuality. The mother was often suspicious that the patient's motivations were deviously sexual; the mother was hostile to any overt sexual interest or flirtation manifested by her daughter.
>
> The patient would react angrily every time her therapist would bring up any sexual content, as if he, like her mother, was implying that she was evil, devious, and sexually preoccupied. Gradually, the therapist became wary of mentioning sexuality at all.
>
> One day, after many months of therapy, while the patient was talking about the sexual attitudes of teenagers, the patient noted that the therapist had not commented on the subject for months. With a sudden sense of clarity, the therapist realized that the patient had intimidated him. Just as the patient had experienced her mother, the patient had behaved toward the therapist in an aggressive, intimidating, controlling, and attacking manner whenever anything remotely suggestive of sexuality was referred to by him.

In this way, the patient had become the "aggressor" with the therapist. This is also an example of projective identification.

Obsessive defenses   To "obsess" is to be preoccupied with or become "stuck" on a particular idea or thought. Sandler and Joffe (1965, 431) observed that defenses can be conceptualized as "special adaptations of normal ego functions"; that is, certain cognitive functions appear with a particular intensity. Denial is related to the processes involved in normal concentration and attention. Repression is related to the normal processes of "clearing the perceptual field and separating the present perception from memories of the past." Displacement can be seen as an application of the ego functions of symbol formation and sublimation (Sandler and Joffe 1965).

The person with an obsessive personality or character style relies upon an exaggerated form of the desire for mastery (an ego function), which appears in the form of an exaggerated attempt to control circumstances. The neurotic defenses of reaction formation, undoing, isolation of affect, and intellectualization are defensive attempts to "master" a difficult or overwhelming situation.

Reaction formation   "Reaction formation" means that an unconscious reaction, feeling, or thought is turned into its opposite. A woman, who hated the ocean and therefore hated all water sports, spoke of her love of water skiing.

A man in his late fifties was hospitalized for a work-up of a GI bleed. The patient made inappropriate sexual remarks, and on more than one occasion exposed his genitalia to the nursing staff and the young female house-staff physician, who had the misfortune to be on call when the patient was admitted (therefore, he became her patient).

The young woman doctor would become distinctly uncomfortable whenever around the patient, and her anger seemed to be clearly written on her face. However, when a seasoned male nurse, offended by the patient's treatment of the young woman doctor, asked the physician how she could be so respectful and kind to a patient who was so disrespectful to her, the young doctor seemed startled and perplexed by the nurse's remark.

What characterizes the young woman's reaction to the patient as a reaction formation is the unconscious nature of her behavior. She did not respond to the nurse with any of the variety of mature (and conscious) responses that might have made sense under the circumstances, like a variation on the theme of "one bad deed does not deserve another." Rather, she seemed unaware of the contradictory nature of her observable anger toward and discomfort around the patient, and her unusually solicitous treatment of him.

Undoing   Undoing is a cousin to reaction formation; in undoing, however, the defended-against thought or feeling actually slips out. The person who has lost control of the thought or feeling then attempts to "undo" the error by means of a counter-behavior.

> A female nurse, who worked on an inpatient psychiatric unit, greeted the male director of the unit on one particular morning by commenting that the color of the director's pants was "revolting." She then left the room. Moments later she reappeared, and noted that she really loved the director's shirt.

The nurse was particularly peeved with this new, arrogant, and not easily approachable director. While he had been on the unit as a director for only a few months, she had worked the unit for fifteen years. The director behaved, however, as though no one knew more than he about psychiatric patients and an inpatient unit, and he made it clear to all the staff, that they were to show him unquestioned respect.

In fact, this experienced female nurse thought that the whole of the new director (not just his pants) was "revolting." Her true feelings leaked out; she then felt a defensive need to "undo" the remark by making a complimentary remark, as if the slight could be retracted.

> In a therapy hour a patient began to refer to his father as a man of "narrow vision." He quickly seemed to catch himself, then adding that his father was a "damn good neighbor." He spent most of the rest of the therapy hour, detailing his father's virtues to his therapist.
>
> At the end of the hour, the patient paused and said, "Whew, what was all that about?"

The patient had offered a criticism about his father; the criticism activated guilt and anxiety, leading to the "undoing" that was manifest in his effusive and yet stilted praise of his father.

Intellectualization   Intellectualization is a common and seemingly efficient defense in which intellectual concepts or the words that are used to describe events are focused upon, serving the function of stifling the emotional significance of the content. The position is rationalized as a pursuit of fairness, wisdom, or the achievement of a "clear vision."

Intellectualization serves the purpose of reducing perceptions and the accompanying intensity of feeling; the situation and the accompanying feelings then become less overwhelming, therefore more containable, and therefore more controllable. For an individual who employs intellectualization as a defense, the "leakage" of emotions seems unmanageable, and/or can be experienced as humiliating. Intellectualization is similar to, if not always combined with, isolation of affect and compartmentalization of feelings.

> Bruce was a middle-aged obsessional male patient, who would repetitively check his stock portfolio and review his money-market balance whenever he felt a welling up of emotion. In the face of an uncertain and frightening internal emotional world (the welling up of emotion), he would turn toward "reality," the intellectual world of concrete, visible, testable external real-world data, in order to reassure himself that all would be well.
>
> On one occasion, Bruce's wife was in a minor but upsetting car accident. A car made a left-hand turn in front of her, ignoring a red signal light. Bruce's wife was not hurt, but she was quite shaken up. She immediately called Bruce on her cell phone. Bruce proceeded to go through a checklist of all the information that she "must remember to get" from the other driver. Bruce forgot to ask his wife if she had been hurt.

Three variants of intellectualization include "reflexive fairness," "reflexive comparison," and "generalization." In reflexive fairness, the intensity of an emotion is attenuated and any personal opinion is minimized; the person who makes use of reflexive fairness must always see two sides of every issue, conflict, or reaction. The primary motivation for reflexive fairness is the need to decrease the intensity of affect, not compassion for or recognition of the other person's point of view.

Another common obsessive defense is reflexive comparison, or the perpetual need to compare. Every circumstance of significance is immediately evaluated through the lens of comparison, and often in relation to an unreachable ideal. The intellectual act of assessing and judging provides a false sense of security.

> A woman in her late twenties immediately began to compare any new man with whom she had a date with a stereotyped set of ideals. She accumulated her ideas about the right kind of man from various movies that she had seen or books that she had read.

Range of empathic capacity, absence of arrogance, and potential for financial success were essential criteria. While this woman had chosen particular character traits that were indeed important, the obsessive focusing on these issues allowed her to remain emotionally distant from any potential man.

Generalization and rationalization are intellectual defenses that serve the purpose of denial, by minimizing the potential affective response. "Everybody feels that," or "everybody thinks that," or "anyone would react in that way" are generalizations and rationalizations that allow a person's particular and uncomfortable feelings to be lost in the mix of the agreement of "everyone" else. That is, a person's feelings are "homogenized" in the service of reducing the quantity of affect that would otherwise be inescapable.

Isolation of affect and compartmentalization of feelings   As with intellectualization, when isolation of affect is used as a defense, an upsetting situation or event and the feelings about that situation or event, or a distressing thought or perception and the feelings about that thought or perception, are kept separated. In this manner, the emotional significance of the event and the resultant potential possibility of being overwhelmed are kept at bay. Isolation of affect appears as an affective blunting or constriction; if emotion is conveyed, it is only in a limited and nonintegrated way.

The terms "isolation of affect" and "compartmentalization" (of feelings) are often used interchangeably; compartmentalization, however, usually refers to the ability to think and maintain feeling in one area while shutting off thought or feelings in another area or areas. Therefore, the person is unconsciously able to "choose" what is bearable.

Ten months into a regular psychotherapy, Jack told his therapist for the first time a terrible story. Jack was called in the middle of the night and informed by an out-of-state police department of the deaths, in an automobile accident, of his steady girlfriend and her infant son. Jack told his therapist that he had never shared this story with anyone.

The next therapy session was filled with intellectual verbiage; no reference was made to the painful event that Jack had confided. In the following session, the therapist attempted to bring his patient back to the awful story. Jack became anxious and quickly changed the subject. Only with many months of work would Jack speak at all about the event. A very, very long period elapsed before Jack was able to return to the overwhelming feelings he had about the abrupt and traumatic loss of the woman and child he had loved.

The story that Jack told was not repressed and was not denied. Jack knew about the story. He simply chose not to think about it (and therefore, not to tell it). The story lived in a separate "compartment," somewhere in his mind. When the story was retrieved from the compartment (that is, Jack told the story to his therapist) the telling occurred with little emotion at all; that is, the "affect" was "isolated" from the story.

In clinical practice, isolation of affect, compartmentalization, and intellectualization are overlapping ideas. Specific identification of which defense is at work is not as important as the therapist's awareness that the presence of these defenses suggest that the patient is frightened of the consequences of allowing certain memories and their accompanying emotions to surface.

MATURE DEFENSES

Humor   In general, humor is a mature defense. Humor is a vehicle through which internal feeling states and/or tension can be released and perhaps acknowledged. The following example illustrates the emergence of humor in the latter part of the treatment as an aspect of the growth attained in the treatment.

> Toward the end of her treatment, Janna was able to joke with her therapist about some of the disappointments she experienced with him, and that were also about him. Janna was aware of her therapist's unwillingness or inability to give her more of what she would have wanted, and aware that some of his inability had to do with his particular character style, a style ironically not so dissimilar to her father's style. Although the joking was done in a soft and good-natured manner, a thread of remaining anger and feeling of being "gypped" was dimly visible in the humor that Janna chose. Both Janna and her therapist knew this; it was something they both accepted as a part of the "endgame" of a generally very useful treatment.

Janna's capacity to engage her therapist in this manner was a reflection of her acceptance of human fallibility, while also acknowledging the "humanity" that she had experienced with her therapist and had consequently been able to find in herself.

Humor can also be used defensively, however, in a manner that is not as constructive as was Janna's use of humor.

Lois had an uncanny ability to make others laugh, and these "others" included her therapist. While initially Lois's therapist found her amusing, and was impressed with her obvious quick wit and verbal skills, with time he found himself perplexed by and eventually irritated with her humor. Gradually, the therapist realized that the humor was made use of as a shield against any emotional state that Lois found difficult.

Lois's history was significant. Her parents were chaotic and primitive people, who engaged in frequent, frightening, physical fights. Lois eventually learned that she could successfully break up the fighting by distracting her parents with the use of her quick-witted humor.

Sublimation   The defense of sublimation allows impulses that would not be wise to act upon, or feelings that would have been difficult to manage, to be channeled into a socially appropriate endeavor or otherwise redirected down a useful pathway.

The gang member who leaves the gang and then establishes an organization that rescues and redirects troubled youths would be an example of sublimation. That is, the aggression that formerly was directed down a criminal pathway becomes redirected into a socially beneficial endeavor. The person who has suffered with lifelong depression and writes a novel about the recovery from depression would be another example of sublimation; that is, the energy that was formally tied up with suffering from the depression and managing its aftermath, becomes redirected down a useful pathway.

Altruism   Altruism can be thought of as a subcategory of sublimation. To be altruistic is to have consideration or regard for the interests of others without regard to what will be gained for the self; altruism is opposed to selfishness or "egoism." The ability to sense the condition of others—that is to empathize with someone outside the self—is probably a necessary requirement for an altruistic act to occur. Altruism develops in the context of self-awareness, and identification with an admired "object" who is altruistic (significant early object, mentor, teacher, etc.), resulting in an altruistic ego ideal.

Boris was self-absorbed and a curmudgeon. He had much difficulty understanding or empathizing with others. He often appeared stiff, rigid, and ungiving, and he was, frankly, downright stingy. In his treatment, Boris displayed all the former qualities as well. He came to treatment only because his wife of forty years made it clear that if he didn't, she would leave him. It was therefore a surprise when Boris told his therapist the following story.

Boris had volunteered to baby sit his grandson, a little boy of two. This in itself was surprising, but the rest of the story was even more surprising. The little boy began to cry as soon as his mother left. Initially Boris felt repulsed by the child's neediness and obvious distress. Suddenly, Boris had a revelation that he knew how the child must feel. He picked his grandson up, held the little boy close for a moment, and then, looking him in the eyes, said, "You must wonder if she'll ever come back."

Boris's mother went out one day when he was six years old. She never returned. Although the mother left during wartime, and the family lived in a part of Europe that was no longer safe, the circumstances of her disappearance were never determined. Boris's father was killed in the war. Subsequently, Boris was raised by a distant aunt and uncle.

In the moment of self-reflection, Boris remembered the dim, awful memories of the time after his mother left. He recalled that his therapist had tried on a number of occasions to speak to him of the pain he must have felt, and the question that must have stood motionless in his mind: "Would she ever come back?" This had never had any emotional meaning for Boris before that moment, with a grandson whom he also loved.

Altruism is a defense because it allows the person who demonstrates the altruistic act to minimize an internal emotional or affective state of helplessness through the act of helping someone else. In this manner, mastery is "achieved" over the state of helplessness.

The empathy and altruism that Boris was able to display to his grandson was an achievement of the treatment. Boris had identified with his therapist's kindness, empathy, and generosity. This identification culminated in his ability to empathize with his grandson's distress, and successfully "sublimate" the pain of his own memories, in the act of altruism toward his little grandson.

True altruism is probably relatively rare. It is always difficult to separate altruism from a person's desire (1) to please a transference figure and thus gain some imaginary approval, (2) to exculpate some guilt, or (3) to gain some form of narcissistic gratification from the altruistic act. The rich benefactor may feel unconsciously (or consciously) guilty about having "plenty." Giving assuages guilt, and provides narcissistic gratification from the acclaim and positive feedback received in response to the "altruistic" act of giving.

Suppression   In contrast to repression, the defense of "suppression" is a conscious act. An impulse, idea, affect, or perception is inhibited, and a deliberate attempt is made to set aside, forget, or no longer think about that which was noticed or acknowledged (an impulse, idea, affect, or perception). Suppression is a common and regular phenomenon. An example of suppression would be the following.

> A man had a fight with his wife before leaving for work, and his wife told him in the course of the fight that she was unhappy with the marriage. Still upset upon arriving at work with several meetings with "huge" clients ahead of him that day, he decided that he had too much work to worry about the conversation with his wife. He would put the disturbing content and feelings aside, and think about it later on, perhaps when he was driving home that evening.

CLINICAL EVIDENCE OF RESISTANCE

Is it always obvious to the therapist when a patient is having difficulty connecting with and expressing thoughts? Resistance is probably always present to some degree, but in every treatment there are times of greater resistance as well as times of less resistance. The periods of less resistance probably do not interfere with the accomplishment of useful work. The periods of greater resistance probably do.

Whether or not a therapist thinks in terms of the concept of resistance, and whether or not specific defenses are identified, change either occurs in a psychotherapeutic process or it does not. The following are general markers that may suggest the presence of resistance, and more specific and obvious manifestations of resistance.

MANIFESTATIONS OF RESISTANCE OR TEMPORARY STALEMATE

Breakdown in the flow of material   Optimally, a psychotherapeutic process unfolds with a natural rhythm (albeit unique to each individual patient) as new material (including significant memories) is presented and feelings are expressed (affects). As this unfolding occurs, the process tends to become increasingly interesting for both patient and therapist. The absence of the particular flow that has become familiar to both patient and therapist is a marker for the therapist that resistance may be present.

The breakdown in the flow may not be immediately and consciously obvious to the therapist. Rather, the slowdown of the usual rhythm may be signaled to the therapist only when a "countertransference" response be-comes evident. Common examples of countertransference responses to re-sistance (on the part of the therapist) include fatigue, boredom, irritation, restlessness, and the inability to concentrate. At times, patients may also ex-perience any of the above as well, and comment independently that their own conversation seems to lack a meaningful process or direction.

Talkativeness   The therapist finds it difficult to get a word in edge-wise because the patient is quite talkative, sometimes flooding the therapist with so much material that finding a theme or themes is difficult or impos-sible. Talkativeness as a resistance must be distinguished, however, from those occasions when the patient just has many pressing things to say and feels that time is short to express all that needs to be expressed. This later situation is usually recognizable because the story that the patient tells makes sense, and the therapist can understand why the patient feels a sense of urgency about completing the full account.

Excessively detailed description   "Excessively detailed description" is closely related to intellectualization and talkativeness, and is often a cover for anxiety of some origin. The most common countertransference reaction to any of these three related defenses is boredom, because the usual affective range that characterizes a story is absent.

> Grant's marriage was falling apart, in part, because he was in-volved in a "messy" affair with a fellow lawyer who also worked in his law firm. Although Grant thought that his wife did not yet know about the affair, he feared that she would soon have access to information that would expose him. Grant was sure that when his wife found out about his infidelity, her motivation to save the marriage would become nonexistent; she would leave him and en-gage him in a disastrous legal battle, in which he would also be threatened with the loss of his children.
>
> Grant tended to fill the hours with an endless discourse about the vicissitudes of his legal cases. He would go on and on, and on and on, about complicated and minute details of legal analysis. He could lull his therapist to sleep. Meanwhile, Grant was not talking about the marriage that was falling apart, the children that he wasn't spending time with anymore, the lover with whom he was endangering his life as he knew it, and the worrisome clues about her personality that would have led any sensible person to "head for the hills."

Silence   Silence is a nonverbal communication, which requires more effortful work on the part of the therapist. The therapist's accurate understanding of the meaning of the silence, and corresponding empathic response, may serve to demonstrate concern for the patient, foster trust, and contribute to the patient's increased understanding of the "multi-determined" nature of silence.

Unfortunately silence can be difficult to understand, because at the very essence of silence is something omitted, as opposed to something being present. It is always more difficult to understand what is *not* there, rather than what *is* there. Additionally, silence can represent a number of emotions, and can appear for a multitude of reasons. A sullen silence may express an emotion such as anger. Another silence may serve to fend off difficult emotions, such as fear or sadness. Suffice it to say that silence is usually an indicator that the patient does not want to talk about "something"; the "something" is not always easily visible to the patient or to the therapist. An exception to this rule is that silence can also accompany the end of a useful treatment. When the end is in sight, there is simply less to talk about.

Avoidance   That which cannot be handled or managed is sometimes avoided. Avoidance may or may not be obvious. At times it will be clear to the therapist that an issue or feeling is not being addressed; frequently it is not apparent that an issue is being avoided, and only in passing will it become apparent that something important is being skirted. In the following situation regarding Bennie, the therapist was forewarned.

Bennie was thirteen years old and had been in treatment for over three years. He came to see his therapist at his mother's insistence, because she was getting remarried (Bennie's mother and father were divorced) and Bennie was very angry about the marriage, and hostile at the time toward his stepfather-to-be. The hostility continued to be a significant issue, but Bennie did form a good relationship with his therapist, and the hostility became less overtly manifested toward his stepfather.

In the past two years of treatment, Bennie had begun to talk more and play less with his therapist. In fact, he seemed to quite enjoy the hours, and the therapist found the flow of talk in the hours comfortable and full. Although his conversation was often more about the many sports activities with which he was involved, Bennie also spoke openly about the conflicts that came up with his mother, father, and stepfather.

On the occasion of the particular hour in which the following vignette occurred, Bennie was unusually quiet. Bennie's therapist asked him if something was bothering him, but he only shook his head and sighed. He said he guessed he just didn't have much on his mind that day. The therapist waited, but nothing happened. The therapist offered a few leads, but nothing happened. Finally the therapist took the plunge:

"You know, Bennie, your mother called me this morning."

The therapist noted the stiffening of Bennie's shoulders and the tightening around his mouth. He felt a moment of hesitation, sensing the pain already in the boy and knowing the pain that continuing the direction of the conversation would inflict. The therapist knew, however, that he'd already made his decision and he knew the decision was a sound one. Bennie was "avoiding" something; something that couldn't be avoided.

"Your mother told me that she passed on some important news to you last night. She said that she didn't know how you would respond to the news, but I gather you were not too pleased."

Bennie continued to sit quietly, but his therapist could see that he was upset.

"She said she told you that she was pregnant."

Bennie spoke now:

"It's not about having a brother or sister. I'd like that. I like little kids."

The therapist responded immediately:

"I know that. I know that you've always been kind of lonely, wished that you had siblings. You've mentioned that before. It's about 'him,' isn't it? It's about your mom and your stepfather, their having a child together. You've never wanted to accept him, and now this. I imagine that that is why you didn't mention it to me."

The anger and sadness was now visible on Bennie's face.

"I'll love the kid (pause)." "But I hate him!"

The therapist nodded.

"The feeling you have about your stepfather being with your mother, it's something that eats away at you. But I never questioned for a moment that you'd love a brother or a sister, Bennie."

Affect as a resistance When "affect is used as a resistance," a particular feeling dominates the affective field instead of another more appropriate and expected response. For example, a good mood might appear in a situation in which sadness would have been the expected emotion. Anger might appear when fear or anxiety would have been more suitable responses to the circumstance or circumstances at hand. Any emotion has the potential to substitute for and therefore deflect another emotional state that is more difficult to bear.

Sometimes a therapist is confronted with an emotional response on the part of the patient that seems superficial or disingenuous, or the therapist experiences difficulty responding to or empathizing with the affective state of the therapist. These reactions may reflect a countertransference response on the part of the therapist. However, these reactions may also suggest that a more fundamental and potentially disorganizing emotional state lies hidden beneath the "affect" that is presented as a "resistance."

Missing sessions Missing a session can happen; sometimes unavoidable conflicts arise. When a patient misses sessions in a manner that begins to strike the therapist as recurrent, and the missing happens without a clear and obvious explanation (for example, the patient has a job that requires frequent and obligatory travel), the therapist should probably wonder about the meaning of the "missing."

Recurrent missing of hours, or the missing of an hour without an explanation that makes sense, may be evidence of resistance at work. Sometimes recurrent missing of hours is a covert method of terminating a therapy.

Lateness to sessions Arriving late to a session is a common occurrence, and for some patients this lateness shows itself to be a constant pattern. Tardiness can be an extension of a lifelong character pattern, or a temporary resistance that ebbs and flows as issues arise, are avoided, then dealt with, or not dealt with and avoided. Arriving late can be a way of controlling the distance between the patient and the patient's difficulties; arriving late can be a way of regulating the intensity of the transference experience.

Secrets The patient who purposefully withholds important information can be challenging, and impossible at times to treat. Paranoid perceptions or even psychosis can be hidden behind the "apparent secret." However, secrecy may also be the result of the intense shame that is associated with the content of the secret, and the shame that would be associated with revealing the secret.

> Barry, a thirty-year-old man who was approximately six months into his therapy, alluded to a secret that involved his steady girlfriend.

Again and again, he would refer vaguely to the secret, in a manner that seemed to invite the therapist to inquire directly, and which seemed to suggest that the topic was deliciously enticing.

Only after several months did the content of the secret come to the surface, and not surprisingly, the secret had to do with a humiliating topic. The tantalizing aura around the secret melted away, and Barry spoke about his inability to consummate the relationship with his girlfriend, and his longtime struggle with impotence. For Barry, the symptom seemed to be proof of his total emasculation. His feelings of shame and the uncertainty about whether any hope existed to overcome the "problem" (the "secret") had for some time prevented this man from making use of the therapy in the service of understanding and change.

Lying   Lying, as with secrets, can have a variety of meanings. Lying that occurs to protect against the experience of shame might be thought of as a symptom; that is, the lie is an expression of an underlying conflict. To tell the truth would be to face embarrassment or shame; to lie is to guard against the experience of these painful affects.

Lying that becomes solidified as a "character trait" is another matter. It is difficult to treat a patient in psychotherapy who does not feel an obligation to tell the truth. A basic assumption of the relationship between patient and therapist must be that it is based on mutual trust. Without this premise, useful work will eventually come to a halt. A patient can always fool a therapist by lying.

Medication use or lack of compliance   When a patient doesn't want to use a prescribed medication, is noncompliant, or misuses a medication, the reason for the deviation from the suggested path is worth exploring and must be explored. As with many other forms of resistance, the underlying reason or reasons can range from the neurotic or character resistances to the psychotic distortions that interfere with the patient's ability to carry out a plan.

Acting out   Acting out can serve as a powerful resistance (Freud 1901, 1914). The phrase "acting out" originally referred to the acting out of transference-related feelings; that is, a patient's transference-related feelings and strivings, instead of being experienced with the therapist and within the psychotherapy, are acted upon outside of the therapy. A simple example would be the seductive young woman who develops an erotic transference toward her male therapist, and "enacts" the erotic fantasy about her therapist (which may or may not be conscious) by involving herself with a married man (or more than one married man) outside of the treatment.

The concept of acting out has enlarged to refer to a more general and nonspecific set of behaviors, which share the common denominator that the therapist views the behaviors as destructive or undesirable (Sandler and Davidson 1973). A factor contributing to the broadened use of the term was the realization that for some individuals, "acting out" is an aspect of a more pervasive character style that is evident within, but also routinely outside of, the therapy. Since it is difficult to distinguish between impulsive behavior that is an "acting out" in response to the transference and impulsive behavior that is consistent with a longstanding character trait, the concept of "acting out" is less useful. Very unfortunately, the term is often used to refer to patients whom the therapist perceives as difficult.

Whether acting out is derived from something that is specifically related to the psychotherapy (the traditional use of the phrase) or is part of a long-standing pattern that is consistent with the person's character, acting out can serve as an obstacle (sometimes a powerful one) to change. Intense and primitive feelings, especially as they surface in the psychotherapeutic process, are not always circumscribed effectively through the use of the language of understanding. Sometimes intense and primitive feelings become discharged not through language, but through action. We call that action "acting out." Acting out may become an enduring pattern in which feelings are removed from the therapy and instead enacted in an experience that drains intensity (such as a steamy, passionate love affair, or a stormy and contentious relationship with a boss, or tender caretaking behavior with some needy soul), but provides no understanding of the underlying conflict that drives the acting out. The gripping quality of the relationship that is assumed in the acting out causes everything else in the patient's life to pale in comparison, including the feelings that are under exploration within the therapy.

In summary, acting out is a complex phenomenon that serves the principle of "multiple function." Acting out can serve as a dysfunctional method of self-regulation or a method of discharging tension, a way to maintain distance in intimate relationships or serve as a method of communication to important objects, or express an enactment of a past trauma that is hidden in the "story" that is told in the specific form of the acting out. Lastly, acting out may function as a displacement away from transference-related desires and feelings that cannot be addressed more directly with the therapist.

WHAT DOES A THERAPIST DO WHEN A DEFENSE IS IDENTIFIED?

Broadly speaking, three options are available to the therapist once a defense is identified.

1. Simply identify and file away the information gained about the patient's primary defenses. This information can be used at a later date when the therapeutic alliance is firm, and the patient is familiar with the concept of defenses and the way in which they serve as a shield against underlying anxieties.
2. Identify and interpret the patient's defense directly. A simple comment can serve to illustrate a defense and its purpose, such as: "You seem to change the subject as soon as something comes up about your son."
3. Identify the patient's defense, but focus on the patient's underlying anxiety, which created the need for the defense in the first place: "You seem to change the subject as soon as something comes up about your son. I gather this is an unpleasant topic, that there is something about your son or about the subject of your son that is uncomfortable or distressing."

For some patients, identification of defenses is confusing or feels threatening. For others, the identification of a defense is helpful, because understanding that a defense is at work becomes organizing, consolidating, and therefore reduces anxiety.

A clever mother, who had had lots of psychotherapy herself, fell into the latter category. She had found it quite useful to understand her habitual defenses, as well as the basic areas of vulnerability that were usually responsible when she became anxious and then invoked her usual defenses. Therefore, when the following conversation with Alexandra, her delightful, then seven-year-old, latency-age daughter came up, she felt that she was well prepared to handle anything (after all, she had worked hard in her treatment, and was familiar with the above principles: identify the defense and decide whether to file it away, interpret the defense only, or interpret the defense and the accompanying underlying anxiety).

Alexandra: *"Mommy, I want to ask a question and I want you to tell me the truth."*

Mommy braces herself. What could the question be?

Mommy: *"What would you like to know, Alexandra?"*

Alexandra: *"I want to know if there is a Santa Claus."*

Mommy thinks to herself, does her little daughter really want to know the answer? She is fairly certain that at seven years old, Alexandra already knows that there is no Santa Claus. And yet the little girl had never seemed before to want to disrupt the magical idea of a wondrous and gentle man who, at least once a year, could make wishes come true ("fantasy" and "repression" are primary defenses of the latency-age years; identify the defenses and then decide whether or not to just file this information away). Does Alexandra really want an answer?

Mommy decides to punt ("address the defense"), and hope that the question will go away.

Mommy: *"Are you sure that you want an answer to that question? Sometimes people ask questions, but they really don't want to know the answer. You've enjoyed Santa Claus and Christmas so much."*

Alexandra: *"I want to know the answer. I'm old enough to know."*

Mommy: *"O.K. There is no Santa Claus."*

Alexandra promptly bursts into tears, and Mommy's heart sinks to the floor. She knew that it was a mistake to say anything to Alexandra. How could she possibly have thought that she knew enough to handle this conversation! She should have said nothing (left Alexandra's defenses of fantasy and repression intact). Faltering now, Mommy tries to take back her words.

Mommy: *"You said that you wanted to know the truth! But perhaps you didn't really want to know and only thought that you wanted to know. Maybe you just think you're too old now to believe in Santa Claus."*

Steadier now, Alexandra looks her mother straight in the eye:

Alexandra: *"No, that's not true. I did want to know the answer. I just didn't know that the answer was going to feel so bad!"*

Alexandra herself points to the anxiety that underlay the defense. How badly she might feel ("feel so bad") to live in a world without her wonderful Santa Claus, and all the magic of those years that she was able to "believe" in him.

SUMMARY

Every therapist weighs and addresses the many different elements of a psychotherapeutic process and makes a choice about the emphasis of a given
treatment for a given patient. Whatever the therapist's style, identification of
specific defenses and consideration of the function of those defenses provides important information and helps to guide the treatment. Defenses coalesce around psychologically significant issues, and therefore help the therapist to appreciate areas of difficulty.

The goal of psychotherapy is not to become free of defenses or to
overcome every resistance. Ideally, psychotherapy serves to create a body of
understanding and a comfortable stability, within which a person has the
freedom to tolerate a wider and more complete array of feelings and perceptions; eventually, even difficult experiences can be integrated in such a
way that they become a part of the "fabric" of a person's life. This endgame
is facilitated by the ability to perceive and acknowledge that which is difficult, shame or guilt provoking, or arouses anxiety, without the invocation of
destructive or psychologically depleting defenses.

REFERENCES AND READINGS

Abraham, J. (1923). Contributions to the theory of the anal character. *International Journal of Psycho-Analysis* 4: 400–418.

———. (1925). The influence of oral eroticism on character formation. *International Journal of Psycho-Analysis* 16: 247–58.

Bellak L., M. Hurvich, and H. K. Dediman. (1973). *Ego Functions in Schizophrenics, Neurotics, and Normals.* New York: John Wiley.

Bion, W. R. (1955). Language and the schizophrenic. In *New Directions in Psycho-Analysis,* ed. M. Klein, P. Heimann, and R. Money-Kyrle. New York: Basic Books.

Freud, A. (1938). *The ego and the mechanisms of defense.* New York: International Universities Press.

Freud, S. (1901). Psychopathology of everyday life. *Standard Edition* 6: 1–290. London: Hogarth Press, 1960.

———. (1908). Character and anal eroticism. *Standard Edition* 9: 169–75. London: Hogarth Press, 1959.

———. (1909). Analysis of a phobia in a five-year-old boy. *Standard Edition* 10: 1–147. London: Hogarth Press, 1955.

———. (1912). The dynamics of transference. *Standard Edition* 12: 97–109. London: Hogarth Press, 1958.

———. (1914). Remembering, repeating and working through. *Standard Edition* 12: 145–56. London: Hogarth Press, 1958.

————. (1923). The ego and the id. *Standard Edition.* 19: 3–107. London: Hogarth Press, 1961.

Gill, M. (1979). The analysis of the transference. *Journal of the American Psychoanalytic Association* 275: 263–88.

————. (1982). *Analysis of Transference.* New York: International Universities Press.

Grotstein, J. (1994). Projective identification reappraised—part 1. *Contemporary Psychoanalysis* 30: 70846.

Haan, N. A. (1969). Tripartite model of ego functioning values and clinical research applications. *Journal of Nervous and Mental Disorders* 48: 14–30.

Hinsie, L. E., and R. J. Campbell. (1970). *Psychiatric Dictionary* (4th ed.). New York: Oxford University Press.

Kernberg, O. (1984). *Object Relations Theory and Clinical Psychoanalysis.* Northvale, NJ: Jason Aronson.

Kissin, B. (1986). *Conscious and Unconscious Programs in the Brain.* New York: Plenum.

Klein, M. (1946). Notes on some schizoid mechanisms. In *Developments in Psycho-Analysis,* ed. J. Riviere. London: Hogarth Press, 1952.

————. (1950). *Contributions to Psycho-Analysis.* London: Hogarth Press.

Kohut, H. (1971). *The Analysis of the Self.* New York: International Universities Press.

————. (1977). *The Restoration of the Self.* New York: International Universities Press.

Malin, A., and J. S. Grotstein. (1966). Projective identification in the therapeutic process. *International Journal of Psycho-Analysis* 47: 26–31.

Pine, F. (1989). Motivation, personality organization, and the four psychologies of psychoanalysis. *Journal of the American Psychoanalytic Association* 37: 31–64.

Reich, W. (1931a). Character formation and the phobias of childhood. *International Journal of Psycho-Analysis* 12: 219–30.

————. (1931b). The characterological mastery of the Oedipus complex. *International Journal of Psycho-Analysis* 12: 452–67.

Sandler, J., and W. G. Joffe. (1965). Notes on obsessional manifestations in children. *Psychoanalytic Study of the Child* 20: 425–38.

Sandler, J., and R. S. Davidson. (1973). *Psychopathology: Learning Theory, Research, and Applications.* New York: Harper and Row.

Thompson, J. M., L. R. Baxter, and J. M. Schwartz. (1992). Freud, modern neurobiology, and obsessive-compulsive disorder. *Psychoanalysis and Contemporary Thought* 15: 483–505.

Tuch, R. H. (1999). The construction, reconstruction, and deconstruction of memory in light of social cognition. *Journal of the American Psychoanalytic Association* 47: 153–86.

Walder, R. (1936). The principle of multiple function—observation on over-determination. *Psychoanalytic Quarterly* 5: 45–62.

Vaillant, G. E. (1977). *Adaptation to Life.* Boston: Little, Brown.

————. (1992). *Ego Mechanisms of Defense.* Washington, DC: American Psychiatric Press.

Vaillant, G. E., M. P. Bond, and C. O. Vaillant. (1986). An empirically validated hierarchy of defense mechanisms. *Archives of General Psychiatry* 43: 786–94.

6

TRANSFERENCE

The ability to understand and handle transference is perhaps the single most important aspect of psychodynamic psychotherapy, and the subject that separates the truly skillful therapist from the adequate therapist. Therefore, it is important for any therapist who practices psychoanalytic psychotherapy to contemplate certain questions.

1. Is the concept of transference fully understood?
2. Are the importance of transference and the enormous value of being able to grasp the way in which transference weaves its way throughout a treatment fully understood?
3. Can the therapist identify transference?
4. If transference is visible, does the therapist know what to do with the transference once it has become evident?
5. Is it possible to formulate a way to communicate to the patient what is "reenacted" through the phenomenon of transference, and in a manner that is understandable to the patient as well? This is not always an easy task.

Although the concept of transference seems comprehensible, the actual phenomenon of transference can be difficult to detect; despite its ubiquity, transference is a highly condensed, highly abstract, often invisible occurrence. The therapist has to know and believe that transference exists, look for it with persistence, and be able, despite its elusive nature, to explain the idea and ramifications of the transference for the patient.

WHAT IS TRANSFERENCE?

From the standpoint of a working definition, *transference is the experiencing of feelings, attitudes, fantasies, behaviors, etc., toward a person in the present, that do not seem to be appropriately directed toward that person, but are a repetition of an experience (or experiences) with a significant person from the past.* These reactions are unconsciously displaced onto figures in the present, thus comparing a person in the present to an internal (within the mind) template. Transference ignores time and space in order to bring together past and present. Old unfulfilled desires become intertwined with current desires; experiences with people from the past become intertwined with experiences of people in the present (Freud 1912, 1915; Balint and Balint 1939; Greenacre 1954; Gill 1982; Zetzel 1956; Sandler et al. 1969).

Complicating the story of transference, transference is not necessarily based on objective "truth" or factual history, but rather is based upon the individual's subjective experience of significant early "objects" (people) and events. More specifically, transference is based upon past interpersonal events as they were (subjectively) experienced at the time; this includes taking into consideration the filtering effect of the developmental needs and the cognitive abilities and capacities that accompany any specific developmental phase of life. That is, the cognitive abilities of an individual during any given developmental period, and the specific needs and struggles associated with that developmental period, will necessarily affect perception. An older child has cognitive capacities that are very different than those of a much younger child; consequently, dependent upon these factors, events will be subjectively experienced in differing ways.

> Jonathan and Christie were sixteen and four years old at the time their father finally succumbed to complications of alcoholism. As adults, although Jonathan and Christie were siblings, each had a very different memory of their father and his death.
>
> Jonathan had many wonderful memories of the father he had loved and shared many interests with before his father's drinking became more pronounced. At sixteen, he was able to recognize that alcoholism is an illness, and that his father had made many attempts to conquer his addiction. He also knew and understood that his father had been sober for fourteen months before his death, and had finally died while waiting for an approved liver transplant (his father had to demonstrate his strength and resolve in many ways in order to be approved for the transplant list, and Jonathan knew this). Jonathan missed his father terribly.

Christie, born much later in her father's life, and at a time when his alcoholism was already well entrenched, had no positive memories of her father. She recalled no special time or moments with him, and her most prominent memories had to do with seeing her father in a hospital room and being repulsed by his smell and appearance. Additionally, Christie's young age at the time of her father's death made it impossible for her to comprehend the larger circumstances of her father's death and life, as her older brother Jonathan had been able to do.

Jonathan and Christie had the same father and lived in the same house growing up, but they had very different objective experiences with and subjective experiences of their father. Many factors enter into the way in which parents and other significant figures in a child's life are experienced, yet all become the precursors for later transference developments. Looking at this phenomenon clinically and theoretically, transference repetition and the ongoing evolution of shifting transference paradigms in a psychotherapy process have the potential to tell a story about the patient's personal history. As might be inferred through the brief story in the above example, Christie and Jonathan had very different transference reactions to men in their later lives, which were based on their experience of their father in childhood and the significant life events that followed.

Transference often contains a fantasy of restitution and fulfillment; a person's life and experience would or could change, if only an essential element that is missing could be obtained (the person has been shortchanged). A transference object is sought, in order that this wished-for restitution be returned to the "true owner" (unconditional love, strength, guidance, approval, etc.).

The unconscious yearning for restitution, fulfillment, "true love," "unconditional love and acceptance," etc., is often a never-ending, powerful motivation that can propel a person from one unhappy, transference-based relationship to another. Christie, above, was an unfortunate example of this.

Christie felt that she never had a real father who had loved her. When she was eight years old and her brother Jonathan was already out of the house, her mother remarried. Christie hated her stepfather. She felt that he was not only totally uninterested in her, but that he was emotionally abusive to her and to her mother.

As she grew into a young woman, Christie became exceptionally beautiful. Consequently, from the time she was a late adolescent, she was always able to secure a boyfriend. The relationships with these boyfriends, some of whom were quite devoted to her, never lasted, however. Christie demanded total attention and dedication from each of her boyfriends, "a never-ending, unconscious yearning for restitution, fulfillment, and true love." Eventually Christie's intense neediness and jealousy of all that her boyfriends were interested in that wasn't about her became so excessive that each relationship successively ruptured, despite the love and devotion that many of the men felt for her and directed toward her.

TRANSFERENCE IN EVERYDAY LIFE

Transference is ubiquitous. People build up a repertoire of what to expect in the present, based upon that which has happened in the past; these "templates" create an anticipatory image of what is to come. The experience of other people becomes less varied and more stereotyped the more transference is present. Transference becomes a significant interference when it begins to affect the capacity to appropriately assess reality! Transference reactions can intrude into intimate relationships; the more significantly transference becomes a factor in essential relationships, the more restricted and constricted these relationships can become, potentially and eventually spoiling them. When in the grip of a transference reaction, the world and the people in it are suddenly seen through the lens of distortion, and reasonable or intermediate possibilities are not necessarily considered. The considerate friend or partner is now unreliable and untrustworthy; the boss ceases to become just a boss and becomes the cruel judge of a person's total worth.

The person who is less subject to being overwhelmed by transference reactions sees many shades of gray. This person knows that an authority figure is just a person with an opinion, and any excessive reaction to anyone is likely to contain an element of transference! The search for examples of transference in everyday life can be interesting and instructive, confirming not only the ubiquity of transference, but also the power of transference to influence choices, and to weave its way (both benignly and malignantly) into all kinds of relationships. Benign manifestations of transference in everyday life can be growth-enhancing. Malignant manifestations are unfortunately usually only malignant, such as the chronic and unfulfilling repetitions that are commonly seen in everyday life.

Joel, a young man who fancied himself a Don Juan, was rejected again and again by the women whom he approached and pursued.

If a woman turned out to return Joel's interest, even if the woman appeared lovely in personality and looks, in short order Joel would find some unforgivable flaw.

The "appealing" women, and the situations in which Joel found these appealing women, were almost always unusually challenging. While driving in his car, Joel would pull up next to a pretty woman and attempt to engage her while both were driving. He would go to a shopping mall, search out the most attractive woman he could find, and try to entice her. If Joel were actually able to initially engage a woman under these circumstances, he would then pursue the woman, tirelessly and relentlessly, often despite considerable subsequent rejection.

A beautiful but aloof and ultimately rejecting woman matched an old template (internal object or "imago") of this young man's mother, whom he had experienced as distant, cold, and rejecting. For Joel, the desperate and endless desire to win over an unattainable woman fulfilled a transference repetition; Joel needed to prove to himself that he could engage a cold and emotionless woman (his mother). Transference brings past unresolved needs, desires, and expectations into the present.

Transference-driven relationships cannot fulfill the unconscious intent or desire, because the past cannot be changed! As long as the transference is acted out, however, an unconscious hope that expectations actually can be fulfilled is sustained, even if that hope is misdirected and unrealistic; the wish to enact old, unsatisfactory editions of stories services the hope of achieving a better revision. If a person is pliable enough to adapt and change, gratification (nurturance, guidance, etc.) can be found in other places. Transference repetition, however, often prevents the development of mature and gratifying relationships. The search for the mythical transference figure, whose presence will (magically) effect restitution for the grievances of the past, interferes with the recognition of potential relationships that might lead to greater stability and long-range fulfillment; consequently, relationships with greater future possibility are sadly bypassed.

In relationships, sometimes in prominent relationships, the power of transference to be both self-destructive and destructive to others can be witnessed.

Carrie developed an intense crush on Stanley, an older man in the department in which she had begun to work. As her erotic feelings (erotic transference) for him continued to grow, Carrie set about the task of seducing him. Stanley was a powerful and prominent partner in the company in which he worked; nevertheless, he had a strong and transference-driven need to be admired for his power and potency.

Carrie's father had deserted the family when she was quite small. Her mother soon remarried a very handsome and successful man who was kind to Carrie but not very involved with her. These circumstances had created in Carrie a (transference-related) need to prove to herself that she could captivate and excite an older man, while at the same time controlling and demeaning that same man in order to reverse her childhood feelings of smallness and humiliation (a consequence of feeling unimportant to her father and her stepfather).

Stanley had grown up with a narcissistically involved mother, whom he constantly attempted to please, prove himself to, obtain love and admiration from, to no avail. In his adult life he found himself constantly in search of adulation, but only from young and therefore unthreatening women.

Mutually intersecting transference desires sometimes bring people together for brief and unfulfilling relationships, or sometimes for prolonged and disastrous relationships; these relationships often do not survive without treatment, because the transference wishes that brought the people together originally cannot be sustained. As these relationships progress and the transference figures melt into ordinary, real people, frustrations accumulate and the relationships deteriorate. Such it is that when the "Phantom of the Opera" takes off his mask, he is no longer an entrancing and powerful Phantom/Father figure, but rather just an ordinary and old man. Transference-driven involvements impair judgment; this is the explanation for the sometimes catastrophic results (Kernberg 1994; Gabbard 1994).

Transference expectations are probably an aspect of all relationships. In healthier relationships, transference repetitions and reactions are less palpable; the partner is more realistically appreciated. In less mature relationships the partner is experienced, especially during periods of stress, like a caricature of some figure or aspect of a figure from the past. Even in less tumultuous relationships, love is probably always fueled by aspects of transference. Until such time as a relationship evolves to a crisis point, at which time flaws become inescapably apparent, the influence of transference can render a person oblivious to the limitations of another person.

Mr. H debated with himself and in his treatment about whether to stay with his wife or seek a divorce. If he left the marriage, would he feel more fulfilled? Mr. H felt very guilty about considering this possibility and he also felt guilty about the many angry explosions he would have with his wife. He frequently wondered aloud: his wife was so much like his controlling, anxious, clinging, and critical mother, had he somehow been responsible for creating the poor situation?

Mr. H's relationship with his mother was profoundly affected by a serious childhood injury, which had occurred during his latency years and engendered great suffering during his late latency and early teenage years. Mr. H eventually completely recovered from his injury, but not before a prolonged and enforced bed rest of almost two years. Mr. H's frightened mother was the enforcer of the bed rest.

In his marriage, Mr. H experienced his wife as overreactive, controlling, demeaning, and emasculating; he would find himself furious in response. The sense of being harnessed (enforced bed rest) by his wife was so overwhelming that Mr. H would retaliate by devaluing his wife, fleeing, or flirting with the possibility of an affair. Ultimately, however, Mr. H would end up feeling sad and empty.

With further exploration, Mr. H was able to grasp the transference meaning of his reaction to his wife. He saw that his anger and reactive devaluation served only to escalate his wife's anger and insecurity; she would then become clingy and controlling, behaviors that Mr. H found absolutely suffocating. Eventually and importantly, however, Mr. H began to realize that his wife was like his mother in very significantly positive ways as well. Mr. H recognized that his loving attachment to his wife was deeply rooted in her ability to nurture him and stand by him, just as his mother had done for him during his long and excruciating childhood ordeal.

The influence of transference, inside or outside of a relationship, can limit the scope of actual relationships, detracting from the closeness that would otherwise be available. It is not uncommon to hear a man or a woman complain that a wife or a husband is more interested in impressing the neighbors than caring for or paying attention to the spouse or the children. Some people have an inexhaustible need for a response from a transference figure, always searching for something or someone else; failing to appreciate what is already "right in front of their nose." The significant other, however stable and reliable, is demeaned and discarded while the person continues to search for a transference ideal (perhaps also in an attempt to discard a depreciated aspect of the self-representation; see chapter

3, "Formulation"). This paradigm is conveyed by the television sitcom "Married with Children." Each half of the couple chronically ridicules and demeans the other half, while always dreaming of an unrealizable ideal that is outside of the relationship.

Desires that are transference derived can also lead to relationships that sometimes have some degree of stability and lead to growth. Examples of such "transforming" relationships—that is, that prompt a person to move beyond him- or herself—abound in literature and drama. These are the *fortunate* relationships with the benevolent older teacher, coach, priest, etc.; fueled by transference wishes and needs, these associations have the capacity to change a person's life (e.g., the film *Finding Forrester*). Unfortunately, such relationships also have the potential to set the naive or psychologically unsophisticated person up to be the victim of emotional, sexual, or financial exploitation. People with substantial unresolved transference proclivity are vulnerable to being hurt again and again, with the end result becoming an increasingly defensive and cynical posture.

TRANSFERENCE AS THE THERAPEUTIC KEY

Transference is expressed in various walks of life: it becomes uniquely apparent in the therapeutic setting and therefore utilizable as a therapeutic tool. The therapist becomes a point of attachment, upon whom the patient's unconscious ideas, experiences, fantasies, and expectations can be elaborated; that is, the therapist becomes the focus of the patient's transference. The evolution of transference is facilitated because of the therapist's presence, availability, and relative neutrality, all of which clear the way for the emergence of transference-based feelings toward the therapist to emerge. Freud (1912) commented, "Psychoanalytic treatment does not create transference. It merely brings it to light."

The eventual value of the therapist becoming the object of transference depends upon the way in which the phenomenon is handled. The occurrence of transference, without analysis of the transference, interferes ultimately with the depth of understanding that might otherwise become possible in a psychoanalytic psychotherapy. Although Freud (1912) was initially thwarted by transference, he realized that the unfolding transference offered a unique opportunity to understand the patient's mind. Transference is a living, breathing, personal history. Transference allows the therapist to understand and reconstruct the influences that were brought to bear upon a patient and came to shape how that patient experiences people and the world, through the revival of transference-driven interactions in the therapeutic space. The identification, understanding, and working through of transference are therefore essential to psychodynamic psychotherapy.

IDENTIFYING TRANSFERENCE

Transference can be expressed in a psychotherapeutic process in a variety of ways. These reactions of the patient and to the therapist may or may not correspond to who the therapist is, but seem to be evocative of someone important from the patient's past. The presence of transference can appear in a patient's behavior, such as an attitude of hostility, fear, or seductiveness that doesn't seem to match the present circumstance. The presence of transference can also be suggested by a patient's words: "I could never work with a person like you" or "You remind me of someone, but I can't think who it might be."

Not infrequently, transference is more visible in the patient's stories about relationships outside of the therapy and other than with the therapist. This may be particularly true in the early phase of psychotherapy, when the process has less momentum and the patient is more reluctant about or resistant to discussing the relationship with the therapist (see below). Transference that is evident outside of therapy may reveal an aspect of the patient that has not been visible in the room with the therapist. For example, one patient was surprisingly diffident and meek with his therapist in the actual therapy sessions, but it became clear that at work this same patient was a bully and a tyrant.

ELABORATION OF THE TRANSFERENCE

Resistance to the Transference/Transference as a Resistance

Merton Gill (1979, 1982), well known for his contribution to the technique of transference analysis, has suggested that the theoretical centrality of transference and resistance analysis in psychoanalysis and psychoanalytic therapy is not necessarily reflected by the comprehensive and systematic pursuit of both in clinical practice. Gill notes that there are two types of transference interpretations:

1. "Interpretation of resistance to awareness of the transference" has to do with a general resistance to the acknowledgment that feelings,

desires, or reactions could be directed toward or are possibly about the therapist, a reflection of transference reactions and transference desires. In this case, the therapist is in the position of trying to find a way to make the implicit transference explicit to an inexperienced or defensive patient, who may become anxious, scoff at, or resent any inference to this effect.

One female patient reacted to her therapist's suggestion that that she might have feelings about her therapist leaving town for an upcoming vacation: "That is the most ridiculous thing I have ever heard in my life." This was a patient whose mother had died suddenly when she was three years old; there was a long subsequent history of handling separations by having "no feelings at all."

2. "Interpretation of resistance to resolution of the transference" focuses on the patient's recognition that the already manifest and acknowledged transference includes determinants from the past, and that the tenacious transference repetition in the present (transference serving as a resistance) holds out little hope of final restitution. Retaliation or satisfaction, vindication or revenge in the present, does not change the past!

To recapitulate, in resistance to awareness of the transference, the consciousness of the presence of transference is what is resisted. In resistance to the resolution of the transference, the transference is tenaciously maintained and the patient is loath to relinquish the hope of realizing transference wishes, or to acknowledge that the transference includes a determinant from the past.

THE TECHNIQUE OF HANDLING THE TRANSFERENCE

Merton Gill has endorsed a number of general technical points regarding the handling of the transference that are worthy of contemplation. The therapist can most rely upon what is directly seen in the room with the patient; therefore, it is useful if possible to allow the transference to expand within the treatment situation. Direct observations of transference reactions and the evolution of transference are the most reliable clues about what went on in the patient's life with significant figures of childhood, what currently goes on in the patient's life, and ultimately what is really going on in the patient's intra psychic life. In addition to serving as a reconstructive tool, the real-time expression of transference is convincing for the patient in a way that perhaps nothing else is.

Clarification and interpretation of subtle allusions to the transference, and/or interpretation of the defensive displacement away from the therapist of feelings that actually are about or do relate to the therapist, are techniques to bring the transference into the therapeutic space. If tactfully and logically presented to the patient, identification of transference emphasizes the safety and value of discussing attitudes toward the therapist, or expectations about the therapist's attitude toward the patient.

> "Todd," new to psychotherapy, repeatedly discussed an incident that had occurred with his new accountant. This accountant had urged Todd to divest himself of certain investments that had been made with another stockbroker a number of years before. Under the influence of the new accountant, Todd came to believe that these investments had been unwise. However, Todd could not bring himself to talk to his old broker, and obsessed about his belief that the new accountant viewed him as a "coward" for his inability to take action.
>
> The therapist wondered aloud if Todd felt that his therapist saw him as a "coward" as well. Initially Todd disregarded this possibility; in fact he thought it was "absurd." After further consideration, facilitated by the therapist's gentle encouragement to contemplate the possibility, Todd realized that he did indeed think, "more than I like," about what the therapist thought of him. He would "hate" the possibility that the therapist thought of him as a "coward."

Some therapists don't believe that the patient's associations have transference implications from the very outset of treatment. Other therapists believe that the patient's associations have transference implications from the beginning and throughout. This difference in perspective may reflect the therapist's "resistance to awareness of the transference" and/or the difficulty in detecting the existence of transference themes with some patients. The ability to visualize and articulate subtle transference themes requires at times great patience, and sometimes great sophistication.

The task of identifying transference is distinct from the decision to clarify or interpret. The decision to interpret transference is determined most importantly by the therapist's assessment of the patient's capacity to understand and integrate the interpretation. Even when transference implications are clear, if material is still forthcoming and there is no threat to the continuation of the treatment, sometimes the therapist might choose to file away a transference interpretation if the setting and timing do not seem conducive to a successful integration of the information.

When a transference theme arises, irrespective of the historical basis, a connection to some aspect of the current situation is usually nearby. Just as the dream is connected to the day residue, so is the transference elaboration connected to something that occurred in the present. Often, when the current stimulus is included as a part of the interpretation, the interpretation makes more sense to the patient. The current stimulus might be as simple and obvious as the sex of the therapist, the manner in which the therapist dresses, or the way in which the office is decorated.

> An expensively dressed woman consulted with a woman therapist for the first time. At the end of the visit she said to the therapist, "I think you are very smart, but I could never entrust myself to someone who wears polyester pantsuits."

One can only speculate as to the meaning of this particular transference reaction on the patient's part, since the treatment did not continue. The consulting therapist had the impression, however, that a significant theme in the patient's life had to do with profound shame about her upbringing in the deep rural South, with her dowdy, obese, and poorly educated mother. Making use of this hypothesis, the polyester pantsuit, "cheap and dowdy," was the stimulus for the transference elaboration.

RESOLUTION OF THE TRANSFERENCE

Once awareness of the transference has been achieved, the resolution of the transference becomes an aspect of the whole treatment. Transference does not just occur, become identified, and permanently subside. The understanding of and working through of transference themes is an evolution. Subtle changes occur throughout a therapy. Transference themes arise and are gradually clarified with increasing precision, but the ability to be aware of the transference is an ongoing process, never completely achieved.

The therapist's tenacious pursuit and understanding of the patient's transference proclivities, combined with mastery and prevention of countertransference responses, is the best protection against a destructive repetition of old patterns that might threaten the treatment prematurely. This process also allows the patient to be treated differently from that which was expected (to have a new experience), thus revealing the transference with even greater clarity. With repetition and psychoanalytically informed exploration, each individual patient can become familiar with the unique set of potential transference reactions, which belong exclusively to that patient.

TRANSFERENCE VARIATIONS

Transference repetitions can be acute or chronic, arising quickly or developing slowly over time. Transference repetitions can be extraordinarily intense, dominating a person's feelings and thoughts, or they can be less intense, having little influence over a person's thoughts or actions.

Most transference reactions are time limited. Remember that any individual can be (in the short or in the long run) in a state of increased vulnerability (stress), creating the culture for greater susceptibility to unconscious longings. This sets the stage for transference repetitions to occur. A transference reaction then occurs, in which a person encountered in the present is similar to an internal representation of a past figure.

> Daniel reported an interaction with a supervisor. The supervisor had made a comment about the difficulty of completing construction projects in the current economic environment. Daniel felt hurt by the comment, wondering if the supervisor was referring to a long and involved architectural project that had been in his charge. The supervisor could be a remote and cool person, rarely complimentary and sometimes unpleasantly critical; these traits were similar to Daniel's lifelong experience with his own father.
>
> Shortly after the supervisor's comment, Daniel had cause to be in a very public forum, at which time this same supervisor praised him warmly about his "excellent work" on the same architectural project. This surprised Daniel, causing him to reflect about his previous reaction and the origin of his incorrect assumption (transference reaction to the supervisor).
>
> Daniel realized that his preconceived expectations (perspective, based on an internal object representation or imago) had affected the way in which he had reacted to his supervisor's remarks. Daniel had personalized, distorted, and then magnified his supervisor's offhand comment; his expectation was consistent with his experience of his father's treatment of him in the past. Although Daniel's father and the supervisor certainly shared some qualities (point of attachment for the transference-based elaboration), the immediate situation was not consistent with Daniel's interpretation.

Transference "reactions" are usually transient, as opposed to the more sustained and intense transferences that coalesce into the "transference neuroses" (see below). Transference "reactions" often drift away when a circumstance is resolved, contact with the object of the transference decreases, or reality prevails (as it did with Daniel).

TRANSFERENCE "CURE"

Transference often appears in the form of the "wished-for" (but "never-had") parent, and the anticipation of restitution within the treatment situation. This phenomenon contributes to the so-called "transference cure." In this circumstance, the therapy provides a "solution" in the form of the fulfillment of certain transference wishes or needs.

Unfortunately, as with romantic involvements that are driven by unrealistic transference wishes, the transference cure is often transient; frustrations eventually arise, leading to the realization that the therapist is not an ideal parental figure either. Even if frustrations do not arise, these kinds of "transference cures" are usually unstable, because they are often dependent upon ongoing involvement with the therapist.

HOW RAPIDLY DOES TRANSFERENCE DEVELOP?

With what rapidity or slowness obvious transference will develop can be an unknown. Transference often becomes visible slowly, especially with neurotic or higher-functioning patients, necessitating that the therapist look for more subtle clues.

> A neurotic patient who said little that reflected a reaction toward the therapist and evidenced no concern about the therapist's opinion, mentioned at the end of an hour that the artwork in the therapist's office closely corresponded to the patient's taste.

This kind of reference might be the first indication of transference at work. In contrast, with patients that function less well (more primitive patients), transference might burst out from the first session onward.

> A patient commented on the therapist's expensive shoes, certain that the therapist was greedy and looking to take advantage of the patient.

A female patient with a male therapist took note of the attractiveness of her therapist and winked, believing that a relationship of more intimacy between herself and the therapist was a distinct possibility.

TRANSFERENCE NEUROSIS

"Transference neurosis" is a term that describes an intense form of transference that evolves during a psychoanalytic experience, replicates the prior childhood neurosis, and in its endurance and power becomes a force within the therapeutic process. Typically, a transference neurosis arises and is visible only in a long-term therapy, such as psychoanalysis. When a patient meets with a therapist four or five times a week, the therapist becomes a cornerstone in the patient's emotional life; this involvement permits the kind of concentration of feelings and emotions on the person of the therapist that allows for the development of the transference neurosis. The frequency and intensity of this kind of a treatment also allows the therapist to explain and demonstrate to the patient the importance and value of reconstructing the "original" neurosis.

The usefulness of an intense and prolonged transference experience, and the utility of the conceptualization of "transference neurosis" has been debated. The phrase highlights a distinct degree and type of transference experience; in this sense, it may be a useful concept. Brian Bird (1972), referring to psychoanalytic treatment, suggests that an intense experience is essential for the understanding and resolution of a neurosis. He also suggests that it can be difficult for a therapist to analyze tenaciously and endure being in the middle of a patient's transference neurosis.

During the middle phase of a treatment in which a transference neurosis has taken shape, transference-based distortions assume a life of their own, becoming less specifically and directly attached to stimuli that have a basis in reality. For example, in order for a transference reaction to occur, something that the therapist does or says has to stimulate a latent reaction on the part of the patient. Once the transference neurosis is set, the linkage between the therapist's actions (or lack of actions) and the patient's reaction to the therapist's actions is less clear. These more enduring transference reactions can activate countertransference correlates in the therapist; as Brian Bird would argue, within the context of the transference neurosis the therapist becomes part of the patient's neurosis and a loss of boundaries between patient and therapist occurs.

TYPES OF TRANSFERENCES

Broadly speaking, transference can be divided into categories or groupings. These groupings can be defined based upon the particular emotional tone of the transference (negative, positive, erotic, etc.), or the type of object transference (father, mother, grandparent, etc.). With respect to the latter, in practice, it is usually an aspect of another person that appears in the transference (part-object transferences) or a needed function that is being obtained through the transference (self-object transference). A loss of reality testing can be manifested in the so-called "psychotic transference."

Categories help to begin to define the particular type(s) of transference(s) that may be operative, and allow for further assessment of the level of functioning of the patient. Patients with primitive pathology are more likely to develop part-object transferences, and rapid and intense transference reactions, and are more vulnerable to developing psychotic transferences. In comparison, neurotic individuals typically have slowly evolving and less intense transferences; these transferences are more likely to have a whole-object quality and to shift less rapidly over time.

Whole-Object Transference

The whole-object transference tends to appear with more neurotic individuals, who react to the therapist in a way that is reminiscent of a parent or significant person from the past. This term is somewhat of a misnomer, since all transference experiences are about "aspects" of a past figure as opposed to the "whole person" of a past figure. Most importantly, when it is operative, transference makes it impossible to see another person in an unbiased fashion. Transference interferes with clarity of vision, and this lack of clarity clouds the lens through which the other person is viewed. Nevertheless, the distinction between whole-object and part-object transferences can be useful. Some transferences have a more distinct quality; the other person is reacted to in a very similar manner as to an enduring and recognizable figure from the past. This is as opposed to the transference in which no clearly recognizable reference to a past figure appears; only fragmented qualities are responded to—that is, the part-object transference.

Part-Object Transference

The most obvious example of a part-object transference/"part-object" relationship is visible with the man who treats women only as sex objects.

The woman's body (or even a part of her body—breasts, legs) is the part object; consideration is not given to the possibility that the woman is a person, and that a person has independent feelings and needs.

> A male patient with a woman therapist spoke long hour after hour about the therapist's various physical attributes; he detailed his wish to travel through her body as though he were on a train, stopping at the various stations (body parts) that were arousing to him. Other facets of the therapist were unimportant to him, even experienced as an intrusion. Not surprisingly, this therapist had some difficulty enduring this transference configuration.

Self-Object Transference

The self-object transference was described by Kohut (1971, 1977, 1980) and elaborated by the many followers of self-psychology (Kohut and Wolf, 1978). The self-object transferences were first identified as primary transference patterns in narcissistically disturbed individuals; Kohut and others have argued, however, that self-object transference is a dimension of all transference. The self-object transference may be more apparent at one point in time. At another time, the self-object aspect of the transference may move to the background, and a more traditional and conflict-based transference will become obvious instead. Self-object needs, and the potential to develop a self-object transference, are present within every individual; even those who are primarily neurotic and have minimal narcissistic pathology can experience a self-object transference.

Kohut (1971, 1977, 1980) described four overlapping subcategories of self-object transference:

MIRROR TRANSFERENCE

The "mirror transference" has to do with the reestablishment, within the transference, of an early developmental need for the acceptance, approval, and confirmation of the patient's self. The therapist is utilized as a "self-object"; the function of the therapist, as self-object, is to strengthen the fragile self-esteem of the patient.

This transference is manifested by subtle (or not so subtle) demands upon the therapist for recognition, affirmation, or praise. The therapist is used exclusively as a mirror by the patient; little appreciation or awareness of the therapist as a separate person exists. Some therapists find this transference taxing, because the therapist feels controlled, encroached upon, ignored, insignificant as a human being that has value and makes valuable contributions; this is especially true when this type of transference becomes intertwined with a merger transference (described below). Recognition of this transference can help a therapist to remain tolerant of and empathize with the patient's situation at this time in the treatment. Kohut suggested that the mirror transference was reflective of an unmet developmental need.

IDEALIZING TRANSFERENCE

This transference expresses the need for a calm, strong, wise, and reliable object (self-object) whose "properties" and presence can be made use of by the patient in order to foster a sense of safety, self-esteem, and well-being; self-worth and value are enhanced in the glow of the idealizing transference. Although generally less taxing than the mirror transference, this type of transference presents certain hazards. Becoming the recipient of a patient's idealization can stimulate the therapist's grandiosity, resulting in the loss of realistic judgment. An idealizing transference can set the therapist up to be a disappointment to the patient, because the idealization is excessive and therefore must necessarily come undone. Last, as with the mirror transference, the therapist may feel irrelevant in this type of transference, because what is attributed to the therapist is obviously exaggerated.

ALTER-EGO (TWINSHIP) TRANSFERENCE

This transference occurs when a reassuring latency or prelatency experience is reestablished. It represents the need to be seen and understood by someone like the self. The alter-ego transference is manifested by the patient's desire to be like the therapist in appearance, manner, outlook, and opinion. The feeling of being "alike" and the sense of sameness allow the patient to feel strong and optimistic. This transference is not unlike the fantasy of the imaginary playmate of early development; therefore, it may play an important role in the acquisition of skills and competence.

MERGER TRANSFERENCE

This is a subcategory of transference, which can be an aspect of any of the above three transference; thus a patient might experience a "twinship merger transference," an "idealizing merger transference," or a "mirror merger transference." It represents the "reestablishment" of a fusion (merger) with the self-object of childhood, through an extension of the self to include the therapist. The therapist is not perceived to have a separate identity; rather, the therapist functions under the patient's control as an integral part of the patient's self. The patient expects the analyst to be completely attuned, to know the patient's thoughts without explanation. A transference paradigm of this type can be extremely frustrating; unfortunately, a significant period of frustrating time is usually required for working through to occur.

> George, a late-middle-aged man, sought psychotherapy because of persistent unhappiness and chronic anxiety. George had a long history of hypochondriacal concerns; for this, he had seen a number of therapists and psychiatrists throughout his life and had consulted many physicians (actually numbering in the hundreds). Typically, George would consult a new physician or psychiatrist and an initial period of idealization would occur, until some conflict arose and the spell of idealization was broken. The conflict would revolve around George's disagreement with and often contemptuous disregard for the physician's opinion, and the relationship would end consequent to an angry argument. George saw most physicians as self-serving and "narcissistic." He himself was a highly opinionated man, who prided himself on his many detailed observations about a vast variety of fields.
>
> While a number of George's ideas were thoughtful and pertinent, many of his notions were naive and extreme, revealing the way in which he greatly overrated his capacities. He would often suggest outrageous hypotheses about medicine that had no known basis in physiology or pathophysiology. In spite of a strong belief in his unique intelligence and gifts, this sad and lonely man often struggled miserably in his occupation as a middle-level manager, resulting in his frequent financial rescue by a kindly and wealthy family member. George had a history of repeated angry explosions that served to ruin most of his favorable work situations. Whenever this would happen, predictably, George would become excessively sure of his own point of view and rigid and angry if his views were challenged.
>
> In spite of his interpersonal limitations, George had achieved a few successes in the distant past. However, by the time he came for his current therapy, George was financially dependent upon his family and harshly critical of himself. In spite of the high value he placed on his intelligence, George could not rescue himself from

the despair he felt about his inability to perform. He often observed that he was an absolute and total failure.

Notwithstanding George's long history of interpersonal difficulties, his new therapist found him somewhat likable and clearly intelligent. Although George was certainly grandiose, he was also intense, needy, and very vulnerable. He spent the early sessions
reiterating how unsuccessful he had been and how unappreciated
he had felt. Many opportunities in his life had become near misses;
this pained and angered him. Unfortunately, it also fueled his intense sense of failure and deep self-hatred.

George spent many hours elaborating his countless health concerns. Expounding upon his personal medical views, he would
elaborate tales of how his concerns had been mismanaged.
George reveled in his own brilliance, attempting to demonstrate
his keen memory and "strut" his opinions in hopes of attracting the
therapist's acknowledgment. Interestingly, the therapist's response
did not seem to matter, as long as the therapist was careful not to
challenge George's opinions or significantly interrupt his mono-
logues. Surprisingly, George's hypochondriacal concerns would
often diminish as a therapy hour progressed; with time George's
somatic preoccupations disappeared altogether.

The therapist liked George and empathized with his distress, but
as time passed the therapist did become frustrated. A growing belief began to form in the therapist's mind that there was little he
seemed to be able to offer George, other than tolerance and the
provision of a place in which George could freely talk. Several
months passed, during which time the "patient" seemed to test the
therapist, perhaps wondering if this "physician," like so many
physicians before, would eventually become fed up and retaliate.

Slowly, George's initial stance and the transference seemed to
change. He began to speak of positive feelings about the therapist
and mentioned that he thought the therapist liked him. He noted
the therapist's furniture and manner of dressing, observing that the
therapist's tastes were similar to his own (something that did not
seem to be the case to the therapist). So ensued a prolonged phase,
in which George seemed to view the therapist as a kind of
"buddy," who shared his ideas, tastes, concerns, fears, etc. The patient frequently began his hour with "we" have a problem, or "we"
probably suspect this, etc. The therapist must think most physicians
are narcissistic, most movies are vacuous, most women are hysterical, etc. George would speak of his discoveries with a sense that
the therapist would share his excitement about a new restaurant, a
new movie, a new book, a new geographic area, or any other in-

terest. The therapist came to be seen as a friend, but a particular kind of a friend: a friend who never disagreed and always shared in George's excitement or disappointment.

During this period, George spoke often of memories of latency-age friends, and a time of life before the divorce of his parents when he was ten years old. Life had been good then. He had had friends and a sense of family, and there were "pick-up" basketball games at the "Y." The therapist felt constrained by this transference experience; he realized that more active questioning and interpretation about the patient's associations seemed only to lead to increasing somatization again, as well as anger on the part of the patient that was difficult to manage. The therapist felt no chance of having input; at times he was irritated at some of the patient's assumptions regarding the therapist's ideas and feelings.

The therapist gradually realized that the many latency memories had a significant "omission" in common. No parental figures were ever present in the memories! There were never any references to a mother or father; George spoke only of times with the guys playing sports, other activities with peers, or detailed recollections about the ambiance of the city streets. The therapist began to realize that George was terrified of allowing himself to care about or to rely upon any parental or authority figure, and this included his physicians. For George, feeling vulnerable or dependent was to experience the emptiness of himself.

Cautiously, the therapist began to refer to the lack of George's memories about his parents. As time passed, the therapist was tentatively able to suggest to George that a connection existed between the one-sidedness and emptiness of his dialogue about current-day figures, and the one-sidedness and emptiness of his relationship with his parents in the past.

Over a time period of several years, the alter-ego, buddy-buddy transference shifted and transformed. A more genuine sense of affection toward the therapist evolved. At the same time, George gradually began to develop a palpable quality of warmth and tenderness. He was able to see and appreciate that the therapist had a life of his own and had different interests; he would refer to the therapist's sailboat or inquire about the therapist's children. The focus of George's insights changed as well. He developed a fondness for several younger friends, and was often quite perceptive about their life struggles. He also became close to a younger sister who had children, and adopted a friendly, uncle-like posture with the children. These relationships were positive and rewarding to George.

A softer and gentler capacity had grown inside George; he could now empathize with others and with himself. George could now speak openly about the disappointments of life and his human failings, without having to disparage himself or defensively extol his capacities in a transparent and grandiose manner.

George had suffered from very significant narcissistic difficulties. A transient mirror transference had first appeared, which quickly shifted to an alter-ego transference. Eventually, an idealizing transference evolved, which gradually melted into a more realistic appreciation of the therapist.

George's fixation at the level of the "grandiose archaic self" was paralleled by the need to merge with a grandiose self-object (to paraphrase Kohut) and was expressed in the transference. With time, the genetic origins of his pathology were reconstructed and George became aware of the failures that belonged to the past. Consequently, a capacity for empathy toward himself and others became a possibility, allowing for the option to appreciate his abilities in the present and pursue a more gratifying life.

For George's therapist, the concept of a mirroring and alter-ego/self-object paradigm was lifesaving for the treatment. It allowed the therapist to accept and understand the enormity of his patient's struggles. It allowed the therapist to comprehend the particular form of the expression of George's developmental needs in the therapy, and the relationship of this expression to the past. The conceptual framework of the mirroring and alter-ego/self-object paradigm also allowed the therapist to tolerate the significant countertransference frustrations that George's pathology engendered.

PSYCHOTIC TRANSFERENCE

While less common, the psychotic transference is infinitely more challenging than transferences seen in nonpsychotic individuals. Reality is distorted, and the therapist is seen purely through the lens of transference; what the patient experiences in the transference is believed to be true.

Mr. R believed that his therapist was sneering at him. He brought this up again and again and no matter what the therapist said or interpreted, Mr. R continued to believe that the therapist was sneering at him.

A male patient developed an erotically tinged transference with a female therapist. Over a period of weeks, the patient spoke of his desire for the therapist, becoming increasingly graphic about what he would like to do with and to the therapist. This seasoned and solid therapist became uncomfortable to the point that she was reluctant to be alone in the room with the patient. The therapist recognized that the discomfort she felt was related to her subliminal awareness of the psychotic content of the patient's thought process. The therapist referred the patient to a male therapist, and the psychotically tinged erotic element receded.

Psychotic transferences can threaten a therapy and are also a poor prognostic variable.

THERAPEUTIC ALLIANCE

The therapeutic alliance describes a phenomenon that is unique and distinct from transference. The value of this concept has been debated; still, many therapists find the concept of the therapeutic alliance a useful way to explain an apparent dichotomy (Brenner 1979; Dickes 1975; Greenson 1965, 1967; Segal 1967). The patient may have intense feelings of love, hate, etc., toward the therapist. This same patient may have the ability to reflect, take a step back, and attempt to understand these intense feelings and reactions— feelings and reactions that would wreak havoc upon or destroy any other relationship. The therapeutic alliance addresses this contradiction: it describes and explains the "working alliance" between patient and therapist that permits the tenacious pursuit of understanding meaning. Understanding meaning is achieved in part by living through, experiencing, and coming to terms with the replay of transference.

The therapeutic alliance creates a neutral territory, a place of safety and trust. Theoretically, the therapeutic alliance is that relationship between the patient's reasonable, analyzing "observing" ego, and the therapist's analyzing "work" ego. While the latter should be a given, the former is an unknown at the outset of any treatment.

As originally conceptualized, the therapeutic alliance refers to a general sense that the patient and therapist can work together in the service of understanding the patient's inner world; it does not refer to transference reactions. The therapist's compassion, empathy, nonjudgmental attitude, and concern facilitate the formation of the therapeutic alliance. Greenson (1965) believed that the therapeutic alliance had the best chance of being established if the therapist shows in his day-to-day behavior a "consistent and unwavering pursuit of insight in dealing with any and all of the patient's material and behavior." Greenson felt that the therapist must be human: sensitive, diligent, straightforward, compassionate but restrained. Zetzel (1956, 1970) thought that the therapeutic alliance recapitulated aspects of the infant–mother relationship. The infant turns to the mother with trust and expectant faith that the mother will try to help; the patient turns to the therapist with some measure of basic trust.

In practice, and complementing Greenson's (1965) advice as above, in order for a therapeutic alliance to develop and be sustainable, a sufficient "match" between the patient and the therapist must be present. A "match" might involve the obvious, such as that the patient and the therapist are the same sex, or have similar backgrounds or come from a common culture (religious, national affiliation, etc.). A match might also arise because of difficult-to-measure intangibles that somehow create a common bond of understanding.

> John was a young man when he first presented for treatment. He had grown up with an alcoholic, unreliable, unavailable, and envious father, who depreciated him. John's mother was quite passive in the face of the father's obvious destructiveness toward the patient, and privately criticized and put John down as well.
>
> John's therapist mentioned her fee at the end of the first consultation. John proceeded to speak of his hopelessness about finding a form of treatment that would be helpful to him. The therapist said he must have had a reaction to her fee. John spoke of the greed of therapists; how would he know whether this therapist wasn't buying her next "vacation house" with his money?
>
> The therapist responded by speaking to the therapeutic alliance; she said that the patient's concerns were understandable. She suggested that one must be cautious when choosing a therapist; the young man should try to find someone who plainly knew what he or she was doing, and seemed clearly able and willing to work hard with him on his behalf.

In the above situation, a transference interpretation might have been something like: "Perhaps I, like your father (or mother) am trying to take from you, drain you, and you will get nothing of substance back in return." Whether to direct a comment toward facilitating the therapeutic alliance or toward addressing the transference, is a conscious decision. Hanna Segal (1967) emphasized that the therapeutic alliance is never independent of transference but instead is an achievement of analytic work and the direct result of addressing the transference. That the therapeutic alliance is an achievement becomes particularly evident with the patient who is difficult to engage, has difficulty with trust, and is hard to keep in treatment. For many patients, interpretation of the transference is essential to the development and maintenance of the therapeutic alliance. The transference must, however, be addressed with the proper tact and timing. No interpretation, including an interpretation about the transference, is ever useful if it cannot be heard by the patient.

SELF-PSYCHOLOGY AND TRANSFERENCE

"Self-psychological" and "classical" views of transference are often compared and contrasted.

In the classical view, transference experiences include certain characteristics:

1. An object relationship: Transference is a form of object relationship based on an internalized image of a significant person from the past.
2. Distortion: Transference is a distortion insofar as the experience of the current object relationship is colored by the memory of a past relationship now played out in the current relationship. Within the current relationship, a "return of the repressed" occurs.
3. Regression: Transference involves a regression because the past becomes perpetuated in the present, reality testing is suspended (to a visible degree), and time sense gets confused (past time and present time).
4. Displacement: Transference means that the past is displaced onto the present (internal image displaced onto a real and present object).

In the self-psychological view, what is transference?

Transference, to paraphrase Stolorow, Brandchaft, and Atwood (1987) offers an opportunity to clarify and understand the characteristics that dominate a patient's way of thinking—that is, the way in which the patient organizes certain types of information. Transference is not simply a regression to or displacement from the past, because transference reflects the continuous psychological attempt to organize present experience and to construct meaning.

The self-psychological transferences (Stolorow, Brandchaft, and Atwood 1987) serve multiple self-object functions:

1. The transference may offer fulfillment of wishes and desires.
2. The transference may provide moral restraint.

3. The transference may help to foster acceptance and adaptation to difficult realities.
4. The transference may help to restore and maintain precarious self-esteem.
5. The transference may be utilized to aid in a defense against emotional experiences that are felt to be dangerous.

Both classical and self-psychology views of transference emphasize the principle of multiple function. Self-psychologists emphasize the functions that transference serves in the present. The self-psychological view does not necessarily view transference as a resistance (resistance to "awareness of" or "resolution of" the transference); transference in the self-psychological view is an evolving process in the present.

The transference experience in self-psychology enriches the patient's emotional life by expanding the psychological structure of the self. Once the treatment ends, the transference experience recedes, but leaves behind a more complex and emotionally enriching experience of the self and of others. These ideas are in contrast to classic analytic thought, in which the emphasis is more on the specific identification, articulation, dissolution, and mourning of the transference, and of those human opportunities and experiences that are past and therefore never will be. In the *Analysis of the Self*, even while still in the language of classical analysis, Kohut (1971) described the impact of interpretations offered in relation to descriptions of the transference. He said that "the meaningful recall of the relevant childhood memories and the ever deepening understanding of the analogous transference experience converge in giving assistance to the patient's ego, and the formerly automatic reactions become gradually more aim-inhibited and more under the control of the ego."

Kohut went on to coin the phrase "transmuting internalization," the process by which change occurs in a psychotherapeutic process, with the gradual accumulation of psychic structures in the context of discovering different experiential possibilities. Transmuting internalization occurs in the setting of a generally empathic process, but at those moments where there are minor empathic lapses or failures on the part of the therapist. If the therapist serves as an empathic self-object in a self-object transference, relatively minor empathic failures, if not overwhelming and if understood in the context of therapy, can lead to growth. Following the non-traumatic, "optimal" frustration of the patient, "transmuting internalization" occurs, leading to the internalization of new experience and the development of new psychological capacity. The therapist does not attempt to frustrate the patient;

disappointments and frustration are inevitable in the therapeutic relationship, just as they are in all human relationships.

Kohut believed that the above-described process leads to the development of new internal psychological capacity (structure formation), whereby the self (individual) is eventually able to execute important self-object functions; even when the self-object is not available, the patient internalizes specific psychological functions that the self-object once performed (therapist). Over time the connection with the self-object is "depersonalized," and the self-object function is internalized and becomes an addition to the self-structure (this is not dissimilar from the internalization and abstraction described in ego psychology). The image of the self-object who provided the function has faded; the capacity is correctly perceived as belonging to the individual.

Is there a way to integrate classical and self-psychological views of transference? Each perspective emphasizes different important facets. Self-psychology emphasizes the accrual of autonomous self-functions and the increasing ability to make use constructively of other people as self-objects. The classical view of transference emphasizes the understanding of the seemingly unending repetition of transference patterns, the development of the capacity to mourn what has passed and never will be, and the relinquishment of repetitive maladaptive behaviors and relationships.

In practice, each perspective is important and probably necessary for the other to occur. Mourning and acceptance of the past is difficult and requires a very significant, empathic human connection (self-object). For the accumulation of new functions to occur, internalization, mourning, and acceptance of the limitations of the past are unavoidable.

Diverse patients bring different needs, conflicts, narcissistic deficits, developmental limitations, etc., to psychotherapy. Pine emphasizes that in all treatments, just as with an individual's development, constellations of difficulties may move to the foreground or to the background at different times during a treatment (Pine 1988, 1989). Paralleling this movement, ideally the therapist has the facility to move among various theoretical frameworks, picking and choosing which transference paradigm most usefully describes the patient's situation.

REFERENCES AND READINGS

Balint, A., and M. Balint. (1939). On transference and countertransference. *International Journal of Psycho-Analysis* 20: 22–230.

Bird, B. (1972). Notes on transference: universal phenomena and hardest part of analysis. *Journal of the American Psychoanalytic Association* 20: 26–301.

Brenner, C. (1979). Working alliance, therapeutic alliance, and transference. *Journal of the American Psychoanalytic Association* (supplement) 27: 137–58.

Dickes, R. L. (1975). Technical considerations of the therapeutic and working alliances. *International Journal of Psychoanalytic Psychotherapy* 4: 1–24.

Freud, S. (1912). The dynamics of transference. *Standard Edition* 12: 97–108. London: Hogarth Press, 1958.

———. (1914). Remembering, repeating, and working through. *Standard Edition* 12: 145–56. London: Hogarth Press, 1956.

———. (1915). Observations on transference-love. *Standard Edition* 12: 157–70. London: Hogarth Press, 1958.

Gabbard, G. O. (1994). Sexual excitement and countertransference love in the analyst. *Journal of the American Psychoanalytic Association* 42: 1083–1106.

Gill, M. (1979). The analysis of transference. *Journal of the American Psychoanalytic Association* 27: 263–328.

———. (1982). *Transference.* New York: International Universities Press.

Greenacre, P. (1954). The role of transference. *Journal of the American Psychoanalytic Association* 2: 671–84.

Greenson, R. (1965). The working alliance and the transference neurosis. *Psychoanalytic Quarterly* 34: 155–81.

———. (1967). *The Technique and Practice of Psychoanalysis,* vol. 1. New York: International Universities Press.

Kernberg, O. M. (1994). Love in the analytic setting. *Journal of the American Psychoanalytic Association* 42: 1137–56.

Kohut, H. (1971). *The Analysis of the Self.* New York: International Universities Press.

———. (1977). *The Restoration of the Self.* New York: International Universities Press.

———. (1980). Reflections on advances in self psychology. In *Advances in Self Psychology.* New York: International Universities Press.

Kohut, H., and E. Wolf. (1978). The disorders of the self and their treatment: an outline. *International Journal of Psycho-Analysis* 59: 414–25.

Levine, H. B. (1992). Freudian and Kleinian theory: dialogue of comparative perspectives. *Journal of the American Psychoanalytic Association* 40: 801–26.

Loewald, H. W. (1971). Some considerations on repetition and repetition compulsion. *International Journal of Psycho-Analysis* 52: 59–66.

Pine, F. (1989). Motivation, personality organization, and the four psychologies of psychoanalysis. *Journal of the American Psychoanalytic Association* 37: 31–64.

———. (1988). The four psychologies of psychoanalysis and their place in clinical work. *Journal of the American Psychoanalytic Association* 36: 571–96.

Sandler, J., A. Holder, M. Kawenoka, H. E. Kennedy, and L. Neurath. (1969). Notes of some theoretical and clinical aspects of transference. *International Journal of Psycho-Analysis* 50: 633–45.

Segal, H. (1967). Melanie Klein's technique. *Psycho-analytic Forum* 2: 197–211.

Stolorow, R. D., B. Brandchaft, and G. E. Atwood. (1987). *Psychoanalytic Treatment, An Intersubjective Approach*. Hillsdale, NJ: Analytic Press.

Strachey, J. (1934). The nature of the therapeutic action of psycho-analysis. *International Journal of Psycho-Analysis* 15: 127–59.

Zetzel, E. (1956). Current concepts of transference. *International Journal of Psycho-Analysis* 37: 369–76.

———. (1970). *The Capacity for Emotional Growth*. New York: International Universities Press.

7

EMPATHY AND
COUNTERTRANSFERENCE

Empathy is an important human ability to possess; it is an essential quality for the therapist who conducts psychotherapy. The effort to understand the patient operates on verbal and nonverbal levels, combining elements of the therapist's knowledge base, life-experience, self-awareness, and
training, in order to find a way into the patient's experience. Empathy is influenced by and dependent upon multiple factors; therefore, an empathic
position can be difficult—at times quite difficult—to achieve.

WHAT IS EMPATHY?

The dictionary defines empathy as "The action of understanding, being
aware of, being sensitive to, and vicariously experiencing the feelings,
thoughts, and experience of another of either the past or present, without
having the feelings, thoughts, and experience fully communicated in an objective manner" (*Webster's Ninth New Collegiate Dictionary*, 1985).

Empathy is an "intuitive" ability to feel into another person, to place
oneself in "another's shoes." Greenson (1960) speaks of empathy as a form
of "emotional knowing," the experiencing of another's feelings, a special
mode of perceiving. He considers empathy to be primarily a preconscious
phenomenon, distinguished from sympathy because it does not contain
the elements of condolence, agreement, or pity. Winnicott (1963) writes
that empathy is a "transitional process," an affective state of sharing between self and object. Olinick (1980) states that "the experience of empathy is the experience of knowing; a feeling of certainty, although at any
given moment one may not be able to specify the derivative of the knowledge or know how to tell the patient what you know." Levy (1985) notes

that empathy is usually preconscious, silent, and automatic yet transient and easily reversible.

Kohut described empathy as a combination of identification and introspection; a way of identifying with the other and then feeling as if in the other's emotional circumstance. Kohut (1959) called this "vicarious introspection." With the use of the psychotheraputic tool of empathy, the therapist comes to know the patient in a different and important way that is distinct from objective analytic assessment, data collection, or psychiatric diagnosis.

EMPATHY IN LIFE

Empathy (along with sympathy) is an aspect of what allows humans to understand, relate to, and feel connected with one another. Reciprocal empathy is part of all healthy relationships, fueling and fostering intimacy. Empathy can also be used in ways that are not benign. Kohut (1971, 1977) and others have pointed out that empathetically derived understanding can be used to hurt, intimidate, control, and terrorize. In contrast, nonjudgmental, nonshaming, and accepting empathic experiences with others, especially with important others, can allow a person to metabolize and endure the disappointments of life, the blows to self-esteem, and the despair associated with loss and personal failure. The experience of empathy is thus taken inside the mind, becoming an aspect of a richer internal world, facilitating the capacity to feel loved and to love oneself, to be soothed and to soothe oneself.

Empathy occurs as a part of the complex interplay between human beings; it doesn't simply follow from the fortuitous pairing with an empathic personality. Psychological factors within a person can limit or block the communication of sufficient information that would allow for an empathic response to occur in the other person. To accept concern is to permit vulnerability. Some people are "allergic" to this phenomenon.

Empathy begins as a parental function, which is vital for a child's emotional development. The "good-enough" mother senses her child's inner predicament; this allows her to respond to her child's needs, most importantly to contain the child's emotional states. With the infant and toddler, this empathic process occurs nonverbally; the mother perceives and responds to the infant's bodily states and cues. Thus, an emotional, intuitive (nonverbal) dialogue occurs, which becomes the foundation for the child's empathic self-understanding and empathic understanding of others. The empathic capacity of the mother and her comfort or lack of comfort with various emotional states will help to determine the emotional states that the child will be able to identify, integrate, and tolerate in later life.

CAPACITY FOR EMPATHY

What contributes to differences in empathic capacity? Empathy probably has genetic and/or temperamental determinants. Some people inherently have greater "emotional intelligence," these people are more reflective, capable of introspection, and aware of and perceptive about others. Empathic capacity normally grows as the child grows, expanding incrementally with psychological development and ongoing neurobiological maturation. The transition from early childhood to latency is accompanied by the gradually increasing capacity for object constancy and beginning ability to feel for others. In adolescence, the increased capacity for abstract thinking expands the teenager's capacity for complex introspection, eventually to culminate in the ability to feel into another person's perspective as well.

Life experiences can contribute to or limit the development of inherent empathic capacity. Losses, other kinds of traumas, and the experience of life predicaments can, dependent on certain factors, "deepen" a person, thus enriching empathic capacity. These factors include the person's own constitutional ego strengths, available "self-objects" who serve the function of helping the person to integrate the difficult and/or traumatic experiences of life in the most useful and adaptive way (parents, teachers, coaches, mentors, physicians, therapists, etc.), and the extent of the trauma and realistic or unrealistic possibility for a functional recovery.

People grow up in different circumstances, and the vicissitudes of each person's life necessarily vary within those circumstances and as a result of chance occurrences. A person who lost a parent in early life might have a substantial ability to understand the depth and complexity of feeling and the long-ranging consequences that this type of event would engender in a person with a similar circumstance. The "middle child" in a family in which "middle" really meant "overlooked" might have unusual antenna for another person who feels that securing recognition was always more difficult than it should have been. One person may have grown up with an alcoholic parent. Another person may have grown up with a particular talent. A woman may have grown up with the gift of extraordinary beauty and all of its attendant prerogatives and stresses. The unique sensitivities that are derived from personal experiences can enhance a given person's particular empathic ability; unfortunately, the opposite can also occur.

Although many of these sensitizing experiences occur early in life, a life-defining experience can occur at any time. Living, with its inherent struggles and disappointments, or a specific and compelling event, such as surviving breast cancer or a myocardial infarction, can deepen or alter character, thus affecting an expansion of empathic capacity.

> Dr. E, a technically able but interpersonally limited surgeon, had lost his mother at an early age. Dr. E could not tolerate any expression of neediness or dependency. He was pleasant but remote, and would work himself to exhaustion. Unwittingly, he could be dismissive or even contemptuous when dealing with a needy patient. This type of situation often occurred in his clinical practice.
>
> After a number of years of a difficult marriage and faced with a potential divorce, Dr. E finally sought psychotherapy at his wife's insistence. Dr. E' s wife complained that Dr. E was emotionally cold, distant, and judgmental; in spite of these complaints, she knew that there was a "tender" part of her husband, and this had kept her with him.
>
> Psychotherapy was initially very difficult for Dr. E. The process required that he talk about himself and in so doing, share himself and begin to rely upon another person. As therapy proceeded, Dr. E eventually did speak about his childhood and the loss of his mother. He saw his mother as an ideal, caring mother; at the same time, however, Dr. E would observe that he "never" thought of his mother and had few memories of anything prior to her death when he was nine years old.
>
> An initial transference configuration appeared in which Dr. E wondered if his male therapist saw him as weak and "henpecked," not really a "man," because he had "submitted" to psychotherapy. With time, however, Dr. E became much more overtly sad. As he shared his sadness (something that he had never done before), memories of his mother, and especially memories of her illness prior to her death gradually came back to him. Dr. E spoke of her slow demise and of her infirmity. He recalled her loss of bowel and bladder control specifically; looking back, he realized how frightening, disturbing, and disgusting this had been to him. With time and "working through," Dr. E was able to recall more painful childhood experiences with his mother; the waiting on her "like a nurse," his frustration with her and consequent guilt about his wish to "get away," and his terrible sadness.
>
> As a result of the psychotherapy, Dr. E became better able to relate to his wife. He could speak of his frustrations with her without feeling "emasculated" by her. Dr. E became able to enjoy his wife's

genuine concern for him, which previously had been threatening and therefore not enjoyable; the enormous difficulty with dependency, and the potential for loss associated with the loss of his mother, had interfered with Dr. E's enjoyment. In his clinical work, the "physician" gradually began to see others in a more complex way. Dr. E noticed that patients were often frightened, and found that he could be reassuring without being saccharine or patronizing. While he was still somewhat stiff, by the end of his therapy Dr. E had softened remarkably. In fact, in the last month of his treatment, Dr. E spoke humorously, and with full recognition of the irony of counseling a colleague who he had felt was insensitive to a patient.

As with a patient, unfortunately a therapist may also have empathic limitations as a consequence of poorly integrated life experiences. This kind of therapist will view a patient's material through myopic lenses. All therapists, of course, have limitations in the purity of their lenses. However, the more spotless and wide is the circumference of the lens, the more able is the therapist to practice the work of psychotherapy empathically and then effectively. Those enriched by greater self-understanding and awareness will "see" infinitely more than those who are not enriched by greater self-understanding and awareness.

Other specific factors may also affect empathy, including variables such as ethnic and/or cultural background, gender, age, or particular hardships or traumas. However, the universality of emotions and self and object paradigms, the ubiquitous nature of human needs and the commonality of many unconscious fantasies and symbols (as revealed in fantasy, dreams, art, and creative works), eventuate in a common language of empathy. Therefore, a therapist may be of a different sex, or have a different cultural or experiential background from that of a patient, and still be quite able to empathize with that patient.

COUNTERTRANSFERENCE

Every therapist has countertransference reactions. These reactions may be minor or significant, conscious or not conscious, acute or chronic, contained or acted upon, apparent to the patient or not apparent to the patient. Countertransference reactions can be made use of in the service of understanding the patient and furthering the therapy, or the same countertransference reaction can be destructive in a variety of ways (precipitating a stalemate, facilitating a premature interruption of treatment).

Countertransference may be defined broadly to include all the therapist's reactions to the patient. Countertransference may be more narrowly defined to suggest a more specific reaction to the patient's transference. The former definition encourages the therapist to be aware that any and all reactions to a patient and/or the patient's circumstances or behavior are worth contemplation; this is the inherent usefulness of a broader definition.

Racker (1953) observed that "countertransference is always present and always reveals itself." A therapist's reaction to a patient can have a particular and unique quality. The therapist's reaction to the patient can be a predictable response that the therapist recognizes to be familiar and to have particular and personal meaning for that therapist. The specificity, degree, and tenacity of a therapist's reaction offers a way of categorizing countertransference reactions.

Predictable (Countertransference) Reactions

Predictable countertransference reactions are the consequence of encountering something in or about the patient toward which most people would respond. This might have to do with the patient's situation. This might have to do with the patient's feelings or behavior, qualities or characteristics, attitude or reactions. The reaction or reactions to the patient's presentation allow the therapist to experience the patient as others do. These predictable responses are therefore reactions to aspects of (or the totality of) the patient's character or reactions to aspects of (or the totality of) the patient's life situation, which may be difficult to bear.

Idiosyncratic (Countertransference) Reactions

Idiosyncratic countertransference reactions occur in response to something about the patient's feelings or behavior, qualities or characteristics, attitudes, reactions, or situation that exposes the therapist's vulnerability. Every therapist has certain unique concerns or sensitivities (vulnerabilities), which can be activated or provoked by a patient. Personal psychotherapy and supervision allow the therapist to become familiar with and understand the origin of these particular countertransference proclivities. These reactions reflect aspects of the therapist's own history or prior areas of psychological difficulty, which are then brought to the foreground by something about the patient.

A male therapist became uncomfortable when a male patient began to describe engaging in sadomasochistic activities with female prostitutes. This therapist had had similar fantasies, coming close to enacting them at various times in the past. He still made use of a sadomasochistic fantasy in order to become sexually excited with his wife.

A female therapist found herself irritable with and intolerant of an older woman patient, whom she found to be "bitchy," self-centered, and vain. This patient reminded the therapist of her own mother who was difficult to be with for similar reasons.

The pursuit of an empathic connection with a patient requires the therapist to review constantly a personal catalog of painful, disturbing, and disequilibrating experiences; this is done in order to find and then momentarily reexperience the corresponding state that will allow the therapist to "find" the patient's state of mind. This task, "regression in the service of the (analytic work) ego," is difficult; challenging the therapist's ability to (in a short period of time) move backward in time and maturity, and then be able to find the way home again.

Countertransference reactions can be short lived or more enduring (chronic countertransference). Sometimes the presence of countertransference is subtle, and therefore may be imperceptible to the therapist. This situation can be particularly damaging to a treatment when the countertransference response becomes of the more enduring, chronic type and is not identified by the therapist.

IDENTIFYING COUNTERTRANSFERENCE

Differences in Posture and Attitude

The position that the therapist assumes with any given patient, and the adherence or variance from that therapist's accustomed style that is present in that position, can be an indicator of the presence (or absence) of underlying countertransference. With every patient, a therapist assumes a slightly different posture ("condition with respect to circumstances; an attitude of mind"—*Webster's Twentieth-Century Dictionary*). This posture or manner is usually a conscious or preconscious attempt to put the patient at ease and facilitate a connection (Sandler 1976). The greater the variance from a therapist's typical posture or habitually comfortable way of being with a patient, the more curious the therapist should probably be about what is being communicated by the patient that is causing the therapist to be subliminally ill at ease.

A very reserved and conservative female therapist found herself being unusually casual with a new woman patient. Casual was quite far from this therapist's habitual style. The therapist began to wonder what it was about this patient that brought out an abrupt change in her manner. The therapist also recognized, that although casual implies comfortable, she wasn't feeling comfortable at all.

The therapist figured out that the patient actually felt threatening and ominous in some ill-defined way. The "casual" response was actually a way of trying to "disarm" the "savage beast."

Dreaming

When a therapist dreams about a patient, a countertransference element is usually active. A concern on the part of the therapist about the patient's state of mind, or material from a recent session (day residue) is often the stimulus for the dream. This type of dream can serve as a useful "communication" to the therapist if it is understood as an unconscious "transference" of information from patient to the therapist and explored through self-analysis on the part of the therapist.

A female therapist had recently begun to evaluate a man in his early twenties, who had dropped out of college in order to "become more acquainted with the real world and its problems." Something about the young man bothered the therapist, but she could not put her finger on the bothersome element. Several weeks into the evaluation process, when the therapist had seen the patient only three or four times, the therapist had the following dream:

> She was at a social gathering. A young man was standing in the corner of the room by himself. There was something "weird" and frightening about the man's appearance. She looked more closely, and noticed that the man's head was tilted to the side, and his bright blue eyes were strangely askew. She felt deep unease.

The therapist was shaken by the dream. As she thought about it, however, she realized that the young man she had recently been evaluating had "bright blue eyes." The eye color was certainly a striking element in the dream, but the therapist immediately knew that another element was even more striking. It was the tilt in the man's head, and the eyes that were "strangely askew."

The day after the dream, the therapist had an appointment with the patient. She realized with a shock that the young man's head carriage was very slightly askew and his eyes were not symmetrical. She now recognized the origin of her "deep unease." The patient's symptoms were not just psychological; perhaps the patient's symptoms were not psychological at all. There was something neurologically wrong with the young man.

The therapist contacted the man's parents and arranged for the patient to see a neurologist. An MRI scan revealed a large meningioma. The man went to surgery and the tumor was successfully removed. Several months later, the young man contacted the therapist. He had returned to college (having explained the circumstances to the school) and was "doing just fine, thanks to you!"

The young man couldn't recall that he had ever wanted to leave his college experience. He found it amusing when he was told after his surgery that he had wanted to "become more acquainted with the real world and its problems." He was "loving being back at school"; in fact, he told the therapist he had decided to make use of his math and science abilities and was now "pre-med."

Forgetting Appointment, Starting Late, or Extending a Session

An error on the part of the therapist that has to do with time, forgetting an appointment, starting late or early, or extending a therapeutic hour carries with it a variety of potential meanings. A therapist may be fatigued, overextended, simply have made a mistake ("sometimes a cigar is just a cigar"), or have made a conscious decision to extend a session. However, it is probably useful for the therapist to be routinely curious about these kinds of behaviors, and at least consider the possibility of an incompletely expressed countertransference reaction. Certainly if a therapist is repeatedly late or repeatedly forgets an appointment or extends a session, especially if these behaviors occur with the same patient, self-analysis or consultation is in order.

Intense Feelings or an Absence of Feelings

Intense feelings toward a patient or the absence of expected feelings on the part of the therapist toward a patient often reflect a countertransference response. Any feeling indicates that something is being stirred within the therapist. An intense feeling therefore indicates that something intense is being activated within the therapist. It is important to note that feelings reflective of countertransference are not only about the negative (i.e., irritation, anger, sadness). Countertransference can appear in positive feelings, such as attraction toward a patient, admiration of the patient, or frank erotic desire. Conversely, indifference—that is, the absence of any feelings toward a patient—is an indication of countertransference.

Meaningful psychotherapy always involves feelings. Therefore, the absence of feeling, or "boredom" on the part of the therapist, may signal a countertransference response to the absence of a meaningful process. This awareness can then signal the therapist to explore the potential reasons for the empty quality and/or lack of affective presence; the lack of affective presence may be in the patient or in the therapist.

Slips of the Tongue (Parapraxes)

When the therapist makes a slip of the tongue, because of the possibility that the slip betrays a countertransference element, it is usually something to contemplate. The phenomenon of being caught by surprise and, depending on the slip, the sudden sense of exposure or concern about the patient's reaction in the moment, can complicate the therapist's ability to react. Later, the therapist can analyze and make use of the countertransference-derived information that may be contained in the slip; the slip may be useful in understanding the mix of the patient and the patient's past, and the therapist and therapist's past. Racker's conceptualization is a useful model with which to understand this particular countertransference experience.

Change in the Therapist's Usual Style of Interpretation or Excessive Use of Genetic Interpretations

A change in the therapist's usual interpretative style, or the excessive reliance on one type of interpretation, should at least arouse a therapist's curiosity about the countertransference that could be in the mix. Any type of interpretation can be overutilized, but the most commonly overutilized interpretation is the genetic interpretation. Genetic interpretations are particularly appealing to the therapist when the patient has an intense transference response that is fully directed toward the therapist. As the patient's intensity grows too difficult for the therapist to tolerate, the therapist attempts to focus the patient on the past, deflecting the patient's reactions and feelings from the present and the therapist. It can be quite trying for a therapist to be with a patient who is chronically angry and accusatory, resulting in the temptation to quickly defuse the situation in this manner (by directing the focus to the patient's past).

Excessive interpretation, especially excessive wordiness or excessive explanation, may express the therapist's underlying anxiety. In an attempt to bolster an inner sense of uncertainty, impotence, or failure by talking more, offering more, attempting prematurely to force an interpretation, or adopting the role of educator more than is appropriate, the therapist tries to quell uncomfortable feelings. The therapist who is just beginning the process of treating patients may be particularly prone to excessive interpretation, because of the attendant initial uncertainty and lack of confidence.

Difficulty Remembering Material

With the beginning of a new hour, it is not uncommon for the therapist to try to recall the content and theme (or themes) of the previous hour or group of hours. With practice, most therapists develop a sufficient "associative" memory; this allows the therapist to link what a patient is talking about in the present to the story of the patient's past as it has been revealed in previous sessions.

As a patient describes a person in an hour, or tells an anecdote about a situation, or describes a certain feeling or predicament, the therapist is consciously and preconsciously sorting through a "Rolodex" of thoughts and associations, in order to find the right "name and number." If this doesn't occur, the therapist's memory and empathic capacity may have been compromised. The therapist's memory, just like the patient's memory, is affected by repression and other defensive functions. These defensive functions can be activated by a patient. When a therapist cannot recall the last session even with associative clues, or finds that a patient has related something several times and the therapist cannot remember having heard the information, it is probably worth wondering what this failure to be able to string a story together is about. For example, painful information about loss or emotional injury can be difficult for a therapist to listen to at times. This may be secondary to the human suffering involved, or it may relate to the specific content of the therapist's own life.

Blind Spots, or Difficulty Finding an Empathic Posture

A "blind spot," or simply not hearing and registering something of importance, is the most difficult countertransference to identify, because this piece of countertransference is manifested in an "omission" rather that a "commission." This situation might come to attention in supervision, in response to some feedback from a patient, when a therapy goes sour, or only after a long period of stagnation has occurred.

The difficulty in finding an empathic posture may be more obvious, but often reflects a deeper, more significant "blind spot." A therapist might notice with a particular patient or at a particular time with a patient, that it is simply too much work to empathize; the thought of the exaggerated effort required should alert the therapist, especially if this occurrence is not limited to isolated instances at which time the therapist is overly tired or preoccupied.

Anytime a psychotherapeutic process is not unfolding and/or working through is not occurring, the therapist might wonder about a limitation of awareness, and what is being missed. The reasonable risk of a countertransference reaction, even in the "well-analyzed" therapist, is an important reason to have some professional forum to discuss treatment cases. This forum could be individual supervision, group supervision, seminars, personal psychotherapy, or all or some of the above.

Models of Countertransference and Its Use

Racker's psychoanalytic model of countertransference is interesting and useful because it addresses the continuous interplay of overempathizing (or overidentifying) and not empathizing enough with the patient (Racker 1953, 1957, 1968). Theoretically, Racker drew from Klein, who stressed the continuous process of the introjection and projection of object representations in all aspects of development, normal or pathologic. Object representations are projected out and modified or reinforced by real, external life experience with others, including with a therapist. These new experiences are taken back in again to either reinforce the patient's internal object world or to modify it. Kleinian thought stresses the constant interplay among the person's internal world, the beliefs and behavior that provoke people in the world to respond in a certain way, and how this continually reinforces internal experience. Psychotherapy attempts to question unconscious assumptions and interpretations of experience by attempting to become aware of (make conscious) the patient's internal world (both cognitively and emotionally) through the perpetuation of these old patterns in the therapeutic relationship. Racker observed that a therapist can replay the patient's old patterns and object relations within the psychotherapeutic milieu, and described this repetition theoretically. Racker made several important points:

1. Both transference and countertransference are *always* present.

2. Countertransference reactions are often the best barometer for determining what is most essential in the psychotherapeutic process. A therapist's countertransference reactions should not be trusted with "blind faith," yet these reactions are a very "personal receiver and transmitter," indicating something about the patient's inner world.

3. Talion law is operative in all countertransference reactions. Every positive transference reaction in the patient is answered with a positive countertransference in the therapist. For every negative transference reaction the patient displays, the therapist experiences a negative countertransference. This observation draws attention to the ease with which a therapist will be pushed and pulled by a patient's reactions.

4. There is a continuous interplay of two types of identification with the patient, called "complementary identification," and "concordant identification." Concordant identification describes empathy (and identification) with the patient; Racker believed that concordant identification was based on positive countertransference. Complementary identification describes the more classic notion of countertransference, as a force that is directed toward the patient and which diminishes the therapist's capacity for empathy. Racker expands this idea, defining complementary identification as a circumstance in which the therapist's attitudes come not only from the therapist's own transference reactions but also reflect the patient's internal, past objects. The degree to which the therapist fails to achieve concordant identification reflects the degree to which the complementary identification will come alive, be acted upon, and create a repetition of the patient's past. Every transference evokes countertransference, thus ensuring a subtle interplay between patient and therapist, concordant and complementary identifications.

5. The therapist's countertransference reactions are important to identify because (to paraphrase Racker) the patient's unconscious is aware of the therapist's unconscious desires. At some preconscious or even conscious level, the patient knows when the therapist dislikes, is intimidated or stimulated by, is angry with, or has other emotional reactions toward the patient, even when these are not verbally acknowledged.

6. The therapist wishes at some level to be accepted, liked, and acknowledged by the patient. Accordingly, the therapist needs and desires the recognition of the patient. A patient can actively frustrate the therapist by direct hostility (mockery, deceit, or active rejection of the therapist's comments) or by passive rejection (such as withdrawal or other distancing maneuvers). These behaviors on the part of the patient provoke the therapist and evoke reactions, inhibiting the therapist and making it difficult to address and confront important issues.

Racker's concept of complementary and concordant identification bring together and allow the therapist to operationalize and utilize countertransference reactions. The model asks a therapist to think about the actual position in the empathic process. Racker's ideas alert the therapist to the dangers of empathy, not just the loss of perspective, but more specifically the possibility of becoming a modern representation of an object from the patient's past.

Empathy and countertransference reactions of all varieties are interwoven in a motif that is always changing, ebbing and flowing, continuously being activated by the patient's unconscious, but also simultaneously being stimulated by the therapist's internal world. An awareness and concern about the empathic process between patient and therapist, as well as a tenacious and persistent pursuit of countertransference reactions, can be a creative and enlightening endeavor, as well as facilitating the process of psychotherapy and the therapist's own introspective process.

REFERENCES AND READINGS

Balint, A., and M. Balint. (1939). On transference and countertransference. *International Journal of Psycho-Analysis* 20: 223–30.

Greenson, R. R. (1960). Empathy and its vicissitudes. *International Journal of Psycho-Analysis* 41: 418–24.

Gutheil, T. G., and G. O. Gabbard. (1993). The concept of boundaries in clinical practice: theoretical and risk management dimensions. *American Journal of Psychiatry* 150: 188–96.

Kohut, H. (1959). Introspection, empathy, and psychoanalysis. *Journal of the American Psychoanalytic Association* 7: 459–83.

———. (1971). *The Analysis of the Self.* New York: International Universities Press.

———. (1977). *The Restoration of the Self.* New York: International Universities Press.

Lewis, J. M. (1978). *To Be a Therapist: The Teaching and Learning*. New York: Brunner/Mazel.

Levy, S. T. (1985). Empathy and psychoanalytic technique. *Journal of the American Psychoanalytic Association* 33: 353–78.

Little, M. (1951). Countertransference and the patient's response to it. *International Journal of Psycho-Analysis* 32: 32–40.

Loewenstein, R. (1957). Some thoughts on interpretation in the theory and practice of psychoanalysis. *Psychoanalytic Study of the Child* 12: 127–50.

Olinick, S. L. (1980). *The Psychotherapeutic Instrument*. New York: Jason Aronson.

Poland, W. (1975). Tact as a psychoanalytic function. *International Journal of Psycho-Analysis* 56: 155–62.

Racker, H. (1953). A contribution to the problem of counter-transference. *International Journal of Psycho-Analysis* 34: 313–24.

———. (1957). The meanings and uses of counter-transference. *Psychoanalytic Quarterly* 26: 303–57.

———. (1968). *Transference and Countertransference*. London: Hogarth Press.

Sandler, J. (1976). Countertransference and role-responsiveness. *International Review of Psycho-Analysis* 3: 43–47.

Ticho, E. (1972). The effects of the analyst's personality on psychoanalytic treatment. *Psychoanalytic Forum* 4: 137–51.

Winnicott, D. W. (1949). Hate in the countertransference. *International Journal of Psycho-Analysis* 30: 69–75.

———. (1963). The development of the capacity for concern. In *The Maturational Processes and the Facilitating Environment*. New York: International Universities Press, 1965.

8

INTERPRETATIONS

How important are interpretations? What do interpretations have to do with change, and how much of the change that occurs in a patient during the course of psychotherapy is attributable to the interpretations that a therapist makes? How important is the content of the interpretation and how specific must the content be in order for an interpretation to be useful? Is it possible to differentiate between what portion of change has to do with the experience of a psychotherapeutic "process" and what part has to do with the specific interpretation or interpretations? An interaction between a patient and a therapist that is grounded in empathy may allow for some developmental growth in and of itself.

The above are difficult questions for any therapist to answer with certainty. Sometimes after the therapy has ended, it is not the blinding insights that are remembered by the patient, but the times when the therapist was experienced as most human or most spontaneous. It is important to mention, however, that even memories of the therapist's human kindness or spontaneity may be analogous to a screen memory, so that a deeper understanding or fundamental theme (which may have to do with a moment of greatest closeness) lies hidden behind the "picture" that is recalled. Perhaps positive memories of psychotherapy are a condensation of a broad psychotherapeutic process as well as specific memories of the warmth experienced in knowing that a therapist is working hard to be of help.

Interpretations are possibly the most essential element the therapist brings to the therapeutic process. When making interpretations to the patient, certain treatment-related questions come to mind.

1. What is the point or focus of the comment?
2. If the point of the comment is clear, what language would be best to use, or how best to phrase what is there in the material to interpret?
3. Is the timing precise enough to say something, and how much of what is understood by the therapist should be expressed?
4. What could the comment ultimately achieve for the patient (assuming all goes well when the interpretation is delivered)? Will the interpretation expand the patient's understanding, that is, will the comment serve to clarify one of the patient's themes (major motif), thus serving to increase self-awareness? Will the comment change the way the patient thinks about others, thus allowing the patient to communicate or relate differently with people? Will the interpretation serve to clarify the past or improve the patient's ability to recall important or previously repressed material, thus facilitating continuity with the past?
5. Most importantly, will the interpretation hurt the patient?

WHAT IS AN INTERPRETATION?

The most classical definition of an interpretation would be that an interpretation conveys the latent, unconscious meaning of the patient's thoughts or actions to the patient. Many theorists and clinicians would argue that interpretations about the transference are the most effective kind of interpretation. "Effective" would imply that unconscious meaning is communicated, with the tact, timing, and clarity that allows for change to be promoted. Prior to the "interpretation" a variety of comments, defined as "intervention," describe the kinds of communications that exist between patient and therapist in a psychoanalytically oriented psychotherapy. Interventions include "advice," "educational comments," "supportive comments," and "clarifications," all of which will be discussed.

WHAT DO THERAPISTS HOPE INTERPRETATIONS WILL BE ABLE TO ACCOMPLISH?

Psychotherapy hopes to allow people to become aware of and understand aspects of inner experience, so that maladaptive behaviors and defenses become less acceptable to the "ego" (that is, become "ego-dystonic"). Interventions and then interpretations facilitate the recognition and definition of thoughts, feelings, behaviors, interactions, repetitions, resistances, transferences, reenactments, etc., in the hopes of achieving an understanding about the underlying meaning of all of the foregoing. As underlying emotions and motives are understood, the patient's incentive to utilize maladaptive behaviors and patterns changes at a conscious/cognitive level. As previous habitual but dysfunctional ways of interacting are understood by the patient to obfuscate real desires, more direct ways of addressing needs becomes a possibility. The following might illustrate this point:

> Paul was a persistently active "Don Juan." In psychotherapy, he realized that his desire to seduce women was derived from the chronic experience of rejection at the hands of his cold and rigid mother, and that his underlying, repetitive, romantic affairs reflected a repetitive need to prove his worth and express his pain and anger. The effect of achieving this insight was that these behaviors become no longer effective or acceptable to him.

Psychotherapy aims to increase flexibility by improving defenses, thus expanding potential options, the effect of which is that feelings and needs can be more directly and realistically addressed. As emotions are more accessible and more easily tolerated, and what is needed is differentiated from what is simply wanted, a person is better able to deal with life and find reasonable gratification. The interactive, interpretative function provided by the therapist, including the capacity to know how to achieve self-soothing, reflection, and self-analysis, ultimately becomes internalized (taken inside the mind) by the patient.

THE COURSE OF INTERPRETATIVE PROCESS

Significant interpretations are built up slowly. Grand interpretations that "strike like bolts of thunder and split stone" are rarely useful, and more often are destructive to the patient and strain the psychotherapy. The achievement of enduring psychological change is more accurately compared to the wearing away of stone. Time and effort are required for the integration of material that is uncomfortable and difficult to accept. As therapists, we slowly direct the patient's attention to areas of concern, as the significance of symptoms or issues of character gradually become understood. A therapist rarely shares all that is known about the patient or the patient's material in any one "gulp."

Rudy was a chronically frustrated and angry person. His character style was such that he habitually dealt with his anger with a passive-aggressive style; more challenging, however, was that he was doggedly resistant to entertaining any possibility that he might be angry, particularly if the anger was directed at his therapist.

Throughout his life, Rudy had harbored grudges toward numerous authority figures; his therapist was simply the latest authority figure on the scene to participate in the same old scenario. While he presented himself as soft, passive, nonaggressive, and unassertive, Rudy was preoccupied with danger and a curiosity about aggressive acts and situations. In fact, Rudy began his therapy with an interest in individuals who had dangerous careers involving potential violence, and dreams of destruction and violence. Once he dreamed of murder and of carrying a smoking gun. In his early treatment, Rudy's dreams were focused on guns as tools of aggression, agents of empowerment, and symbols of sexual potency.

For quite a long time, the best that Rudy's therapist was able to do was to clarify that he seemed preoccupied with the topic of aggression. One day Rudy began to talk about the way he hated getting stuck in traffic jams; how unbearable he found it to have to be "stuck in a place, unable to get anything from being there." Somehow in this moment, the therapist was able to say that perhaps Rudy thought this same way about being stuck in the room with her (the therapist), particularly if he thought that she was giving him nothing. Rudy was silent for a long time. Finally he shifted uncomfortably in his chair and the therapist realized that Rudy was trying to hide the fact that he was crying. The therapist remained quiet. Slowly Rudy began to speak, his words labored. He said that it was always like that with his father; the long silences at dinner, the long silences in the car, the way in which he felt as though his father didn't notice that he was alive and at the same time was always so punitive toward him.

This sensitive and tactful therapist thought long and hard in this moment about whether to say anything. So many previous attempts to engage Rudy in a reflection about himself had failed. Even when she decided to take a chance, she elected to bring the interpretation into the transference, rather than specifically referring to Rudy's relationship with his father or trying to tie the transference to the genetic interpretation that lay behind it. Taking into consideration this patient, who so badly needed to be rebellious with any figure of authority, the therapist's carefulness allowed Rudy to come to the more significant and fundamental genetic interpretation by himself; somewhere (in his mind) he knew that his relationship with his father was filled with pain and distress. In this way, Rudy was able to allow insight while still preserving his dignity.

THE INEXACT INTERPRETATION

Glover's (1931) concept of the "inexact interpretation" is a clever and provocative idea, especially worth calling to mind when contemplating the reason why a patient might *prefer* a particular interpretation or interpretations. The inexact interpretation refers to a partially correct interpretation, which is favored in lieu of a more accurate and complete interpretation; by accepting the partially correct interpretation, a deeper, more significant interpretation is avoided.

Trends in "pop psychology" offer the most obvious example of how certain "pat" interpretations fade in and out of vogue, much like the "number-one song" on the radio. "Codependency" had its heyday as a pat and popular interpretation. While the word had some usefulness, it also became a buzz word that could be adhered to tenaciously, providing ample resistance to more accurate and less flattering interpretations.

> Pammy, a very spoiled and unmotivated twenty-year-old girl, was enraged with her therapist for daring to address her entitled behavior. In the next hour, Pammy informed her therapist that she was quitting the treatment with her current therapist because she had discovered "the problem" and had found "a new therapist who would *really* be able to help her." Her new therapist was a "recovering codependent."

Patients and therapists alike at times utilize "incomplete" interpretations. The incomplete interpretation is not the same entity however, as the "inexact" interpretation; the incomplete interpretation is understood by both patient and therapist together to only be "on the way" to a more complete or fundamental interpretation. That an interpretation is "inexact" becomes particularly obvious when a person latches onto the interpretation as though it were sufficient to obviate the need for any further understanding. For example, "Fred" was very fond of telling his therapist that any behavior in which he engaged "was understandable" (and therefore in his mind, acceptable) because his "parents were so awful" that they had "robbed [him] of his childhood."

The overutilization of inexact interpretations can be apparent in the beginning of a treatment with a patient who has been in a prior treatment and/or who has become familiar with "self-help" books. In an attempt to find an explanation for an uncomfortable situation or feeling, a certain perceived enlightenment can become "beloved." It is always wise for the new therapist to keep in mind that explanations do not become entrenched without reason, however. Pammy clung to her "codependent" explanation to avoid examining or coming to terms with unappealing aspects of her character, a good reason for a therapist to meet the challenge of Pammy's inexact interpretation with a certain amount of resolve. The problem is that inexact interpretations can also be retained because they serve a "transitional object" function or act as a "life raft"; in this case, the inexact interpretation serves to hold the owner of the interpretation afloat until such time as a better rescue boat not only comes along, but also proves to be more reliable and durable (the therapist).

THE POWER OF INTERPRETATIONS

The interpretation has power because the psychotherapist has importance. If the therapist had no importance, the interpretation would have no more significance than the daily astrological reading would to someone who didn't subscribe to astrology. It isn't only patients who sometimes attribute "powers" to the psychotherapist. People in general will not infrequently joke with a therapist about whether the therapist is "reading my mind." Fantasies regarding the therapist's omniscient capacity are both comforting and discomforting.

> Dr. Pearl, a psychiatrist, had occasion to take a ski vacation with his good friend and colleague, Dr. Emerald, also a psychiatrist. Following a vigorous day of skiing, the two friends decided to assuage their aching bones with some time in the sauna at their lodging. The sauna was full of rowdy and very sociable men. The conversation moved rapidly from telling tales about the day of skiing, to telling raunchy jokes and off-color stories about personal experiences. The two psychiatrists quickly joined in with the conversation. Time went by, with all enjoying the merriment, until someone in the assemblage asked Dr. Emerald what he did for a living. Dr. Emerald, "less than on his toes" after his long day of exercise, replied that he was a psychiatrist. The silence that followed was deafening. Eventually people seemed to loosen up somewhat, but the mood of the group was decidedly altered.

The interpretation has potential power because it represents the understanding of meaning, and the understanding of meaning opens up the possibility of inducing change in a person. Changing a person can lead to changing a person's life.

> Rudy (described previously) eventually understood, through interpretation, that the passive-aggressive and rebellious stance he maintained in the world had a meaning. The meaning had to with the rage he suppressed continuously in order to exist around the father he feared, and the pain and wish for revenge and restitution that were consequent to his father's disinterest in him. Rudy understood, also through genetic reconstruction and interpretation, that his father's experience in a prison camp during the war had damaged his father irretrievably, and that these events had nothing to do with Rudy's worth or capacity.
>
> Rudy went back to school. He discovered that he was actually quite good at science and math. After a year of taking college courses in junior college, he applied and was accepted to an excellent four-year college. During his junior year in college, Rudy did community service at an animal shelter. He loved the animals. He frequently told his therapist that working with animals was the perfect job for him because the animals were always so loving and appreciative to those who tried to help. He had gotten to the point in his treatment where he could even laugh at his previous defenses. He would joke about the fact that he wasn't about to "mess" with the "authority figures" in the animal hospital, because the authority figures were all magnificent big dogs and he knew he was no match for them!
>
> Rudy applied to and was accepted to veterinary school. He went on to become a professor of animal surgery at the veterinary school at which he was trained. He married, and some years later began a family of his own. Rudy appreciated quite well the power of interpretation to change a person's life.

THE DELIVERY OF AN INTERPRETATION

Winnicott (1951) said that interpretations should not be suddenly released, but owing to analytic preparation, should be experienced as something the patient has always known. This is not the easiest of tasks for the therapist to accomplish. Will the patient be surprised by the interpretation? Will the interpretation be *expected*: "I sort of knew that you were going to say that." Or will the interpretation be totally *unexpected*: "Not only is that off the wall, but I am really offended by what you said!" Can the patient integrate, sufficiently enough to make the interpretation worth offering, what is suggested by the therapist?

A patient may respond in a manner that the therapist had not predicted even when the conditions in which the interpretation was offered seem optimal. Failures in empathy or precision occur; an interpretation can be experienced as unempathic because the timing of the interpretation was poor, the wording of the interpretation caused the patient to feel criticized or humiliated, or the interpretation was just plain inaccurate. All of this becomes visible when the interpretation is offered. Hopefully the patient will be able to explain to the therapist that the interpretation was hurtful or seemed to miss the mark and both patient and therapist will then be able to proceed to explore other options.

Context matters when an interpretation is suggested. The nature of the current climate of the transference will affect the receptivity of the patient, especially if the interpretation is difficult to accept. For example, if a patient has hostile feelings toward the therapist already, an unwelcome (however accurate) interpretation may be perceived as or used by the patient to avoid understanding, perhaps by attacking the therapist. Such it was with Pammy, described above. Pammy wanted and expected her therapist to indulge her, as her parents had always done before; Pammy also knew on some level that her therapist wanted her to work in the treatment. This was something that Pammy had not done much of before, and did not want to do in the present or the near future. She made use of any interpretation that was in the neighborhood of her self-indulgence to talk about her therapist's "unprofessional manner and insensitivity to her needs."

Some occurrences become difficult to interpret because of the specific sensitivity that is often associated with these events. For example, people often find parapraxes or slips of the tongue uniquely embarrassing. Kohut (1970) suggested that parapraxes should not be directly interpreted because of the associated narcissistic vulnerability; the slip often leaves the owner of the parapraxis feeling exposed and mortified. This embarrassment does not need to be amplified by a therapist. Of course, not all slips need to be avoided. If the patient finds the slip amusing or notices the slip and wonders about it, then the exploration of the parapraxis can become a collaborative and interesting (and therefore not mortifying) experience. Otherwise, the parapraxis should probably be filed away in the therapist's memory bank, and the meaning contemplated for another and more appropriate time.

Another, perhaps slightly less vulnerable, arena of occurrences has to do with the territory of interpreting the dream. One patient told her therapist that she had many dreams all the time but could not bear to share them; she was so sure that her therapist could see in the dreams things that she could not see. Additionally, dreams often contain embarrassing elements. These are difficult to report unless the climate between patient and therapist has been well established to be one of safety and trust.

Sometimes it is tempting to point out a particular behavior on the part of the patient that is symptomatic or exemplifies a character trait. This is always something to think twice about before proceeding. Focusing on some behaviors or character traits, whether by the therapist or even by the patient, may stimulate shame.

> Joe had a long history of provoking arguments with coworkers. He was keenly aware of this old pattern, which had landed him in trouble with fatiguing predictability. Whenever Joe reported another argument from which he seemed helpless to refrain, he felt a deep sense of mortification and shame that he had been unable to stop himself, which further promoted his belief that he was defective. Consequently, Joe's therapist could not find a way to engage Joe in the process of curiosity about his behavior.
>
> Eventually the therapist could see the meaning of Joe's pattern of provoking arguments so clearly that she felt Joe surely must be close to seeing it as well. She made an interpretation about Joe's profound sense of shame about the ADHD that had remained undiagnosed throughout his childhood. She pointed out the repetition in Joe's adult life of his childhood pattern of not being able to control his inattention and impulsivity, and the shame that would always follow from his loss of control. Joe looked at the therapist and blinked several times. He hesitated only for a moment longer and then spoke softly. He said that he knew in his heart that what the therapist had said was true.

THE IMPORTANCE OF "TACT"

"Tact," which is the ability to perceive intuitively or know what might be a helpful or sensitive thing to say, operates silently but is an essential prerequisite for an interpretation (Poland 1975). Derived from the "ability to put oneself in another's shoes" or to "feel" what another person would feel (that is, to "empathize"), tact implies an understanding of the potential narcissistic

vulnerability of another person. The use of tact allows the therapist to protect the patient's self-esteem, while at the same offering or introducing insights that have the potential to be difficult, or painful, or injurious. Tact is
what allows a therapist to gauge what should or should not be shared with
or said to a patient. At times, to say too much can be tactless and only hurt
the patient. At other times, to say too little can be tactless when honesty
would be more respectful to the patient. Sometimes, saying nothing or saying nothing of consequence is rationalized as thoughtfulness or politeness,
but actually confrontation or directness would have been more tactful than
saying nothing. The thoughtfulness or politeness in this case is not tact but
"pseudotact" (Poland 1975).

THE ROLE OF ABSTINENCE

The principle of abstinence continues to evoke much debate (Stolorow,
Brandchaft, and Atwood 1987) despite assuming the position of a fundamental psychoanalytic concept. Abstinence suggests withholding and even
moral restraint, but what really is abstinence in a psychotherapy setting and
what is the role of abstinence in interpretation? Where did this notion come
from and why?

Abstinence in a psychotherapeutic process means that the therapist
abstains from a certain type of involvement with the patient. By maintaining a certain consistent distance from the patient, not routinely reinforcing
or supporting the patient without investigation, but always in search to understand "what makes the patient tick" (see chapter 3, "Formulation"), the
therapist remains in a "neutral" position. The clinical practice of abstinence
is never absolute but relative, and always subject to the circumstances at
hand (which may have to do with the patient or with the situation). Some
patients need a positive or friendly response from the therapist; other patients find any warmth or friendliness on the part of the therapist to be intrusive and/or seductive. Abstinence defines the boundary. The giving of
advice is limited, sharing of personal information by the therapist is mostly
discouraged, participation in the patient's extratherapeutic activities is selective and always carefully measured, and advice is only offered when really necessary and always within the boundary of the therapist's field of
knowledge.

An additional reason for the rule of abstinence is that abstinence serves
the function of providing a place in which fantasies and perceptions can be

elaborated. In everyday life, when fantasies and perceptions are shared with another person, discomfort in the other person may occur, which may cause the other person to put an end to the elaboration. Offering a "problem-solving" response can also block the elaboration of the fantasy or perception.

Abstinence does not mean that the therapist has to be cold, distant, or uninvolved; these qualities are never a useful addition to any therapeutic interaction, but a persistent attention to the "boundaries" between the patient and therapist is always implied.

Freud thought of abstinence as a therapeutic tool and rule. He modeled the analyst after the unemotional and detached surgeon; however, this somewhat cold representation was in contrast to his own therapeutic demeanor. On occasion Freud fed patients in his office, had them to dinner, praised them, and even helped them financially. Why then did he develop his belief in the rule of abstinence?

Certainly one motivation for the necessity to attend to a rule of abstinence had to do with the destructive sexual, business, or otherwise personal involvements between therapist and patient that occurred in Freud's time, and still occur today. Unfortunately, some therapists do use or have used patients for sexual pleasure, as a vehicle to secure business deals, or for other favors that are personal for the therapist and contribute little or nothing to the patient; these occurrences have the potential to leave enduring scars on vulnerable patients. The rule of abstinence defines a boundary so that the therapist does not express romantic feelings for the patient, does not have sex with a patient, does not cultivate an extratherapeutic relationship for the sole purposes of the therapist, and always scrutinizes the motive for any contemplation about nontherapeutic involvement.

Abstinence protects both the patient and the therapist. Freud recognized from his own experiences that a potential danger was associated with intense feelings toward a patient. Even very positive feelings toward a patient can be less than constructive if a therapist's ability to evaluate a patient becomes consequently colored, or rescue fantasies about a patient get out of hand. Additionally, a patient's reactions or feelings toward or about the therapist can be narcissistically gratifying (for the therapist); a therapist might use a patient for self-serving reasons, often without conscious knowledge. In practice, each therapist tries to achieve a humanistic balance between friendly support and unwavering adherence to integrity and neutrality; these qualities must always accompany the responsibility of having license to make use of the "tools" of the psychotherapeutic process. Interpretation is one of those tools.

TYPES OF INTERVENTIONS

Include the following:

> Advice
> Educational
> Supportive
> Clarification

Advice

Advice is commonly dispensed in many types of therapy; however, advice can be the most problematic type of comment provided to a patient. In the first place, a therapist has a domain of expertise, the value of which is sought when a patient presents for a consultation and/or for ongoing treatment. No other area of expertise is being consciously solicited by the patient, no matter how many other areas or fields the therapist has mastered outside of the psychotherapeutic space. In the second place, no matter how logical or reasonable may be the advice offered, to give advice may be to inadvertently ask of the patient something that seems unbearable or impossible; the result is that the patient feels ashamed because of a resultant perceived incapacity. Thus, in the service of trying to be of assistance and better a patient's circumstances, a patient might be advised to confront a friend or a boss, or to leave a poor relationship. Obviously, when safety is an overriding issue, the therapist's advice or intervention has a clear-cut and unarguable motivation (for example, in the case of the individual who is with a dangerously abusive spouse); without such a clear-cut indication for advice, the therapist may discover too late that what looked like fertile ground for intervention was really ground not ready for planting. Many a therapy has been brought to a close because a well-meaning therapist offered well-intended but ill-advised advice.

The giving of advice to a patient is relatively easy for a therapist to do; the problem is that the therapist doesn't have to live the life that is affected by whatever advice is given. The patient lived the life that existed before the therapist ever appeared on the scene, and the patient will live the life that exists long after any advice on the therapist's part is put into play; this is a valuable and sobering thought. A patient may not follow the "best" course because the patient simply cannot do it; a patient may not follow the "best" course because "the course" is really not the best.

When a patient asks for advice, the inquiry may indicate a wish to satisfy some other but less apparent need; this need may have nothing to do
with the advice that is directly solicited. Advice, as with all interventions,
occurs in the context of a transference. Patients have feelings and needs that
are directed toward the therapist; advice, for example, can feel to the patient
like a form of parental concern or nurturance. Advice is this context is not
necessarily unhelpful as long as the advice is solely in the area of the therapist's expertise. However, the offering of advice does not usually fulfill the
need for nurturance in the long run, and is therefore not a substitute for
eventual interpretation of the transference in a psychoanalytically conducted
psychotherapy.

The frequent giving of advice by the therapist may preclude the expression and development of the patient's ability to think independently;
Winnicott (1960) would refer to the development of the "true self." If the
therapist only gives advice, the patient may attempt to follow the therapist's
lead without any real understanding of the knowledge base or thought
process involved that allowed the therapist to come to the decision that was
offered in the form of advice. The goal of psychoanalytic psychotherapy, ultimately, is for the patient to "internalize" a thought process that allows the
patient to come to decisions that make sense for the patient, or to be able
to put together a plan that would lead to the gathering of sufficient information to allow for the best decision that can be made under whatever circumstances might prevail.

It is worth remembering that to give advice means to give counsel or
information, to render an opinion. Therefore, when making a decision to
dispense advice or to refrain from offering advice, the therapist usually first
contemplates certain questions.

1. What does the patient really want and need?
2. If the patient has a sense of what action is needed or required, what
   interferes with taking action, and is the interference reality based or
   neurotically based (a psychological conflict precludes taking effective action)?
3. If the patient cannot figure out what action is needed or required
   (which might include taking no action at all), what stands in the patient's way? Is the difficulty reality based, that is, has insufficient information been collected or is the information not available that
   would allow an informed decision to be made? In this case, the
   therapist's "advice" may be an important aspect of the gathering of

information, especially if the therapist is specifically consulted as part of the patient's effort to do diligent "research."

If the difficulty that the patient faces in arriving at a decision is not about a reality issue (a reality issue would include a lack of adequate information with which to make a decision) would the giving of advice by the therapist be wise? As mentioned above, advice can interfere with the task of understanding the psychological obstacles that may stand in the way of the patient being able to visualize a sensible pathway and make a decision.

> Charlie was a thirty-year-old businessman whose job involved frequent dealings with a number of more senior bosses. One of Charlie's bosses turned out to be particularly harsh, denigrating, excessively hostile, and perhaps even bizarre. Charlie frequently brought up with his therapist the nuisance and burden that dealing with this boss had become. At times, the situation was so difficult that Charlie thought perhaps he should quit his job. Charlie contemplated confronting his boss, but worried that any response to a confrontation would be worse than the consequences of either staying and doing nothing, or leaving. Charlie would try to solicit advice from his therapist. What should he do? Should he leave or stay, do nothing or do something?
>
> Charlie's therapist felt that to give advice under these circumstances would be unwise. The job was an excellent position in an uncertain economy and Charlie had a family to support. To confront the boss might be a disaster, because the extent of the boss's disturbance was not something the therapist could assess. Furthermore, the therapist thought that Charlie himself already knew all that the therapist was thinking, so what was it really that Charlie was asking? The moment that the therapist asked himself this question, he knew exactly the answer.
>
> One of Charlie's most significant issues in psychotherapy had been his great need to prove himself "manly." Charlie would often engage in activities that were somewhat puzzling and distressing to his wife; eventually what became apparent was that all the activities had the same effect for Charlie because all of the activities shared a common theme. Whether the activity was skiing double–black diamond slopes or learning to skydive, each of Charlie's activities made him feel like "more of a man." Charlie knew that he couldn't afford to lose his job and he knew that it would be unwise to confront the boss. He simply felt that the "manly" thing to do would be to "take a stand."

Charlie's therapist never gave advice about this matter, but he did tell Charlie something, and he told Charlie that an "interpretation" was hidden in the words. The therapist said, "Sometimes to be a "man," one has to do first and foremost what is wise." Charlie knew immediately what his therapist meant. Charlie's father had been a macho bully who had told Charlie throughout his life that to be afraid to take a chance was to be a "wimp." Charlie's father took many chances, and most of them were unwise. Charlie made the decision to stay at his job, and he quietly and without distress relinquished the idea of confronting his boss.

Educational

"Educational comments" are exactly what is implied by the phrase. Educational comments are an attempt to enhance the patient's understanding of the workings of the mind, through the means of educating the patient about the factors involved in understanding what "makes a person tick." Through introducing the patient to an understanding of the "language" of the mind, emotional and psychological issues become more understandable. Particularly for the patient who might be new to the process of a psychoanalytically conducted psychotherapy, educational comments are especially useful as long as the comments are delivered with "tact" (neither pedantic nor patronizing).

An educational comment may be as simple as, "People sometimes try to keep busy in order to avoid the awareness of being sad." Another educational comment along the same lines might be, "People often do things for reasons of which they are unaware." Each of these comments is an attempt to introduce the patient to an aspect of the "language of the mind." The first comment is an introduction to the idea that "defenses" can exist and operate silently (that is, out of awareness). The second comment refers to the concept of the unconscious and unconscious motivation.

Supportive

Supportive comments are often useful, sometimes essential, and certainly appear in every therapy. However, supportive comments can also be experienced by the patient in a multitude of not so useful ways. These include:

1. The comment feels demeaning, because it feels pedantic or patronizing.

Mary, four weeks postpartum with her second child, spoke to her therapist about her concern that she was crying all the time and found herself not wanting to be with her baby at all. The therapist assured Mary that this was "not an uncommon feeling" and that "everything will be all right." Mary felt that her therapist's comment was patronizing and demeaning. She was quite serious about her feeling that something was very wrong with the way she felt, because her first postpartum period had not been at all the same. Mary went for a consultation with another therapist and her postpartum depression was diagnosed. Four weeks later, now on an appropriate antidepressant for her condition, Mary was back to her old self.

2. The comment feels useless, because it is either incorrect or of no benefit.

Mary, in the example just given, felt that her therapist's comment was both incorrect and of no benefit; for both of these reasons, the comment was useless to her. Mary knew that she was in need of specific help; support seemed completely insufficient given her circumstances, and therefore to Mary, the therapist's comment felt completely unempathic.

3. The comment contributes nothing to the patient's understanding.

Mary, again in the aforementioned example, was desperate. She was frightened that she should never have had another child; perhaps the reason that she felt as she did was evidence of this. How could she, who had always loved children and thought that she wanted "at least four of them," be so uninterested in her baby? The therapist's comment did nothing to help Mary resolve the questions in her mind, because she did not think her uncomfortable feelings were either previously typical of her or typical of other young mothers whom she knew.

When the bottom suddenly falls out from beneath a patient's self-esteem, or excessive anxiety erupts because of a specific event, or an intolerable conflict arises for which no immediate resolution is at hand, or for whatever immediate reason a person's ability to function adequately suddenly fails, a supportive comment may be not only appropriate but kind. On occasion, a direct interpretive comment that addresses the psychological origin of a failure of self-esteem, an escalation of anxiety, or an enhancement of conflict helps to restore or consolidate the patient's equilibrium. At other times, the immediacy of a situation and the critical need to ensure a rapid restoration of functioning necessitates an alternative technique; sometimes, the patient simply requires a "vote of confidence." This is the function of the supportive comment. So it was for "Jennifer" with her psychoanalyst.

> Jennifer had long wished that she could go to medical school and become a psychiatrist. Unfortunately, however, Jennifer was "phobic" about mathematics. Finally she had convinced herself, with the help of her psychoanalyst of four years, to try to take the necessary prerequisites for application to medical school. The night before her final exam in "Advanced Calculus," the last exam in the last required course she needed to complete, Jennifer panicked. She told her analyst that she "just couldn't do it!" Her analyst, without a moment's hesitation, said to Jennifer, "You can do this Jennifer, and someday, I'll be voting for you for President of The American Psychoanalytic Association." Jennifer's panic subsided, and several weeks later, she began her application process to medical school with a "straight A" average in math and the sciences.

A therapist hopes to facilitate the patient's autonomous capacity to resolve conflict, maintain self–esteem, and assume direction in life. At times, a therapist's own reactions may play a role in the overutilization of supportive comments, particularly when the therapist is feeling helpless, overwhelmed, threatened, etc. Offering supportive comments may help a therapist feel less impotent in the face of a patient's pain. The most useful comments are those that are specifically directed, with a clear-cut intent in mind. Unsophisticated comments such as, "I know everything will work out," "I know you are a good person," "Things will get better," etc., often miss the boat. On the other hand, sophisticated supportive remarks are made possible, actually for the most part are only possible, because of the therapist's understanding of the forces that drive or motivate the patient ("dynamics").

> Brian had very mixed feelings toward his terminally ill father. He had felt deep resentment toward his father, and for this reason had for many years avoided almost all contact. During the process of psychotherapy, Brian had developed a deeper understanding of his father's character and the influences that had created who his father had become. Consequently, the beginnings of a relationship between father and son had begun. Tragically, it

was in this time period of renewed possibility that Brian's father's rare and aggressive cancer was diagnosed. Seemingly overnight, Brian watched his father sink into a coma, suffer a respiratory arrest, and become intubated and placed on a respirator. Brian was thrust suddenly into the position, as the executor of his father's living will, of deciding whether or not to disconnect the respirator and let his father die.

Brian knew that turning off the respirator was what his father would want, but he was paralyzed by confusion, anxiety, conflict, and guilt. He could not make a decision. It was at this juncture, as the days threatened to turn into weeks of indecision, that Brian's therapist elected to intervene. He said to Brian:

> *"I know that you have had very mixed feelings toward your father, and these feelings have at times included periods of intense anger. However, the decision to turn off the respirator at this time in your father's life, when your father has no chance of further useful life before him now, and all who have knowledge of the situation have advised you so, seems totally and really only, decent and humane."*

In times of human loss and greatly difficult circumstances, direct human support is sometimes the only appropriate and meaningful course of action. Thus, the loss of a loved one, the discovery of a serious illness, a disastrous or heart-rending change in life circumstances, necessitates compassion before interpretation about more complex unconscious meanings. Perhaps Shakespeare grasped and phrased this best when he said, "Honest plain words best pierce the ear of grief" (*Love's Labour's Lost*, Act 5, Scene 2).

Clarification

To "clarify" means to make or become easier to understand" or "to make or become free and clear from impurities" (*Webster's New Twentieth-Century Dictionary*). The elucidation or illumination of a patient's feelings, ideas, perceptions, or motivations is the goal of a "clarification." The gradual identification of the patient's predominant feelings or concerns is an essential building block of the house that is eventually the whole of the psychotherapy process. Clarifications are the result of the therapist's ability to recognize common threads within the patient's associations. Clarifications reflect back to the patient or assist in the effort to put into words what seems to be on the patient's mind. Clarifications attempt to direct the patient's attention to a potential idea or theme that might be a precursor to a more complete understanding or interpretation. A clarification "lays the groundwork." The ability to decipher thoughts and then put those thoughts into language is an essential aspect of the psychotherapy process.

Simple, direct comments such as the following are examples of clarifications:

> "You seem to be saying that your father was pretty uninvolved in your life."
>
> "You seem to be talking about the fact that it's burdensome when your kids and your husband are needy at the same time."
>
> "You seem to be talking about all the ways in which you have felt defeated lately."
>
> "You seem to be saying that you were excited about your acceptance to law school, until that conversation with your mother."

INTERPRETATIONS

Include the following:

> Comments that Address Resistance or Defense
> Transference Interpretations
> Reconstructions or Genetic Interpretations

Resistance and Defense

In spite of the fact that a patient usually seeks treatment in search of help, forces within the patient can impede the patient's ability to make the most use of the available resource of the treatment and the therapist, thus serving to defeat the process of change; we call this "resistance." "Defenses" are mechanisms that are used by the ego, and serve the purpose of protecting the person who makes use of the defense against potential danger. Defenses operate unconsciously, and can be adaptive or maladaptive. Identification of resistance in psychotherapy allows the patient to wonder what it is that the patient would rather avoid thinking about or discussing in the treatment.

Identifying the characteristic defenses that a person makes use of and what precipitates the mobilization of these defenses allow both therapist and patient to wonder about hidden underlying emotional currents (latent content) that necessitate the employment of the defensive arsenal. With time, specific defenses may be linked with specific feelings, events, or constellations of events. In movies about the old West, the audience always knew where the dead body was because the buzzards hovered above the scene of the crime.

1. "Jill" would be especially kind to those who had hurt her feelings or angered her ("reaction formation").
2. "Jack" would become completely immersed in a new sporting activity, buying all the latest equipment and taking lessons as often as possible, whenever he was depressed about the loss of his latest affair ("hypomanic" defense).
3. "Tanya" would become ecstatic about a new girlfriend, certain that this was the "best friend she'd ever had," until the new friend disappointed her in some, perhaps minor, way; then she would reject the new friend absolutely and turn to the next wonderful new friend with equal and similarly intense emotion ("splitting").

"Billy," eight years old, still had "accidents" at school. He would fail to go to the bathroom in time and wet his pants. For this reason and others, he was seeing "Dr. T" twice a week. On the latest occasion of having an accident at school, Dr. T gently brought up with Billy that it must have been hard for him when his classmates teased him about his wet pants (which Billy's mother had reported to Dr. T). Billy, in characteristic fashion, replied, "It wasn't hard. I just pretended I didn't hear them and then it didn't bother me at all!" ("denial").

Dr. T, who had heard this before, gently persisted and interpreted the "resistance": "Perhaps it is hard to talk to me about your wet pants because it makes you feel so bad, just as it makes you feel bad when your friends at school tease you."

Billy immediately shook his head and promptly covered his ears with his hands. Dr. T thought for a moment. He was quite sure that Billy had heard what he'd said, and quite certain that addressing the resistance was "on the money." Dr. T continued, now with an interpretation about the symbolic function (latent content) of Billy's symptom, hoping to get underneath the "defensive denial."

"Even though it makes you uncomfortable to be teased by your friends at school, I think that it is worth it to you to wet your pants, because you are so angry. You are angry at your Mommy and Daddy for getting a divorce, and angry at your Daddy for being so hard on you when your Mommy is not around. Last night you stayed at your Dad's house and he was hard on you about your soccer game. Perhaps this is your way of showing both your Mommy and your Daddy how powerful you can be with your pee,

just as you could be powerful with your pee when you were a little boy."

At this point, Billy promptly took his hands off of his ears, picked
up a ball in the toy box on the shelf, and hurled it as hard as he
could at his therapist. Dr. T deftly caught the ball in his hand, and
just as he did so, noted the secret smile of unspoken acknowledgment that crossed Billy's face.

Ego psychology emphasizes the utility of interpreting resistance or defense, before interpreting latent content (or the underlying anxiety). With
some patients, this tactic seems particularly useful. For the obsessive, so reluctant to lose control, gradual, sensitive delineation of defensive patterns allows for a graduated tolerance for greater vulnerability, opening the door to
face underlying feelings and conflict. For a patient who is acutely overwhelmed and in need of rapid access to understanding, speaking more directly to the underlying feelings or conflict may be important. Most essential is to keep in mind what the patient can tolerate and integrate, as
opposed to what would be overwhelming and frightening.

Dr. T felt that Billy's symptom had continued long enough. His use of
the symptom served a defensive function to ward off his pain and anger, and
the meaning of the symptom was close to undeniable. Billy's ability to move
along the developmental continuum was being impacted by his insistence
upon staying a little boy, and making use of a little boy's "weapon." To be a
little boy was to hold on to a time that was prior to his parent's divorce.

TRANSFERENCE INTERPRETATIONS

Transference interpretations are an essential element of psychodynamic psychotherapy (the concept of transference is explored in chapter 6, "Transference"). Expectations and desires arise in all significant relationships, "transference" describes the appearance and expression of these expectations and
desires in interpersonal interactions and relationships. Transference-based or
transference-driven expectations and desires can be mildly to extremely unrealistic, and can give rise to destructive and unfulfilling relationships, or
damaging and impetuous behaviors within relationships.

Dynamic psychotherapy attempts to provide an environment in which
transference, with all of its many manifestations, can be mobilized within the
treatment and systematically analyzed. Additionally, the therapist in a dynamic psychotherapy hopes to be able to provide the patient with a respect

and appreciation for the tremendous power that transference can exert and evidence.

Through the fostering of the development of transference, the historical origins of certain habitual expectations and reactions can be clarified and understood. Thus, in the context of a psychotherapeutic relationship, the reality of past and present circumstances are more fully appreciated and potentially mourned, clearing the way for an acceptance and enjoyment of other human possibilities. Through an understanding of individual and unique transference proclivities, and the intensity that a transference experience fosters in a psychotherapeutic process, the patient becomes more adept at recognizing, and therefore better able to negotiate, the transferences that occur in everyday life.

Transference interpretations can be frightening to some patients. If the psychotherapy is not frequent enough, safe enough, or sufficiently intense to make transference interpretations about the therapist understandable, the utilization of "displaced" transference interpretations may be more prudent and tactful. Thus, the patient's transference reactions to people other than the therapist are clarified instead.

If the decision is made that it would be useful to the patient to try to clarify a manifestation of transference with the therapist, a simple idea can be offered: "I'm wondering whether you might have some of that feeling toward me." In this manner the patient's attention is redirected, allowing the patient to look for a connection between the feelings in the story being told and the relevance of the feelings in that story toward the therapist. The transference interpretation takes the clarification one step further, drawing a connection between the patient's feelings toward the therapist and similar feelings toward a significant person in the past. Thus, the idea above would be extended to include, "I'm wondering whether you might have some of that feeling toward me now, and it is so close to the way you have so often described feeling about your father when you were growing up. Even now, when you are around your father, some of that feeling comes back again, just as I think you felt it with me a moment ago."

GENETIC INTERPRETATIONS, RECONSTRUCTION, AND PERCEPTION OF THE PAST

As transference becomes clarified and interpreted, patient and therapist connect present and past experience (as in the interpretation above). The therapist's understandable discomfort with the transference-driven affects or behaviors on the part of the patient (anger, erotic desires, etc.) that become directed toward the therapist can precipitate a rush to the genetic half of a transference interpretation. Premature genetic comments may defuse the intensity of the moment, but at the sacrifice of the full affective experience that is often necessary to convince the patient of the existence of the transference repetition and the authority that it assumes and imposes upon the patient's perceptions.

Once the therapist has addressed and not sidestepped the possibility that the patient may have feelings about the therapist, interpretation of the transference repetition and the genetic antecedent will have more command.

Ben, so atypically aloof and unemotional for such a young person (Ben was just seventeen years old), began one day to speak of his deep sense of aloneness. As his eyes began to well up, he caught himself and said, "I'm sure you don't want to hear this babble."
The therapist replied,

"I feel so often that you keep your distance because you are so unsure of my interest, and yet it has seemed so obvious to me lately that you were feeling sadder than I've seen you for awhile. I've wished that we could talk about that because the feeling of aloneness would fit with your sadness."

Ben shifted in his chair, his body position suggesting that he was clamming up again. The therapist regretted for a moment that he had spoken as he had; perhaps he had said too much, or had he said too little? The therapist settled on the latter possibility and spoke again:

"You know, Ben, you never know where you stand with your father, and can never trust that any offer of closeness will not be snatched away again in the next moment. I can understand then that it would be difficult to tell me about feelings that are quite personal. I wouldn't want to tell someone something personal either, unless I thought that that person really cared about me.

Perhaps with me as with your father, you are always left wondering whether I really am concerned about you at all. To think that I don't care and yet you have to sit and talk to me, that would be pretty awful. It would be pretty alienating I suppose, and leave you feeling quite alone, as you described today. I know that you have talked about the great sense of aloneness you have had growing up. You live with your dad since your mother died. After she was gone, he became so inaccessible. We have talked about how your dad has never been the same since your mother's death."

GENERAL RULES ABOUT THE DELIVERY OF THE INTERPRETATION; THE "ART" OF INTERPRETATION

1. Most interpretations should be reasonably short and concise.
2. Interpretations should always be worded in a manner that is respectful of the patient. Were the roles to be reversed, and the therapist would not like to hear the interpretation about to be delivered, it is probably best not to present the interpretation.
3. Usually it is best to avoid formulaic or intellectualized interpretations; they have a way of coming back "to bite" that only serves to illustrate the reason to stay away from these kinds of interpretations. Those patients who have been subjected to formulaic interpretations tend to use recognizable hallmark phrases that are of no practical value.
4. The patient's own unique methods of symbolism, which include metaphors and phrases that have personal but definite meaning for the patient, may be particularly useful when phrasing interpretations. A man who experienced women as demanding, greedy, and ultimately useless would often say, "The screwing one gets is not worth the screwing one gets." This descriptive phrase became a humorous shared communication between this man and his therapist, coming to represent those things or people or experiences that would have meant so much to the patient, but to secure them involved a price too high to pay.
5. The avoidance of becoming drawn into using the patient's defense or defensive style in the delivery of an interpretation is sometimes an effort of will on the part of the therapist (Loewenstein 1957). The patient's defensive style is sometimes "catching." Inadvertently, the therapist begins to employ the patient's own defense in the interpretations offered. Examples would include the defensive volley that can result in a debating and argumentative process with an obsessive person, or the covert or overt contemptuous battle that can occur with the borderline patient who also happens to be intimidating and demeaning to the therapist.

Dorothy, an extremely erudite and articulate but cynical woman, reluctantly came to treatment. Dorothy could be vivacious, charming, and entertaining; however, just beneath the surface simmered a pot of anger and contempt.

The therapist began to notice that his interpretations to Dorothy were beginning to sound unlike his usual self, worded with an imperious and embellished style that he would have found repugnant had he heard it from another therapist. Upon reflection, this therapist began to realize that he had adopted the patient's style; without conscious awareness, he had found himself replicating the superior and contemptuous flavor of her speech.

6. When it comes to interpretation, the less (rather than the most) important themes (conflicts, narcissistic vulnerabilities, character styles or traits, etc.) provide a safe starting place, especially with a patient who is new to the process of psychotherapy. Focusing on more significant conflicts and vulnerabilities in the beginning of a therapeutic relationship can be overwhelming, leading to an excessive activation of defenses, which can drive a patient out of therapy.

7. Caution is warranted when considering the delivery of a substantial interpretation prior to a long absence from therapy, because time would not be available to assess the impact of the interpretation. The impact is only worrisome, of course, if the response to the interpretation is not positive, but this is often an unknown at the time the interpretation is suggested (Greenson 1967).

8. An interpretation can be more helpful if made when feelings are "alive"; an interpretation is most likely to make sense and therefore lead to change if it occurs when the patient is emotionally engaged. If the session lacks significant emotional intensity, the memory of a similar emotional reaction will sometimes suffice.

The therapist of a depressed and unhappily married thirty-five-year-old man was unable to elicit the intensity of feeling that the therapist knew the man had about his wife. Feeling, however, that an interpretation was called for, and the moment would pass if he said nothing, the therapist said:

> *"I know that you say you are not currently upset and angry with your wife as you have been so recently in the past, but I think you were afraid to say anything to her because you are so afraid she could leave. It was so terrible for you in the past when your first wife left and you became so deeply depressed."*

For the more seriously disturbed patient, such as the borderline patient or the psychotic patient, the rule of interpreting when feelings are alive is probably best modified. When delivering an interpretation to the "brittle" patient, the effort to keep the patient integrated takes precedence over the goal of "achieving conviction" (that is, the patient is convinced of the interpretation); intensity of emotion may be more fragmenting than integrating for the patient who is struggling to keep from being swallowed up by thoughts and feelings.

TIMING

The choice about the timing of interpretations varies greatly from therapist to therapist, and may be dependent upon the theoretical framework employed (for example, a Kleinian therapist might use transference interpretations very early). With most patients a rough sequence occurs, moving from interventions (advice, education, support, clarification) to interpretations (resistance/defense, transference, genetic-reconstructive). Certain situations will demand a change in the sequence, however. A patient who rapidly develops dangerous acting-out behavior or an intensely negative reaction that threatens the therapy requires more direct and rapid interpretation. The early stage of treatment usually involves more instruction, support, education, and clarification. The middle stage of treatment sees more resistance and transference interpretation. The late stage of treatment involves more genetic interpretation/reconstruction.

HOW DOES THE THERAPIST KNOW IF
AN INTERPRETATION WAS ACCURATE?

This important and complex question cannot be answered simply. Listed below are several markers that allow a therapist to deduce whether an interpretation was useful or not:

1. The verbal agreement that an interpretation sounds correct is useful, but may not predict the enduring impact of a comment.
2. The recollection of a new (not previously heard) memory, or an enhanced ability to explore an important previously recalled memory, often provides evidence of an interpretation's utility.
3. The spontaneous recollection of a dream following an interpretation suggests that the interpretation was meaningful; dreams are easily forgotten because the material associated within the dream often sits on the repressive border. The freeing of repression, leading

to the expression in a dream of previously unacceptable thoughts, indicates the usefulness of the interpretation.

4. The expression of a new feeling or "affect" provides evidence that an interpretation was accurate.

5. Occasionally a correct interpretation can markedly and suddenly decrease anxiety, much like what happens to a balloon after being punctured by a pin.

6. The partial reliving of a prior experience, complete with the emotions that were present at the time ("abreaction"), gives evidence of the power of an interpretation. This kind of reaction is most visible with posttraumatic situations. In practice, however, unless the emotional experience is particularly dramatic, the abreaction is indistinguishable from "new" affects.

7. Occasionally, a sudden change in behavior will signal the evidence of the power of an interpretation. Acute change occurs infrequently, however; substantial change requires time, repetition, and working through.

8. The "ah-ha reaction," much more commonly seen in the movies, does occasionally occur in therapy. With the "ah-ha reaction," the light goes on and emotional and cognitive awareness occur.

9. "Acting out" can occur in response to a correct interpretation, especially with the adolescent patient; an interpretation can be accurate but also can activate a state of being overwhelmed.

GUIDELINES FOR SELF-DISCLOSURE: SELF-REVELATION AND CONFRONTATION

The issue of "self-revelation" (that is, what personal information a therapist does or does not reveal to a patient) has frequently been a contentious topic within psychoanalysis. Freud left a powerful imprint on the field, emphasizing dispassionate analysis and the rule of abstinence. However, from the early days of psychoanalysis to the present time of a more consumer-oriented and less authoritarian culture, various positions have been advocated. Some recent proponents regard the utilization of self-disclosure as a therapeutic tool.

Lewis (1978) delineated particularly useful guidelines regarding self-disclosure. First and foremost, the therapist must be human, genuine, and true to the self; within these parameters, disclosing highly personal information is unnecessary. "Highly personal information" does not include the simple questions that are often posed by patients. These simple questions are usually intended to flush out whether or not the therapist is likely to be able to understand the patient's experience (former category), or how much information is necessary to provide in order for the patient to explain a thought process or a story (latter category).

In the former category, common questions include:

Do you have children?
Do you see children?
Are you married?
How long have you been in practice?
Have you seen people like me before?

In the latter category, common questions include:

Have you read (a certain) book?
Have you seen (a certain) movie?
Have you ever been to (a certain) place?

One frequently asked and emotionally significant question fits into both categories above. This question is designed to elucidate both how much information will be necessary to provide, and whether or not the therapist can really comprehend the way the patient feels. However, the question is also an appeal for "*hope*"; that is, has the therapist "been" where the patient is now, and did the therapist survive and/or recover from that state? The question is: Have you ever felt the way I feel?

For other patients, questions may be "loaded" in a manner that cannot be fully assessed by the therapist at the time the question is posed. Lewis suggests that the more personal the information that is requested, the more caution and reflection the therapist should exercise before making a disclosure. As a sound general rule, the more urgently the therapist feels compelled to make a disclosure, the more closely the therapist should examine the motive. A strong desire to share personal information is probably rooted in a countertransference reaction. While these reactions can provide much "food for thought" for the therapist, "acting out" on the part of the therapist by proceeding to share the information probably will not be very helpful to the patient. Lewis also suggests that the most useful disclosures are those that provide feedback to the patient about the patient's impact upon the therapist. While in theory this suggestion may have a point, in practice, the caution, tact, and grace that are essential for this kind of feedback to be successfully delivered are difficult to achieve.

REFERENCES AND READINGS

Glover, E. (1931). The therapeutic effect of inexact interpretation: a contribution to the theory of suggestion. *International Journal of Psycho-Analysis* 12: 397–411.

Greenson, R. (1967). *The Technique and Practice of Psychoanalysis,* vol. 1. New York: International Universities Press.

Gutheil, T. G., and G. O. Gabbard. (1993). The concept of boundaries in clinical practice: theoretical and risk management dimensions. *American Journal of Psychiatry* 150: 188–96.

Kohut, H. (1970). Narcissism as a resistance and as a driving force in psychoanalysis. In *The Search for the Self,* vol. 2, ed. P. H. Ornstein. New York: International Universities Press.

Lewis, J. M. (1978). *To Be a Therapist: The Teaching and Learning.* New York: Brunner/Mazel.

Loewenstein, R. (1957). Some thoughts on interpretation in the theory and practice of psychoanalysis. *Psychoanalytic Study of the Child* 12: 127–50.

Poland, W. (1975). Tact as a psychoanalytic function. *International Journal of Psycho-Analysis* 56: 155–62.

Stolorow, R., B. Brandchaft, and G. Atwood. (1987). *Psychoanalytic Treatment: An Intersubjective Approach.* Hillsdale, NJ: Analytic Press.

Strachey, J. (1937). The nature of the therapeutic action of psychoanalysis. *International Journal of Psycho-Analysis* 15: 127–59.

Winnicott, D. W. (1951). Transitional objects and transitional phenomena. In *Through Paediatrics to Psycho-Analysis.* New York: Basic Books, 1975.

———. (1960). Ego distortion in terms of true and false self. In *The Maturational Processes and the Facilitating Environment.* New York: International Universities Press, 1965.

9

WORKING THROUGH

Philosophy is perfectly right in saying that life must be understood backward. But then one forgets the other clause—that it must be lived forward.

—Kierkegaard, *Journals and Papers*

DEFINITION

Working through is an important but unfortunately imprecise term that is meant to refer to the psychic or emotional work that is required for the psychotherapeutic-interpretative process to effect meaningful internal change. Various explanations of the term "working through" have been offered. Some writers emphasize the process in which the therapist offers interpretations: the patient overcomes resistances to the interpretations via psychic "work," and with the gradual acceptance of repressed material, the patient is liberated from the grip of repetition. Others emphasize the internalization of functions that are experienced within the psychotherapeutic process: an enhanced observing ego, the capacity to self-analyze, or the development of self-soothing capacities would be examples of these functions. In practice, working through is a complex process, requiring emotional work on the part of the patient. Psychic energy is utilized in order to identify significant themes, each of which requires individual attention. The identification of recurring themes is an integral aspect of psychoanalytic psychotherapy; as themes recur, associated feelings recur as well. With time, the recurring themes are gradually evaluated and understood and lost possibilities are mourned, resulting in the gradual acquisition of greater internal freedom.

Working through, as an aspect of the psychotherapeutic process, begins in the first session and can be observed throughout the therapy. The ability to identify aspects of working through during a treatment is important for many reasons, but one of those reasons is to restore confidence that the treatment is still moving. Especially during those periods in which there is apparent or relative stagnation, and particularly when symptomatic change is not apparent, identifying the micro-elements of the working-through process can signal that internal movement is still taking place.

Is Identification of the Elements
of a Working-Through Process Accomplished
Only by the Intuition or Feel that Is Derived from Experience?

Intuition or "feel" certainly can provide important feedback about the presence or absence of working through. For example, broad counter-transference reactions such as boredom, irritation, or fatigue, that are not usually experienced with a particular patient, can be reflective of resistance or of a stalemate in the process; conversely, when these reactions are absent and the therapist feels interested and engaged, the presence of a working-through process is suggested. This may be an unreliable tool, however; for example, a patient can be interesting and engaging as an aspect of a transference/countertransference phenomenon or enactment, and yet without an interpretation of the phenomenon or enactment, working through is not being achieved.

OBVIOUS MARKERS OF WORKING THROUGH

These more obvious markers of working through include events that do not occur every day, but when present, do provide an opportunity to evaluate the status of the working-through process, or provide evidence that working through has occurred. Contacts with family, separations from psychotherapy, and new relationships provide an opportunity to evaluate the status of the working-through process. Symptomatic change provides evidence that working through has occurred.

Contact with Family of Origin

A man asked a friend, who happened to be a psychotherapist, "How do you know when you have had enough treatment?" Skeptical about psychotherapy, the man was nevertheless intrigued by the possibility of what he might gain from insight. He spoke about how every visit home to visit his parents was painful; his unresolved and ambivalent feelings regarding his family seemed obvious. The psychotherapist friend responded: "Perhaps one measure might be the ability to visit one's parents without untoward painful feelings." Visits to parents or close family members are not always painful, especially if the visits are infrequent. However, these kinds of visits often stimulate a variety of emotions that otherwise remain distant from the self— that is, in the "background." Visiting home brings emotions into the "fore-ground." The man mentioned in the previous example was unable to work through his own mixed, confused, and painful feelings about his parents.

> One individual, shortly before he was to go home on a vacation to visit his parents, became painfully preoccupied with the possibility of a nuclear holocaust. This went on for a number of days, until gradually, in the context of a treatment situation, he grew to understand that the focus on a holocaust was related to the upcoming visit home. His preoccupation reflected unconscious anger and despair, and the anticipation of the awful void that he would experience upon seeing his parents.

Homecomings and special holidays can activate a variety of feelings about members of the family of origin. Underlying ambivalence may be exposed. The direct experience of rage, love, envy, jealousy, or competitiveness may be surprising or disturbing. The awareness that certain needs will be left unfulfilled can be quite distressing. Different people (and different patients) will have different degrees of awareness of these feelings. Often psychotherapy increases an individual's sensitivity to and appreciation of the feelings that occur before, during, and after visits home. Memories and old emotions are rekindled with each visit; these memories and the reexperiencing of old emotions often result in changing perspectives upon subsequent visits, and contribute to the reconstruction of a person's early life. The decrease in the intensity of the patient's response with each visit home is a barometer of the patient's working-through process.

Separations from the Therapist

Treatment interruptions can be brief in duration, such as those caused by vacations (the patient's or the therapist's) or holidays; treatment interruptions can be of longer duration, initiated by the patient and for either internal reasons (a wish to take a break) or external reasons (change in life situation). Treatment interruptions provide another opportunity to assess what portion of that which the patient and therapist had wanted to accomplish, has been accomplished, and what portion has not.

Treatment interruptions often serve to bring the transference into sharp relief. For example, one patient may feel that the therapist was to "glad to get rid" of the patient; another patient may not have that thought at all. The complete absence of feelings surrounding a separation from the therapist, particularly if the treatment has been important and in process for some time, may indicate a resistance in the patient to feelings in the transference.

Breaks from therapy offer an opportunity to see how the patient experiences separation. Feelings of loss and abandonment will be experienced or defended against in a manner that is likely consistent with the patient's sensitivity to loss and separation. Breaks from the treatment can bring to the surface difficulties with separation, and can reactivate the process of mourning in a person who is still resonating with respect to loss or trauma. Paradoxically, separation may be experienced as liberating. Either way, a separation allows the patient, at least temporarily, to cope with feeling and memories, and achieve insight independently. In this manner, separations often reveal the existence of a more reliable and integrated sense of self and competence, which would be an index of working through. Alternatively, separations can serve to highlight the work that remains to be done; this does not mean that working through of other issues has not been accomplished.

New Relationships

A common reason for coming to treatment is a difficulty with relationships, usually in the arena of romantic relationships. Therefore, when a patient who has difficulties in relationships is in a treatment situation and initiates a new relationship, a series of questions come to the therapist's mind. Is this relationship going to be the same as or different from previous relationships? If this relationship is different, how is it different? Is it more realistic? Is it more gratifying? How great or small a role do unresolved wishes and needs play in the evolving relationship? Is this new relationship a repetition of previous dysfunctional relationships, or is the patient sufficiently freed from the influence of the past to command "free choice," that is, "free" from unconscious determinants? Although no one is ever completely freed from the past or from the tendency to repeat that which is familiar, some repetitions are more frustrating or damaging or dangerous than others. As the working-through process unfolds, a progression from less

constructive and unsuccessful relationships to more constructive and successful relationships should occur.

Symptom Diminution

The diminution of major symptoms is usually, but not always, evidence
of working through. However, sometimes symptoms can disappear abruptly
as a function of a "transference cure" without true working through; in this
case, the symptom (or symptoms) usually recurs.

Tillie was not a young woman when she came to treatment for the
first time in her life. She was not a "therapy kind of person," but
she had come to the end of a long line of medical doctors who had
worked up her symptom. She had now been referred for a psychiatric evaluation.

Tillie had intermittent difficulty swallowing. Sometimes her
throat felt so close to closing up completely that she didn't eat
for days, afraid that she would choke on anything that wasn't
liquid. Tillie's swallowing difficulty had been extensively worked
up by every competent professional within reach and beyond,
because Tillie didn't have to worry about the expense of the
work-up. However, no physical reason for the symptom had
been ascertained.

Tillie's interactions with her doctors became the predominant focus of the initial hours of her treatment. She struggled with her expectations of her doctors, her disappointment about and anger toward her doctors for their failure to help her, her feeling that no
one understood her fear that eventually, if no one could help her,
she wouldn't be able to eat at all. Tillie didn't talk about herself
outside of her symptom. She provided little information about her
current family or her past. She wasn't interested in exploring "what
was long gone"; nothing else was wrong in her life that wouldn't
be fixed by getting rid of her inability to swallow.

Somewhat unexpectedly, and within a few short weeks, Tillie's
symptom disappeared. However, the therapist went on vacation, and
the symptom reappeared. Tillie decided that she could now go away
on a trip and the symptom came back while she was gone. The reappearance of the symptom during separations signified the dependence of Tillie's symptom relief on the therapy and the presence of the
therapist, and demonstrated the lack of working through.

After a few months, during which the above pattern repeated itself one more time, Tillie did agree to talk about issues other than

her symptom. Tillie's parents were killed in an automobile accident when Tillie was four years old. She was raised by her maternal grandmother, who died at the age of sixty-four; Tillie was thirteen-years-old at the time. After her grandmother's death, Tillie went to live with various relatives until she was able to go away to school. On her eighteenth birthday, she found out about the trust. Her grandmother had been a very wealthy woman, and Tillie was the beneficiary of her estate. At the time of consultation with her therapist, Tillie had just turned sixty-four years old.

Even when symptoms do improve because true working through has occurred, the slowness of resolution of some kinds of symptoms that a patient brings to psychotherapy makes symptom resolution a poor short-term marker of working through in a therapeutic process. Some symptoms, on the other hand, do resolve themselves in gradual yet observable pieces. Actually, Tillie's recognition that the resolution of her symptom was in some way tied to the psychotherapy and that her past might actually have some meaning for her, was a micropiece of working through. Tillie recognized that symptoms mean "something" and that for her, that "something" was related to her relationship with the therapist.

MICRO-ELEMENTS OF WORKING THROUGH

In addition to the more obvious indicators of working through described above, less obvious indicators of a progressing psychotherapeutic process exist as well. What follows is a description of those less obvious indicators, or "micro-elements" of working through. In practice, many of these less obvious elements overlap.

Emergence of "New" Emotions

New emotional experiences or the experience of new emotions often provides the first evidence of progress in the working-through process. "New" emotions are actually only new in a relative sense. The emotion itself may not be new; emotions or emotional experiences can be repressed because of conflict surrounding the emotion, and/or because the overwhelming nature of the feeling precludes an adaptive integration at the time. What is new is the ability to feel that emotion more deeply.

Any emotion can become represented in a new way. From sadness to elation, from anger to love, these new emotions can become a powerful part of the emotional ambiance of the therapy experience for sustained periods of time. The appearance of a "new" affect often occurs again and again. With each new discovery of the same "new" emotion, awareness of and comfort with this new affective state becomes more freely available.

New affects are inseparable from the retrieval of memories and the mourning process that will be discussed below, because affects are part of memory; that is, part of a memory is the feeling that is attached to the recollection. In practice, the memory itself may follow behind the experience of the "new" emotion; therefore, the new affective experience is useful because it is a signal that something is happening in the treatment and that the associative material arising in the therapy is meaningful.

New emotions usually emerge slowly within a psychotherapeutic process, and only with time, grow to a have a powerful presence. However, new emotions can appear seemingly suddenly, when actually, sufficient preparatory work has been accomplished to allow the patient to tolerate the affective state.

> Rebecca initially sought treatment because of an "inability to feel." Within the first few visits, she reported the following story. She had seen a movie about a man who, having disassociated himself from his family for many years, returned to attempt to make peace with the family only much later in his life and at a time when he was already quite ill. Rebecca and her girlfriend had spoken about the movie on the way home, and she had told the girlfriend that the movie was rather boring. As Rebecca and her friend continued to talk about the movie, inexplicably Rebecca felt an overwhelming sadness and began to cry.
>
> This "new" affective experience was startling for Rebecca, and initially she had little understanding of what had caused her to feel so sad. However, over the next several sessions, Rebecca's associations began to focus on her parents and her childhood. With time, it became clear that her sadness related to these memories. Rebecca had felt about her parents very similarly to the main protagonist in the movie. She had not, however, gone back to attempt a reconciliation with her family, and had always assumed that she probably never would.

Rebecca's sadness was hidden out of her awareness (repressed); in the process of psychotherapy, and stimulated by a movie that resonated with her personal experience, her sadness became evident.

Emergence of Memories

The emergence of new memories is often evidence of a working-through process. Alternatively, in a fashion similar to the appearance of new emotions, "new" memories may be recollections of actual old events that have been "forgotten" or, more specifically, repressed. Some of these memories may be dramatic and obviously traumatic in nature. Others may be much more subtle; only with repeated examination do the meanings become clear. Some memories have a "screen memory" quality; these memories are particularly significant because of the fact that a screen memory is "like a picture that tells a thousand words."

The vignette that follows recalls "J. C." who first appears in chapter 1. It provides an example of a traumatic memory that emerged in therapy in a dramatic way:

> J. C., in the midst of an evolving erotic transference with her male therapist, began to talk of wanting to see a woman therapist instead. The male therapist tentatively suggested that perhaps the patient might be having some uncomfortable feelings toward him; he could understand that if these feelings were present, they might be difficult to talk about and the young woman might feel that it would be easier to talk with a woman. The patient neither confirmed nor denied any such feelings during the hour.
>
> J. C. reported a curious incident in the next session. Her husband had expressed an interest in lovemaking by slipping his hand between her legs and fondling her from behind, a gesture of approach that was familiar to both of them. However, abruptly, the young woman had slapped her husband, and with a vehemence that had startled both of them. J. C. couldn't imagine what had seized her. Without recognizing the connection, the young woman then reported a memory that had come to her in the interim between the previous session and the current session. She hadn't thought of the memory since her early teens, probably around the time of the death of her father. She recalled, with obvious distress, that her father used to touch her in inappropriate ways; he would touch and sometimes fondle her breasts. This aspect of her father had seemed to be in contrast to his professional stature and power, financial success, and social standing in the community.
>
> The recovery of the young woman's memory about her father was pivotal. It marked the beginning of the deidealization of her father. The young woman had been engaged in a desperate attempt

to emulate her father professionally, believing him to be the model of what a person would aspire to be. Another part of her really saw herself differently and wanted to move in another direction. As repressed recollections of this other less admirable and deeply disturbing aspect of her father came back to her, the young woman was able to free herself from the need to be like her father (identification with the aggressor), and pursue a much more gratifying career path.

The next vignette illustrates the emergence of a less dramatic but nevertheless painful memory. This vignette has more of the "screen memory" quality described above.

The patient, Harold, was an obsessive middle-aged man. Harold recalled the following memory after his therapist commented that Harold not infrequently seemed quite reluctant to reveal things about himself, almost as though he expected to be attacked or humiliated. When Harold was about thirteen years old, he asked his sister about a girl at school one day at the dinner table; he happened to have a crush on the girl. Before his sister could answer, his father turned to him, and Harold recalls his father saying, "So, the boy has a crush on a girl. Look at that. My boy is finally interested in girls. I didn't know that my boy was interested in girls."

Harold felt humiliated by his father's mocking tone and words, and resolved never to tell his father or anyone else again about his love interests or relationships. The memory remained imprinted as an image in his mind, serving the principle of "multiple function," or the "picture that tells a thousand words." It became a commentary about the relationship between father and son (the father's competitiveness with his son), the father's character (the father's insensitivity), and Harold's sensitivity to feeling shame.

As is evident in the two preceding vignettes, memories often arise in the context of an evolving transference. What may be recalled first is either the memory or the associated affect. Obsessive personalities tend to remember the story, but without the associated emotion. The emergence of memories gives evidence of psychological motion. Memories that emerge in psychotherapy may be simple and obvious in their significance, or complex and not quickly or easily understood. The process of understanding memories is an important and ongoing part of psychotherapy and is an aspect of working through.

Increased Continuity with the Past

"Continuity with the past" is closely related to the recall of memories and emotions, but it implies an additional degree of "fluidity" with memory; the past can be recalled, reexperienced, considered, and accepted. The ability to achieve continuity with the past provides comfort or consolation, because memories and their attendant emotions enrich experience, even if that experience is at times unfortunate. The memory of having survived difficult experiences can be fortifying in times of doubt; the people who were present along the way to guide, support, and teach are remembered in times of need. The comprehension of life as a story that has themes and is explicable expands the individual's capacity to appreciate human experience and to achieve inner peace. As Shakespeare said, "What is past is prologue" (*The Tempest,* Act 2, Scene 1).

To have continuity with the past means to have the awareness of having been affected by the past and to recognize the likelihood of such an influence again. Continuity with the past is something that develops only gradually; the life history is pieced together, certain themes begin to stand out, and mourning begins, with the realization and acceptance that certain opportunities may have passed forever. The following vignette illustrates this point.

Bradley was an emotionally distant and successful businessman, and the head of his own company. The growth of the company was stymied at the time Bradley entered treatment, because Bradley could not bring himself to borrow money. He had a deep and unalterable fear that he would feel dependent on and enslaved by any lender to whom he might turn. In therapy, Bradley came to realize that the fear that stood in his way in business, infiltrated his life in the social arena, and affected his capacity to have a close relationship that was both loving and sexual.

Gradually, Bradley relaxed his guard. As he became more involved in his treatment and felt closer to his therapist, Bradley began to recall memories of an older couple, a man and his wife who had functioned as parental substitutes throughout his childhood. The husband of the couple was a tough but caring man who had taught Bradley about nature and taken him backpacking. This man had obviously cared greatly about Bradley, in contrast to his narcissistic, self-absorbed father, and his passive mother who had lived in awe of his father and defined herself through her husband's (Bradley's father's) success.

   When Bradley went away to college, he abruptly cut off the relationship with the older couple. With the surfacing of memories
of the relationship with the couple in the treatment, Bradley felt
impelled to find the couple again. Twenty-five years had passed,
however, and to his great distress and with deep sadness, Bradley
reported to his therapist that his search had found them both dead.
Bradley realized that his remote style and consequent inability to
rely upon or feel dependent upon anyone, sorrowfully, had driven
him to sever ties with these wonderful people.
   As the work of the therapy continued, Bradley came to understand that his contact with the couple had been a double-edged
sword. While he had loved both the man and his wife, these people had also served to remind him of the emptiness of his relationship with his own parents. It was a bit like going to the home
next door as a child and discovering that it seems warmer or more
inviting than one's own home. This discovery is both appealing
and saddening as it is a reminder of what one doesn't have.
Bradley further came to understand that this pain had compelled
him to distance himself from the couple, move on, and end the relationship. Bradley realized that while this solution had temporarily ended his pain, ultimately he had deprived himself of a very significant and nurturing relationship.

The memory of the older couple now became a bittersweet but also
important memory, a memory that Bradley could recall without depression
or denial, a reminder that relying or depending upon people is an aspect of
human existence and not a fatal flaw.

   The continuous interplay of past experience and memories with present experience and perceptions is a phenomenon; it is not in and of itself
unhealthy. The following vignette demonstrates a healthy ability to accept
the past and its mark upon the present.

   Paul reported to his therapist that he had experienced a fleeting
   sense of restlessness while coaching his son's Little League team. He
   then had a memory of his grandfather, a gentle and kind man, who
   had loved watching his grandson (the patient) play baseball. Paul's
   grandfather had been a frequent presence in his young life. Paul felt
   a sense of sadness, and then quickly went back to coaching.

   This vignette is also an example of "nostalgia." Nostalgia is a "longing
for something far away or long ago" (*Webster's Twentieth-Century Dictionary*);
it has to do with the sad sweetness of valued memories. Memories are sad

because the good experiences of the past are gone; memories are sweet because the experiences of the past were good. Nostalgia acknowledges both the capacity to have good memories and feel sadness about that which is lost. Beyond the sadness associated with the passing of good experiences, the sadness associated with nostalgia may also weave in other "losses" that are inseparable from the loss in the nostalgic memory.

In the vignette above, Paul's recall of the memory during the Little League practice was actually a condensation of multiple bittersweet losses just prior to and into his teen years. Paul's grandfather had died during Paul's teen years; the loss was especially painful because Paul had loved his grandfather so much. Paul's father was transferred to a job in another city. Only later did the rest of the family join the father. The move to join the father was welcome to Paul because he missed his father; the move was unwelcome to Paul because he left permanently behind the neighborhood (and the baseball field) of his childhood.

Preoccupation with nostalgia, or a persistent belief that the past was special in a way that cannot be matched in the present or the future, can prevent working through and stalemate a treatment or a life. This preoccupation is captured by the phrase the "good old days."

Changed Patterns of Dreaming

The character of a patient's dreams and the pattern of dreaming can change during a therapy. Ella Freeman Sharpe (1937) made a number of observations about this. The number of dreams that are remembered increases during therapy, particularly in those people who have dreamed sparsely before. Repetitive dreams are dreamed less often or stop altogether. Generally, dreams become more concise and more gratifying.

> A middle-aged, obsessive man reported at the beginning of his therapy that he had never had a dream. Seven months into the treatment, he spontaneously reported a dream; by the end of therapy, he reported frequent and rich dreams.

Leaving aside these broad changes, dreams often provide evidence of the small incremental changes that demonstrate working through. New themes can appear in a form that is "visible to the naked eye" (that is, the patient or the therapist can now make out the dim outline of the theme) for the first time in a dream. Old themes can appear in a manner that suggests that change is occurring; the themes that become elaborated in dreams are often the first harbinger of change. As the treatment progresses, dreams tend to become more gratifying, less frightening, more under-standable, and more useful and interesting to the patient. The dream begins to function for the educated patient as a "communication to the self," a method of pulling to the surface thoughts and feelings that are sitting just outside of awareness.

> Flora, a sixty-year-old woman, came to therapy burdened and un-happy. Her husband had recently recovered from a debilitating ill-ness, which although now resolved, had left Flora physically and emotionally depleted. Flora was tormented by recurring night-mares of violence and destruction that had started while her hus-band was ill. As her frustration, fear, resentment, feeling of depri-vation, anger, and associated guilt regarding her husband's illness were articulated and understood, Flora's nightmares ceased. The content of her dreams began to shift, and the manifest content of the dreams began to include scenes that were clearly associated with Flora's childhood. Memories, particularly of a father whom Flora had both idealized and profoundly resented, opened the doorway to a deeper layer of understanding of the feelings that had driven Flora into treatment.

The ability to utilize a patient's dreams increases as the therapist, and then the patient, become familiar with the unique style and pattern of the patient's dreaming. Dreaming may dry up and then reemerge, or a patient's dreams may have a particular flavor and then change as a new theme arises, the transference shifts, an interpretation is made, and the effort of working through is again apparent.

> A woman who prided herself on self-control, took no interest in men, and denied any positive or negative feelings about her fam-ily, had two significant dreams. In the first dream, the woman was angrily throwing objects at her sister. In the other dream, she was intimately involved with a man. Both of these dreams reflected something that the woman could not consciously imagine, and would not openly admit even if the thoughts were conscious.

Dreams with repetitive thematic material often change, and recurrent dreams often stop altogether in the context of psychotherapy. Recurrent dreams, especially those that have a long history, endure because a core theme (which may be about an aspect of the self or about a significant ob-ject relationship) or event (trauma) is encapsulated in the dream. As the working-through process proceeds, repetitive dreams provide a fascinating chronicle of the delineation, evolution, and eventual resolution of the core theme or event. The following case provides an example of a transformation of a traumatic dream over the course of psychotherapy:

> Margie was a middle-aged woman who had a childhood history of cruel sexual abuse. Consequently, she had a long history of difficulty in close relationships and severe sexual inhibitions. She also had developed a self-defeating personality at best, and at worst a significantly masochistic character.
>
> Margie dreamed of cold, dark, wet spaces, and the accompanying feeling was one of terror.

Thus, the traumatic event was represented by the cold, dark, wet space, condensing her experience of the sexual abuse and representing her fear of and deep sense of alienation from people.

> The recurrent nightmares were so intense that Margie was at times afraid to sleep at night. However, the dreams would appear and then disappear. During the treatment as well, the dreams would appear and then disappear, leaving Margie always uncertain about when or if she could sleep without being afraid.
>
> As Margie became more involved in the treatment and began to feel more at ease with her male therapist, for the first time a pattern to the frequency of the dreams began to emerge. With her increased comfort and feeling of closeness to her therapist, the nightmare clearly came more frequently. The therapist pointed out to Margie that she seemed to associate terrible consequences with feelings of closeness or with the wish to be able to depend upon someone.
>
> With time, the nightmares became more detailed and specific circumstances and feelings were detailed in the dreams, which seemed clearly to be "nightmare-like" memories of the sexual abuse and its accompanying emotional terror. Gradually, as the connection between the nightmares and the memories was explored, the dreams faded away. However, on those occasions in which Margie felt erotic desires toward or the wish to be dependent upon her therapist or any other man, the nightmares briefly resurfaced. The association between the wish to allow closeness with a man or actual feelings of closeness to a man, and the return of the nightmarish dreams, was certainly a demonstration of the enduring power of Margie's previous trauma.

Dreams serve as a chronicle of the expanding internal psychic world of the patient and as a barometer of change. As therapy proceeds, a therapist often sees more obviously the dream constellations previously presented; as above, the dream particularly assumes the function of a communication to the therapist and/or to the self. This in and of itself is an example of working through, because the ability to make use of the dream as a communication to the therapist or to the self is evidence of the formation of the "self-analyzing" capacity.

Evolution in the Repertoire of Usual Defenses

The pathway to changing a defensive style involves the recognition of and shift from less useful defenses to the utilization of more mature defenses, and the recognition that defenses tend to be employed in response to a particular set of stimuli. The set of stimuli that will or usually provoke or set in motion a defense or defenses are unique for every individual. The person who has more mature defenses and an understanding of those factors that tend to provoke a protective response (in the form of a defense) tends to be more relaxed, and more available not only to listen to the thoughts and opinions of other people, but also actually to be curious about other people's thoughts and opinions.

> A woman realized that when she found herself being excessively kind and solicitous toward her husband or to others, she was usually actually angry. As she became aware of this particular defensive style (reaction formation), she was able to consciously note these episodes of excessive kindness and solicitousness, and wonder what it was that had irritated or annoyed her.

As the themes of the internal world of a patient become accessible and are put into words, and feelings and perceptions are understood and therefore become less threatening, certain behaviors or defenses become "ego-dystonic" (or "self-dystonic"); that is, these defenses no longer seem fitting or appropriate or "syntonic." The woman in the above case grew to see her overly solicitous behavior as disingenuous. As she became aware that her actions served the purpose of defense, the use of reaction formation became less acceptable to her, or ego-dystonic; with a greater awareness of what she felt and of her internal processes, came an increased ability to speak more directly to her concerns. As a person becomes less defensive and more able to appreciate an internal process, an enhanced awareness of the self and others follows.

Increased Awareness

Awareness increases incrementally. Sometimes the increments come in small bits, akin to finding only one new piece of a three-dimensional jigsaw puzzle even though many hours and many weeks have passed in the effort. With time, however, a series of small achievements coalesces, and a big section of the jigsaw puzzle becomes visible.

Patients usually develop a growing awareness of themes, through the small elements at first; for example, a particular need is expressed consistently, the experience of envy surfaces repetitively, the complicated nature of feelings about sexuality becomes recognizable, or a particular and consistent reaction to a certain type of person becomes evident. Patients may point to a theme at arm's length; the therapist is alerted to a theme that shares a resonance with the patient through an association to a movie or a book, or the struggle observed in a friend or colleague or a loved one. Whatever the method of approach, gradually certain themes or feelings arise with greater regularity, allowing the therapist the opportunity to illustrate the centrality of the theme or feeling. The following vignette illustrates the process whereby a patient gradually became aware of and accepted her sexual desires and needs.

Hilda had grown up in a large German family, in which she was the youngest and only daughter among many older brothers. Her mother was critical, controlling, and almost paranoid about her daughter's behavior, particularly sexual behavior. The mother was constantly vigilant, making frequent comments about the dangers of sex and seeming to believe that her daughter was capable of trying to usurp her husband or sons by sexually seducing them.

During the beginning phase of therapy, Hilda spoke of the students in a seminar that she was teaching. She was extremely critical of the flirtatious behavior between the women and men in the class. At first, Hilda only occasionally alluded to the issue of the sexual behavior of college students and their preoccupation with sex, but with time she returned to stories of flirtation and sexuality more and more frequently. The topic took many turns. Hilda would focus on society and the preoccupation of men with sexuality. She talked of advertising and how advertisers used sexuality to both sell and advocate "loose sexuality."

With gentle clarification on the part of the therapist, Hilda's focus began to shift. She talked about the "crushes" of little girls and little boys. She spoke of a niece who had a crush on her older male cousin. Gradually, Hilda was able to acknowledge her interest in a relationship and its attendant sexuality. She realized that her pre-occupation with the sexuality of others had something to do with her own preoccupation. Ultimately, Hilda realized that the judg-mental attitude toward sexuality was really her own, developed from her childhood experience with her mother and her father.

The awareness of a heightened focus or intensity that is directed to-ward certain thoughts and feelings is the first piece of a working-through process. This "associative preoccupation" often becomes more intense be-fore it becomes less intense, and is an aspect of the working-through process. The preoccupation diminishes as feelings are unearthed and new perspectives are integrated, allowing for a greater awareness and more real-istic appreciation of the self and of others. Hilda recognized that the preoc-cupation with sexuality and sexual themes was really about her own preoc-cupation, and that she didn't have to feel ashamed or guilty about her thoughts. Increased awareness is often about themes that have to do with sexuality (as above, in Hilda's case) or aggression. Kernberg (1992) writes that the recognition and acceptance of expectable anger and aggression is a difficult life task and part of the midlife process, occurring in full only with the maturity of midlife.

Decrease in Naïveté

Naïveté diminishes during the course of psychotherapy; this has to do with a change in the defensive repertoire. Naïveté is a combination of lack of experience, lack of education, and most importantly, denial, as reflected in the adage "hear no evil, see no evil, speak no evil" (see chapter 5, "Re-sistance and Defense"). The diminution of naïveté denotes working through. This diminution is recognizable because naïveté commonly results in a person finding him or herself in distressing situations in the world be-fore it is worked through, because it so commonly evolves in therapy, and because the absence of naïveté can be relatively easily identified. The loss of naïveté may at first open the door to a range of difficult feelings, including repulsion or revulsion, cynicism, or despair. Ultimately, however, the loss of naïveté is protective, because the defense interferes with reality testing.

Increase in the Range and Stability of the Observing Ego

Therapy awakens and enhances the capacity to step back and objectively assess a situation and oneself without becoming overwhelmed by feelings and without shying away from that which is difficult; that is, to possess an "observing ego." The growth of an observing ego is often evidenced in the calm reflection and acceptance of the necessity to look at or observe oneself that appears with comments such as:

> "I was thinking about my reaction to what you said in the last hour. I realized that it was in excess of what was deserved. I know that you didn't mean it the way I decided to hear it."
>
> "I thought about your question, what it was that shifted my mood this week, and this is what I realized . . ."
>
> "It was difficult for me when you said that I struggled with envy. I don't like to think of myself as an envious person; however, I see that it is true."

As therapy proceeds, the growing capacity of the observing ego is reflected in an increasing ability, even in the heat of passion or a powerful emotional reaction, to step back and ask the question, "What is going on?"

Existential Crisis

As defenses become less strangulating and anxieties more accessible during the process of psychotherapy, a patient is required, by virtue of what is learned, to reevaluate what is and is not, might be or might not be fundamentally valuable. Thus with increasing awareness, the individual in treatment reassesses the values upon which self-esteem, and judgments of others and of the surrounding world were based. During this process, a subjective "crisis" of faith can occur: values, goals, the basis of motivation in life, and identity can suddenly or not so suddenly become unclear, not unlike the stereotypic "midlife crisis." This can be a minor experience or a profound experience, and is often accompanied by confusion, questioning, a subjective sense of being lost, and a feeling of loss.

With time, and the examination of and understanding in treatment that allows a reappraisal and reconstruction of the life that has been lived, stability is restored; values, goals, and priorities—what is motivating and that which creates a sense of identity—are discovered or rediscovered. The existential crisis then typically passes. This reappraisal may or may not be obvious to an outside observer, but it should be evident to the therapist and is an aspect of working through. The actual reconstruction eventually should be obvious to both patient and therapist and is an indication of the readiness for termination.

The following example captures the quality of an existential crisis:

Eliana asserted with sincere and great despair, "I will never be first violin, and if I am not, then life is not worth living!" For this woman, who had a very significant talent and had worked all her life in pursuit of this difficult and at times elusive goal, the contemplation of the above was a crushing and yet potentially realistic conclusion. As Eliana's understanding of herself grew and expanded, she came to realize the degree to which she had based her whole life on the eventual achievement of a position that would make her "first" and earn her fame. The pursuit of fame and being first was Eliana's quest. This quest was largely derived from a belief that was rooted in the past (reappraisal and reconstruction). Eliana believed that securing fame was the only road to finally pleasing her father and earning his indisputable love and respect. Ensuring a "first" position in "something" was the only way to locate final restitution for a life that had been lived always "second" to a brother who was older and more valued than any girl in her family could ever be.

Most existential crises or identity crises are subtle. However, at times the degree of confusion and loss of the previously defined idea about the self informs the therapist of the patient's existential crisis or identity crisis. This is illustrated in the next vignette:

Gregory valued his independence, viewing himself as self-contained and autonomous. He was contemptuous of those who asked for attention or caretaking. During therapy, Gregory realized that underneath his self-perceived independence was a profound sense of deprivation and feeling of neediness. As he became increasingly able to acknowledge his own needs and the part of him that yearned to be cared for and taken care of, his exaggerated independent posture gave way. Temporarily, he felt disoriented and unsure of his perceptions and judgment; his view of himself and others was in flux.

With time and hard work in his treatment, Gregory began to see himself in a more complete way. Ultimately, Gregory was more able not only to articulate his needs directly, but to do so in a way that increased the likelihood that his needs would be fulfilled. He became able to share with his wife a vulnerable and dependent aspect of his inner self. He found that his wife was accepting and tender, an experience that Gregory had never imagined possible. This led to a profoundly meaningful new experience of feeling loved.

Reappraisal of the Superego and Ego Ideal

A clear sense of morals and ethics, and a set of goals and aspirations, are probably essential criteria for psychological stability to be reliable; therefore, these complex functions are a fundamental aspect of who a person is and who a person comes to be. Working through is observed in the evolution of a stable set of morals and ethics, and the definition of reasonable and achievable goals and aspirations. Psychotherapists see less self-acceptance or greater self-acceptance, less self-criticism or more self-observation and consequent criticism of the self, less guilt or more guilt, and less perfectionism or greater self-demands, depending on the direction in which the patient needs to move in order to achieve "maturity" and character.

Reappraisal of the superego and ego ideal as a manifestation of working through is illustrated in the following vignette.

> Mary was a middle-aged businesswoman who found herself unable to attempt any task that she couldn't perform with exceptional ability. Many potentially enjoyable tasks, such as tennis, painting, writing, etc., were precluded, because Mary could not tolerate performing at a beginner's level.
>
> A minor but nevertheless significant turning point occurred in the third year of treatment, around Mary's attempt to learn to bake. When Mary baked her first batch of cookies and the cookies were terrible, she wanted to give up on baking immediately. A part of Mary was, however, ashamed, not only of the defective cookies but of her reaction. She now recognized that the reaction was childish. Mary again attempted to bake cookies, and this time with better results. She gave the cookies to a number of friends and was amazed to receive many compliments on her culinary skills.
>
> This seemingly minor achievement had a different quality than Mary's major achievements; the differences qualify this occurrence as an indication of working through. Mary pursued an effort that was in uncharted territory, in which Mary was clearly a novice, and in which her initial results were imperfect; a loosening of Mary's view of herself and standards were required in order to persist with the baking. Additionally, Mary recognized that to stop baking just because she couldn't make a perfect cookie was foolish and childish, and that this was not an admirable side of herself. Lastly, the baking had an additional significant and hidden meaning. Mary had previously disdained any obvious demonstrations of frank femininity, and baking was for Mary a distinctly feminine activity. Therefore, the choice to pursue the activity of baking was

also reflective of working through in the arena of Mary's comfortable identification with her own femininity.

Mourning

In much wisdom is much grief: and he that increaseth knowledge increaseth sorrow (Proverbs 1:14–15).

In the course of a good psychotherapy, mourning is inevitable. For some patients, the task of mourning is difficult and may become insurmountable. Borderline patients in particular tolerate loss and mourning, or what Masterson (1981) has called "abandonment depression," poorly. For these patients, but also for many other patients, the ability to withstand the state of mourning may be the most significant achievement of psychotherapy; moving forward in life requires that what has been or what will never be is accepted, mourned, and moved past.

When a patient who has begun the process of psychotherapy becomes more despondent, it is possible that the patient is experiencing an evolving depression (major depression). What appears as depression may, however, be the sadness (mourning) that becomes more evident as a patient comes in contact with and is more able to accept that which has been lost. Mourning and depression are not the same entity. Mourning involves the temporary "loss of love of the world"; melancholia involves the "loss of love of the self" (Freud 1917). Mourning may involve considerable sadness, which is associated with or linked to an experience of loss or disappointment; mourning is not, however, associated with the excessive self-condemnation or pathologic feeling of responsibility that characterizes melancholia (depression).

There are three broad and overlapping types of mourning evident in psychotherapy:

1. Mourning for the loss of a more ideal possibility:
   "If only I had this or that, then life would have been or now would be different."
2. Mourning for the loss of a previous character, experience of the self, or identity:
   "I am not who I thought I was."
3. Mourning for the losses that are inevitably the consequence of illness or psychopathology:
   "If only this hadn't happened to me."
   "If only I had behaved, coped more effectively, or reacted differently my life would be in a more secure state."

Mourning for the Loss of a More Ideal Possibility

The empathy, understanding, and connection that are part of the therapeutic relationship can set in motion for certain patients the challenging and painful process of mourning for that which was not available in the past. This happens in the context of what Freud (1916) referred to as the "special kind of love" whereby education occurs; the individual mourns the loss of a less than ideal past (Freud 1916), and accepts the fate that is inevitably each person's destiny.

The process described above is embodied in certain kinds of comments:

"If only someone had encouraged me to pursue my education."
"If only someone had told me what to do."
"If only someone had stopped me,"
"If only I had had different parents."
"If only she (or he) hadn't died."

Mourning for the Loss of a Previous Character,
Experience of the Self, or Identity

Mourning for the loss of a previous character, experience of the self, or identity is simply another way of articulating the group of concepts subsumed under the categories of increasing awareness, existential crisis, and change in the quality of the superego (ego ideal). The experience of sadness is derived from the requirement to give up perceptions dearly and previously held about the self in order to move on toward greater maturity.

> Darin mourned the loss of his old self-image. He had romantically defined himself as a drug-using rebel, a James Dean look-alike, who refused to conform to the bourgeois society in which he was "forced" to live. He disdained the "corporate man" and identified with the blue-collar worker (like his father), but actually unconsciously envied the former and viewed the latter (his father) as a failure.
>
> During the course of psychotherapy, Darin assumed more responsibility and in so doing evidenced his obvious competence and began to feel the desire to be competitive and successful. While driving to work one morning and listening to the Grateful Dead at full volume, he was suddenly overtaken by the recognition that the music and its associated image of the drug-using "Deadhead" had little to do with who he really was. Ultimately, Darin

came to see the old James Dean image as a "lie." With this insight Dean also realized, sadly, that the James Dean image had in part been constructed in order to serve the purpose of denial. Hidden behind the image was Darin's awareness of his significant abilities and successes that had far surpassed those of his father. The pain and sadness associated with the perceived loss of his rough and "edgy" persona was also the pain associated with the more complete acknowledgment of his disappointment with his father.

*Mourning for the Losses that Inevitably Are
the Consequence of Illness or Psychopathology*

The losses that occur as a consequence of psychopathology or frank mental illness become more recognizable with the improvement that occurs as a result of good treatment or a medication response. Therefore, that previous conflicts or problems of character have sequelae, or that illness has morbidity and may profoundly and perhaps permanently affect life experience, has to be dealt with and accepted in some way and at some point.

Donnie, an able and ambitious woman, married an impotent and unambitious man whom she controlled and dominated. After several years had passed, during which time she had been unhappy with many aspects of her life, Donnie sought psychotherapy.

After a period of intense and difficult work, Donnie gradually came to understand that she had married her husband for pathologic reasons. She needed to dominate a man and thus had dominated her husband. Her need to dominate served as a defense against a yearning for an involved father figure, as well as against a fear of involvement with and dependence upon a man who might disappoint and hurt her as appreciably as her father had.

Several years into the treatment, Donnie sadly discovered that she was in a sorrowful position. She was married to a man on whom she could not rely and whom she did not love, with two small children in whom she was invested, and with a strong philosophical aversion to divorce. She recognized that her own "psychopathology" had led her to make a "choice" (to marry her husband) that was really not a choice at all, because the action was the result of motivation outside of her awareness.

Donnie elected to stay with her husband for a number of years. When the children were in their middle teens, she met a man whom she did respect, upon whom she could rely, and with whom a strong sexual bond existed. Donnie left her husband and coped with the difficulty of her children's anger toward her for the breakup of the marriage. Her choice was no longer motivated by forces outside of her awareness, but was an informed decision that represented the "lesser of two evils." Donnie chose finally to leave the marriage at a time at which the children were old enough to be less vulnerable, at a time at which she felt strong enough to manage her guilt, in order to finally live with and in the experience of genuine love.

Realistic self-acceptance is always "a mixed bag." Maturity never feels quite as does the magnificent experience of the adolescent or the narcissist when admiration is immense and near at hand. The capacity to accept the limitations of mortality poses an inevitable timeline, limiting what can be accomplished, experienced, and attained. Donnie understood this at the end of her treatment. This understanding enabled her to solidify and carry out the decision to live the last half of her life with someone she loved, and at a time when she herself finally was capable of loving in return.

> The web of our life is of a mingled yarn, good and ill together, our virtues would be proud if our faults whipp'd them not, and our crimes would despair if they were not cherish'd by our virtues." (Shakespeare, *All's Well that Ends Well*, Act 4, Scene 3)

Understanding and Observation of Transference and Its Manifestations

The process of working through can be observed in the evolution of the transference, and though the observation of the patient's grasp of transference and its manifestations within the treatment and in the patient's relationships in the outside world. Ideally, transference comes alive within the therapeutic relationship and is explored and understood. Early in the treatment, the patient develops an awareness of transference and a beginning appreciation of the significance of transference through the process of education and interpretation on the part of the therapist. As working through progresses, different elements of the transference arise, predominate, evolve and are "worked through" to resolution (see chapter 6, "Transference").

Awareness of Transference

Early in the therapy, movement is evidenced by the patient's growing awareness of transference, a gradually increasing capacity to discuss its significance, and early delineation of more specific transference reactions.

A patient, in the beginning phase of a treatment, reported a fantasy that she would arrive at her therapist's office, only to discover that her therapist had moved without telling her or leaving a follow-up address. The freedom to allow for and share the fantasy was a micro-example of working through. The patient's eventual grasp of the relationship between the fantasy and the loss of her father to cancer when she was seven years old (transference) was evidence of an additional piece of working through.

Transference in Evolution

Early in the treatment, transference paradigms may be clear and obvious, or subtle to the point of not being recognizable or discernable. Transference and its evolution are typically less obvious in less intense treatments, and are sometimes initially less apparent in the treatment of higher-functioning patients. However, in most treatments, especially once the treatment has progressed past the early period, a range of transference reactions are evidenced.

Rosie began treatment with a male therapist when she was nineteen years old. By the time she completed her treatment at the age of twenty-seven, she was engaged to be married to a wonderful man, and established in a career that had the potential to bring her considerable success and financial security. Over the many years of treatment, Rosie experienced many transference reactions to her therapist.

Initially, Rosie had a crush on her therapist and developed a variety of romantic fantasies about him. The romantic fantasies gradually shifted and gave way to a concern about her therapist's reliability and, ultimately, concerns that he would abandon her. Rosie then began to feel "indebted" and "addicted" to her therapist; she felt like she was the "therapist's slave." She then began to resent her "male therapist," who was "probably like all those disgusting and worthless men." She felt that her therapist was uninterested in her; she must be repulsive to him; he would never choose her as a mate, even if he had the freedom to do so.

In the final phase of the treatment, Rosie realized that her therapist was "just a person, and not a God," but that he was also a person who had been enormously helpful to her and to whom she felt gratitude. She was also able to recognize clearly that her therapist had deep affection for, as well as a deep and abiding respect for her work in the treatment and for the person she had come to be.

Diminution in the Intensity of the Transference

Working through involves not only the recognition (awareness of the transference) and evolution of the transference in the treatment, but also the eventual diminution of the intensity of the transference as resolution occurs. Diminution of the transference refers to the lessening intensity of transference reactions and the increasing capacity of the patient to place transference reactions in perspective as working through occurs. With the dissipation of transference intensity, the therapist may feel less constrained or imprisoned by the patient's transference expectations; therefore, the therapist feels more human, more relaxed, and less burdened during the hours with the patient. With the dissipation of transference intensity, the patient often becomes aware of the therapist's realistic human qualities and limitations, and the constraints imposed by the parameters of the treatment situation. This recognition allows the patient to turn increasingly to skills and talents within the self.

Rosie's treatment, described above, is an excellent example of the diminution and resolution of the transference.

Claiming the "True Self"

> To thine own self be true, And it must follow, as the night the day, Thou canst not then be false to any man.
>
> (Shakespeare, *Hamlet*, Act 1, Scene 3)

Winnicott's (1960) idea of the "false self" and the "true self" is a simple concept, which can be made use of as a marker in the psychotherapy process for the development of the solidity of the self. For Winnicott, the "false self" is unconsciously set up to be the self that is perceived by other people and interacted with as though it were the real self, but this false self feels intrinsically inauthentic. The person who is occupied by a false self subjectively feels apathetic, experiences a sense of unreality and futility, and lacks spontaneity and aliveness. This lack of vitality has been described by Heinz Kohut (1971) and Alice Miller (1981).

This excessive or unconsciously derived "false self" results in and creates false relationships and fails in intimate relationships, because the tension between false self and true self is more exposed and therefore less manageable the more intimate a relationship becomes. The "adaptive" and consciously chosen "false self" that appears in the ability to utilize manners, to be tactful, to be "political," and to disguise true feelings, when such behavior is useful or necessary, is not the same entity as the unconsciously chosen false self that is referred to above.

In order to make important life decisions and engage in intimate relationships, contact with the true self is necessary to facilitate wise choices that are authentic and genuine, consistent with and faithful to the real self. The false self may, in contrast, employ socially dictated norms or an impersonal checklist in order to make important life decisions; this may not be the best way to choose a lover or a career.

The following vignette describes the transformation of a woman patient in her early twenties, as she discovered the difference between her false self and her true self:

> At the beginning of treatment, Marla was histrionic, flirtatious, and made up like a Las Vegas showgirl. She thought she wanted to be a professional singer, but seemed unable to take the required steps to facilitate such a career. She felt depressed and struggled to make friends generally, or to find a suitable boyfriend specifically. To the therapist, Marla seemed sad and empty, and somehow distant and untouchable.
>
> Marla had never known her father. Marla's mother was a hysterical woman, who had lost her own mother when she was very young. The mother was extremely beautiful and took great pride in her attractiveness; the mother was also physically unaffectionate, remote, and despised any demonstration of neediness or dependency. Marla's mother had imagined that her daughter would someday be a debutante, a socialite of poise and loveliness. Unfortunately, Marla was plain in appearance and socially timid. With her mother as a model and guide, however, Marla eventually approximated her mother's wishes but in an inauthentic manner; she became frenetic and over-the-top in a "Las Vegas showgirl" kind of way.
>
> In the course of the treatment, Marla came to understand that her mother had wanted Marla to become a mirror image of the impression that the mother wanted always to create herself. This, Marla came to realize, was impossible. In Marla's "painted-on state," she was a foolish caricature of the mother's beauty; a miserable facsimile of a woman she could never be.
>
> Early in her treatment, Marla had remembered an incident from her childhood. This memory was perplexing because on the surface it seemed positive, but Marla's subjective recollection of the episode was that it felt sad. The memory was of coming home from school after being teased by her classmates for being overweight and ugly. Marla's mother consoled Marla by telling her that she

was attractive, and that the other children must be jealous. The patient repeatedly referred to this memory, and gradually came to understand the memory as a microcosm of the patient's experience of an important aspect of her relationship with her mother. In reconstructing the memory, the mother's emphasis on her daughter's beauty came to be understood by the therapist and the patient as the mother's need to have a beautiful daughter to fulfill her own fantasy. The mother lacked the capacity to see her daughter as she was, because of the mother's inability to connect with her own experience. This limitation of the mother had led the patient to distrust her own inner experience and to distrust her perception of others, particularly of her mother. Marla's mother acted as if she were supportive, but her mother's behavior did not feel supportive to Marla as a child.

Marla changed substantially. She learned to recognize and appreciate her own special qualities. The makeup came off and she cut her hair. She began to take tennis lessons and discovered that she was quite good at this. The tennis became a regular workout, and through the tennis Marla met a group of friends. Marla discovered that there was more to life than looks. She went back to school and studied to become a speech therapist, a profession she had learned about through one of her tennis friends. Another tennis friend, a man she met during this time as well, eventually became her husband. He was very aware of Marla's intelligence, appreciative of her many capabilities, and supportive of her career choice.

Marla discovered her energy and vitality in the evolution of the congruence among her life goals, personal relationships, and her true and authentic self.

Changing Perception of Others

An individual's perception of others can become deeper, more sophisticated, and more complex during the process of a psychoanalytically conducted psychotherapy, and in fact, this is one of the goals of such a process. Stereotypical depictions of or reactions to other people are less frequent and bothersome; the heroes and villains that so often plague the neurotic's life become farther and fewer between. Although this change in perception pertains to people at large, it is most evident and most useful when applicable to the important people in the patient's life.

Wilma was a middle-aged professional woman. Early in her treatment, she railed against her "inept," "inhibited," and generally "pathologic" husband. The patient could give an endless recitation of her husband's limitations. As the treatment evolved, Wilma was gradually able to appreciate the origin of her husband's difficulties and to recognize his many valuable qualities. Wilma recognized that she had played a significant role in bringing about the exaggerated presence of her husband's weaknesses and in burying his strengths. Wilma realized that she could be a "barracuda" and that her husband was vulnerable. She began to see that the very vulnerability in her husband that she had previously so disdained actually contributed to the tenderness and sensitivity that her husband brought to the relationship with her, and that these qualities were in point of fact quite valuable to her and contributed to her own stability.

The most problematic of all perceptions may be the perception of parents or other primary caretakers, because early object relations become a part of the fabric of the mind and lay the groundwork for subsequent transference reactions, more chronic transferences, and internalized aspects of the self. Psychoanalytically oriented psychotherapy aims not to blame but to understand, reconstruct, and put into context the qualities, characteristics, and limitations of the people with whom the patient is involved or with whom the patient must be involved because of necessity (a boss who is disliked, an ex-spouse with whom children are shared). Parents are included in this list. Working though is often expressed through the patient's ability to grasp, understand, and perhaps empathize with the parent or parents' choices and outlook on life, even if this outlook is substantially different from the patient's own.

Patients often ask this question of the therapist: "Does one have to forgive one's parents?" The answer to the question is complicated because we inevitably identify with our parents. Coming to grips with elements of our parents is therefore an aspect of coming to grips with ourselves.

Shift from Internal Preoccupation to Outward Orientation

With working through, a gradual increase in the ability to be aware of, listen to, and empathize with others occurs. Paralleling many of the elements described above, the patient gradually develops an ability to "put oneself in the other person's shoes." Greenson (1967) gives an example of a man in analysis who was petrified of having sex because of performance concerns. A pivotal point in the treatment and a demonstration of this aspect of working through occurred when, in the midst of intercourse with a woman with whom he had become romantically involved, the man suddenly realized that the woman was fearful about the adequacy of her own "performance" as well.

Reconstructions

An essential psychoanalytic principle is that experiences from the past live on in memory, and therefore have the potential to influence thoughts and actions without a person's conscious awareness. Some patients grow to view or understand the past in new ways during a psychoanalytic psychotherapy, because psychotherapy provides an opportunity to question the belief systems and old familial myths that are an aspect of the internal roadmap. These "reconstructions" allow for modernization of the old maps. Sometimes this process is very dramatic, as illustrated in the following vignette:

> Ralph was a middle-aged man who had never been able to maintain a relationship with a woman, in spite of dating a number of women who appeared to be both likable and appropriate for him.
>
> Ralph was a perfectionist. He had high expectations of himself and the women with whom he became romantically involved. After a period of time, Ralph found every woman selfish and insufficiently giving. In addition to his frustrations with women, he also had a long history of anger and disappointment with physicians, whom he perceived as unreliable, ignorant, and arrogant.
>
> Ralph's childhood history was notable. His mother died after a sudden and brief illness when he was eight years old. His mother was subsequently idealized by Ralph's father, his much older siblings, and accordingly by Ralph. In reality, however, he had almost no memories of interactions with her.
>
> Ralph's memory of his childhood was overshadowed by his deep sense of inadequacy; his recollections clustered around his inability to perform academically, his social awkwardness and consequent lack of success with girls, and his weak athletic abilities. In contrast, Ralph imagined his mother to be spunky, brave, able, and entrancing, and insisted that he and his mother were particularly close until the time of her death. Therapeutic exploration revealed over time that Ralph's insistence upon the closeness between himself and his mother was largely based on history related to him by his father and his own need to imagine his mother as having cared deeply for him; he had few independent memories of close or warm moments with his mother.

By the third year of psychotherapy, Ralph had become increasingly in touch with his deep underlying sadness. In the context of attempting to renew a relationship with a past lover (one of many that he had previously rejected), for the first time, Ralph began to recover a series of memories about his mother.

Ralph reported a dream that reminded the therapist of another dream that Ralph had told him about. The dream had occurred on the night after Ralph's return from summer camp, shortly before his mother died. This vivid dream, which Ralph had often reflected upon, was an indelible memory of his childhood, a contrast to his otherwise sparse and hazy memory. In the childhood dream, Ralph was in a vast stadium, like a baseball stadium; however, the stadium was completely deserted; his only feeling in the dream was a vague uncertainty and anxiety. As Ralph had reflected on the dream in later years, he was aware of the "aloneness" of the dream scene.

In the hour in which he had reported the initial similar dream, Ralph went on to speak of the frequency with which he found fault with women. The therapist suggested that perhaps his experience with his mother had not always been so positive either. He pointed out that the dream in the stadium antedated his mother's death, and yet it was a stark and lonely dream. Ralph was silent for a moment. He spoke about a television documentary that he had seen about a group of doctors who had gone to Russia to provide free surgical care to infants and children, and how touching this was. He spoke of watching the mothers and observing their intense connection with and protectiveness of their children. Ralph began to cry softly.

After several minutes, Ralph told the therapist something that he had never mentioned before. Ralph said that in his twenties, he had learned from a relative of his father that his mother had tried unsuccessfully to abort the pregnancy with him, and that she had turned his care over to nannies for most of the time prior to her death. He had never believed this story before, but now he vaguely recalled that it was true. Additionally, Ralph told the therapist that he had long suspected that his mother's "brief and sudden" illness and death had actually been a suicide.

This new perspective about his mother, although quite painful for Ralph, was an epiphany. This "reconstruction" allowed Ralph to recognize that maintaining the idealization of his mother had protected a benign image of her at a significant cost to himself. In order to maintain the image of his mother as "ideal" and therefore unmatchable and irreplaceable, Ralph had to allow the real women in his life to carry the old deep rage and disappointment

that he actually felt toward his mother, thus making his current relationships impossible. Additionally, Ralph was always braced and
ready to leave a relationship before the relationship could leave
him. He wasn't about to leave himself open to abandonment and
the predictable and consequent suffering that would be his lot in
this event again.

Many families have myths; the myths are often brilliant, fervent, passionate, crazy, and creative, and exaggerated, apocryphal, and untrue, and
serve to obscure and therefore protect against underlying truths. The myth
sometimes proves to induce destructive and painful consequences, which in
the end far exceed whatever pain would have been endured with the truth.
Ralph mourned deeply the loss of the myth about the beautiful and devoted
mother who merged with him and in so doing allowed him to feel whole.
Ralph earned, however, the love of a real flesh-and-blood woman in place
of the myth. He stayed with the woman with whom he had become rein-
volved and it was a good relationship for Ralph.

Shift in the Derivatives of Gratification

Another shift in the course of psychotherapy is the development of the
capacity to "decathect" the libido from "infantile objects," or the development of the capacity to achieve fulfillment through the exercise of real skills
and in interaction with real people. This is in contrast to fantasized possibilities for the self that have little real hope of becoming realized (wanting
to become a rock star without being able to carry a tune or play an instrument) or the pursuit of ideal relationships that do not exist or are a repetition of imagined and/or exaggerated images of figures from the past. A goal
of psychotherapy is to enable the patient to find fulfillment, or at least the
satisfaction of mastery, in and from the world of real possibilities and currently available objects rather than from illness and its associated symptoms.

SUMMARY

Working through is the "work" of therapy, and work does not occur without exertion. The effort to achieve understanding and insight, the increasing acceptance of the past, the appreciation of reactions and feelings in the
self and in others, the integration of the realities of life, and the numerous
trial attempts within the context of therapy to experiment with more adap-

tive ways of relating to others, to the self, and to the world are all aspects of working through.

Many of these small elements become increasingly recognizable as the work of the treatment progresses, and working through gradually occurs and is revealed to both the patient and the therapist.

REFERENCES AND READINGS

Brenner, C. (1987). Working through: 1914–1984. *Psychoanalytic Quarterly* 56: 88–108.

Brodsky, B. (1967). Working through. *Psychoanalytic Quarterly* 36: 485–96.

Freud, S. (1914). Remembering, repeating and working-through. *Standard Edition* 12: 145–56. London: Hogarth Press, 1958.

———. (1916). Some character types met within psychoanalytic work. *Standard Edition* 14: 311–33 London: Hogarth Press, 1957.

———. (1917). Mourning and melancholia. *Standard Edition* 14: 237–59. London: Hogarth Press, 1957.

Greenacre, P. (1956). Re-evaluation of the process of working through. *International Journal of Psycho-Analysis* 37: 439–44.

Greenson, R. R. (1967). *The Technique and Practice of Psychoanalysis*, vol. 2. New York: International Universities Press.

Karush, A. (1967). Working through. *Psychoanalytic Quarterly* 36: 497–531.

Kernberg, O. (1992). *Aggression in Personality Disorders and Perversions*. New Haven, CT: Yale University Press.

Kohut, H. (1971). Some therapeutic transformations in the analysis of narcissistic personalities. In *The Analysis of the Self*. New York: International Universities Press.

Kris, E. (1956). The recovery of childhood memories in psychoanalysis. *Psychoanalytic Study of the Child* 11: 54–88.

———. (1976). On wanting too much: the "exceptions" revisited. *International Journal of Psycho-Analysis* 57: 85–95.

Loewwald, H. (1972). On internalization. *International Journal of Psycho-Analysis* 54: 9–17.

Masterson, J. F. (1981). *The Narcissistic and Borderline Disorders: An Integrated Developmental Approach*. New York: Brunner/Mazel.

Miller, A. (1981). *Prisoners of Childhood*. New York: Basic Books.

Novey, S. (1962). The principle of "working through" in psychoanalysis. *Journal of the American Psychoanalytic Association* 10: 658–76.

Orgel, S. (2000). Letting go: some thoughts about termination. *Journal of the American Psychoanalytic Association* 48: 719–38.

Parkin, A. (1981). Repetition, mourning and working through. *International Journal of Psycho-Analysis* 62: 271–81.

Schur, A. N. (1994). *Affect Regulation and the Origin of the Self.* New York: International Universities Press.

Sedler, M. J. (1983). Freud's concept of working through. *Psychoanalytic Quarterly* 52: 73–98.

Shane, M., and E. Shane. (1984). The end phase of analysis: indicators, functions, and tasks of termination. *Journal of the American Psychoanalytic Association* 32: 739–72.

Sharpe, E. (1937). *Dream Analysis.* London: Hogarth Press.

Stewart, W. A. (1963). An inquiry into the concept of working through. *Journal of the American Psychoanalytic Association* 11: 474–99.

Valenstein, A. (1983). Working through and resistance to change. *Journal of the American Psychoanalytic Association* 31: 353–73.

Winnicott, D. W. (1958). The capacity to be alone. In *The Maturational Process and the Facilitating Environment.* New York: International Universities Press.

———. (1960). Ego distortion in terms of true and false self. In *The Maturational Processes and the Facilitating Environment.* New York: International Universities Press, 1965.

10

TERMINATION

All therapies end sooner or later, whether or not the ending was planned. Ideally, endings occur when both patient and therapist have some reasonable sense that what can be done has been done as satisfactorily as possible. Therapies end in many variations, including those in which the terminations occur when things are still seemingly unresolved.

It is possible that most terminations actually occur at a point of resistance during which time the aggravation or sacrifice simply outweighs the anticipated gain. When people feel better, the motivation to gain self-knowledge diminishes, because therapy does require a time commitment, a financial investment, and the psychic energy necessary to face that which is difficult within the self.

Hopefully, people leave therapy with an experience of internal growth and an appreciation of the value of psychotherapy. Some people will return to therapy again at a later time, when the challenges of life and changing circumstances and opportunities bring up issues that were previously unrecognized or unresolved. Psychotherapy hopes to open up the developmental process, thus allowing the person to continue to grow and change. This does not exclude the possibility of stumbling or hitting a developmental impasse. The enlarged capacity to utilize others, including a therapist if need be, is of great adaptive value. While returning to therapy is not a goal of treatment, acceptance and awareness of the limits of personal perfection, and therefore the ability to make use of a therapist and the process of psychotherapy again when circumstances prevail, is a goal of psychotherapy.

In most treatments, both therapist and patient develop a sense at some point that the time has come to end the treatment. Conviction regarding the timing of termination often begins as an intuition, usually paralleling working through and achievement of the goals previously delineated.

Whenever the prospect of termination arises, whether as a mutual decision of patient and therapist, mandated by business or life circumstances, or because a patient leaves prior to completion for emotional or impulsive reasons, certain questions come to mind. Where does the patient stand in the scope of the psychotherapy process: is the ending or termination phase at hand? What has been achieved? What has not been achieved? Is it even possible to accomplish what has not been accomplished?

In order to answer the question "Where does the patient stand in the psychotherapy process," a revisitation of the dynamic formulation is necessary. What was the therapist's initial understanding of the patient, and what assessment was made about what needed to be accomplished in the work of psychotherapy? What has changed and what has not? What has been worked through and what has not? From the vantage point of termination, both therapist and patient should have the ability to piece together in a coherent manner what it was that "made the person (patient) tick."

Understanding is accrued through the work of psychotherapy, made easier along the way by the patient's diminished defensiveness and increased ability to tell a personal story. A therapist's preconscious awareness of his or her increased facility and ease in the empathic process often informs the therapist of the possibility of termination; things now just "make sense." Additionally, this awareness typically relates to the passing of the "middle phase," in which more is required of the therapist. Regrettably, as the element of hard work decreases for the therapist, the possibility of a termination is heralded.

Looking backward from the point of view of the termination phase, the phases of psychotherapy become more apparent. When the treatment has been more intense or more frequent, the phases are that much easier to distinguish from one another. Treatment is usually divided into three broad phases. These phases are the opening phase, the middle phase, and the termination phase. Each phase is characterized by certain elements, with the middle phase being perhaps the least distinct.

OPENING PHASE

During the opening phase, an environment of safety and trust must be established in order for the "work" of therapy to be possible; this is called the establishment of the "therapeutic alliance" (see chapter 6). Freud noted (1913, 109) that "an effective transference" and a proper rapport with the patient must be established, "before we can make interpretations." Sterba (1934) observed "the effective factor in interpretation lies in the division of the ego into an experiencing portion and an observing portion." The latter is the result of a combination of "positive transference, and identification with the analyst." In the opening phase, a fundamental positive feeling about the therapist must occur, in order for the "observing portion" of the patient to be mobilized.

Ornstein and Ornstein wrote, "the opening phase is characterized by the patient's unconscious efforts to seek or to 'locate' the analyst . . . to assess his emotional availability and to define his limitations" (1985, 41). The therapist, to paraphrase the Ornsteins, must become attuned to the patient's self-experiences, and appreciate the resistances that stand in the way of the patient "finding" the analyst. Resistances reflect lifelong defensive patterns, developed to protect the self from "retraumatization." The patient's confidence in being understood, and recognition of the possibility of seeing things differently, becomes a motivation for psychotherapy (Ornstein and Ornstein 1985).

During this early period, the therapist gathers the data that is necessary in order to develop a dynamic formulation through empathic listening and a directed and psychoanalytically informed inquiry (patient's chief complaint, factual history, object relations, etc.). Initial themes begin to coalesce, sometimes with great clarity. Wishes toward and expectations of the therapist and of the treatment begin to appear. Sometimes these wishes and expectations appear in fantasies and dreams. Transference reactions (as opposed to more enduring transference themes) may be immediate and obvious; the genetic root may or may not be difficult to discern. If transference reactions are not obvious, at least the initial stance of the patient toward the therapist (attempting to please, seduce, provoke, alienate, remain distant or unattached, etc.) can be observed.

Therefore, a positive connection with the therapist and the experience of being understood, the development in the patient of the capacity to step back and be observant about the self, and the hope that it is possible to view the self, other people, and experiences differently, are important assets for entry into the middle phase.

MIDDLE PHASE

Sometimes the middle phase is only recognizable in retrospect. Whatever had characterized the opening phase no longer seems to apply, and suddenly everything seems much less clear. Transference reactions are not as easily recognized and obvious themes have melted away into more ambiguity. The therapist begins to wonder what might be going on in the patient, and finds the struggle to put it all together greater. The middle phase is a time in which therapy becomes an experience as well as an intellectual endeavor. Transference breathes its subtle effect. The effort on the part of the therapist to maintain an empathic contact with the patient is complicated by complementary and concordant countertransferences.

Gradually, transference themes come together; the patient experiences the therapist in certain more enduring ways that echo more convincingly figures from the past. These habitual transference related reactions may be more bothersome to the therapist (see chapter 6 on alter-ego transference). Additionally, transference patterns evolve and give way to other transference paradigms as working through occurs. For example, the transference may shift from a more predominantly positive feeling about the therapist to a feeling that is more negatively tinged, or from the expression of predominantly maternal desires toward the therapist to wishes and desires that are more paternal in nature.

Understanding of the genesis and utility of the patient's "character" (the habitual way in which a person relates to the world and other people) is a task of the middle phase. Delineation of the structure of the superego becomes an area of focus. What is the nature of the patient's moral code and system of ethics? What are the patient's goals and aspirations: where did these goals and aspirations come from and what was their path of evolution? Formulating an understanding of the patient's sexuality is also a task of the middle phase. How solid is the patient's sense of masculinity or femininity? What kinds of sexual fantasies does the patient have, and what do those fantasies mean with respect to the patient's object relations and ideas about gender and the implications of gender?

For the therapist, the middle phase is hard work. Enduring the patient's strongest and most difficult emotions can be taxing, especially when those emotions are primitive or universal (rage or depression). Understanding, containing, and making sense of countertransference reactions is effortful. Breakthroughs occur when the therapist or the patient has a moment of clarity or sometimes an epiphany, and suddenly, some piece of the puzzle makes sense.

During the middle phase, patience is a necessary and desirable quality for the therapist to have mastered.

TERMINATION

With planned endings, the termination phase includes a period during which the therapist and patient examine the patient's readiness for termination and then make a formal decision to set the date. This decision becomes then in its own right, a useful stimulus for material that helps to finalize the therapy, or conversely to clarify a lack of readiness for termination. Thus, a decision to stop becomes a test of readiness and an impetus to finish what has remained undone. The absence of any reaction or feeling about the decision to end a therapy, or a desire to leave a treatment immediately without any discussion about the ending, raises the possibility of a defensive desire to run away from the consequences (imaged or not) of leaving the treatment by avoiding the experience and exploration of reactions and feelings associated with the event. Leaving a treatment has a meaning for each patient, whatever that meaning might be.

Patient and therapist would both often like to avoid the painful and/or disappointing aspects of termination. If the therapist knows the patient well and has in some way participated in the patient's life and decisions, an emotional investment in the patient's well-being exists. This connection must now be relinquished, like the final departure of a child from home. Termination also clarifies for the therapist what has been accomplished, and what has not. This bittersweet experience unmasks the therapist's own worries about personal limitations and value (of the work or of the self). Hopefully, these kinds of questions and concerns will dissipate with adequate reflection on the part of the therapist; if they do not, the result can be an avoidance of thinking or talking about the issues of endings and leavings, even when the time is clearly at hand.

Since much variation in the termination experience can occur, what markers are useful to follow in order to assess readiness for termination?

Dreams Themes

The usefulness of dream content in assessing readiness for termination has long been observed in psychoanalysis. As described in chapter 9, dream content often changes during psychotherapy. Dreams may become less tormenting, or less repetitive, or more gratifying. Dreams may demonstrate new solutions to old conflicts, or signal a rapprochement with and freedom from figures of the past. Dreams can become an adjunct, an avenue of communication to the self, a tool of "self-analysis."

In the following example, freedom from an old, stereotypic authority figure or adversary is demonstrated in a patient's dream.

Mr. J lived in the shadow of a famous, able, but domineering and critical father, who had been dead for many years. The following dream occurred shortly after a business success.

> Mr. J dreamed that he had done well on an examination and a professor congratulated him for his fine work. Mr. J then saw his father, who said nothing and went on his way. Momentarily, Mr. J experienced a sense of disappointment, but he also felt "okay" and proud of his performance.

Mr. J's dream expressed and acknowledged an intense feeling that he (the patient) could never please the voice of his father inside his head (internalized object relation), yet at the same time Mr. J remained able to feel satisfaction about himself. He was able to do this in part by turning to a more benevolent internal object in the figure of the professor, presumably representative of the therapist.

Mr. J sought treatment initially because he was never able to sustain a positive feeling about himself. He had always compared himself to his father, and felt that he had never been able to live up to his father's standards. Consequently, Mr. J had been doomed to endlessly catalog his achievements, an effort to rescue himself from despair.

In spite of his lifelong sense of failure, Mr. J had many talents. He also had a great capacity to empathize with others, and an enormous desire to understand himself. This dream was the end product of much psychotherapeutic work, demonstrating a vastly expanded observing ego, a richer internalized object world, and a sufficiently positive self-representation.

During the termination phase of another patient, Mr. K, the following dream demonstrates the resolution of conflict-ridden and guilty feelings about an internalized object (introject).

> Mr. K deeply resented his well-meaning but narcissistic and obsessive father. Mr. K was plagued by feelings of guilt, and had a chronic inability to mourn his father's death. After much psychotherapy, this patient had a simple dream. Mr. K was walking down a hallway, and found that he was walking next to his father. He put his hand on his father's shoulder and said, "I love you." His father smiled and they parted ways as the hallway divided.

The patient was deeply moved by this dream and experienced a profound sense of relief. The dream represented Mr. K's ability to mourn the loss of his father through the means of restitution in his mind of the best of his father's qualities. This image of his father became part of Mr. K's internal world ("internalized"), forming a more positive and comforting voice, which Mr. K could then turn to in times of need (internalized object or "imago").

This last example is of a dream that repeated itself throughout the treatment of Ms. L. The elements of the dream changed over time, as Ms. L worked through and resolved her conflicts, came to accept a reality that she could not change and had to live with, mourned the loss of what she could never have, and found reasonable gratification in her life nevertheless.

> Ms. L had a repetitive dream in which she was sent by her mother to a certain bakery in order to get a particular cake for a special occasion. A key repetitive element of the dream was that Ms. L was always very anxious about performing this task. What if she were unable to secure the particular cake for which she was sent because the line at the bakery was too long and the store closed before she got to the front of the line?
>
> As the treatment progressed, the dream began to change. Ms. L began to shop for herself (not on assignment from her mother), and sometimes Ms. L's therapist was the baker behind the counter. During the termination phase of the treatment, Ms. L dreamed that she went to the bakery and actually got her cake; while it was not exactly the cake she wanted, it was "good enough."

Freedom from Internalized Objects (Second Individuation)

As suggested in the previous examples, the freedom from the less than useful aspects of parental figures that reside in the mind as internalized objects is a goal of psychoanalytic psychotherapy. Shakespeare said poetically:

> That nature which contemns its origin
> Cannot be bordered certain in itself.
> She that herself with sliver and disbranch
> From her material sap perforce must wither,
> And come to deadly use.
>
> (*King Lear*, Act 4, Scene 2)

The Ability to Manage and Integrate Disappointment and the Deidealization of "Magnificent Figures"

Disappointment is probably an aspect of concluding any therapy, since the result is usually not perfect (Rangell 1982). With termination, the patient is more clearly able to see the limitations of the process and of the therapist. A useful marker for termination is that these disappointments are accepted (deidealization of "magnificent figures" occurs) and the patient moves on, somewhat like the adolescent's deidealization of the parents. If the patient can view the therapist more realistically and at the same time maintain an appreciation of that therapist's contributions, the groundwork for a more realistic acceptance of others and of the self is laid (Novick 1982, 1990). An ending of this kind, without excessive anger or depression, correlates with a later ability to accept and enjoy others. This is as opposed to an endless search for the "perfect" friend or lover, or a manifestation of an unresolved search for an idealized ("magnificent") transference figure. If disappointment is not addressed during the termination phase, a disruptive aftereffect may be the result, occurring after termination and taking the form of an enduring devaluation of the therapy and the therapist, others, and the self (Rangell 1982).

Mourning the Loss of the Therapist as a Real and Transference Object

Hopefully, the therapist has been concerned and thoughtful; in some circumstances, the therapist may actually be the most consistently involved person in the patient's life (Loewald 1988). To leave therapy means to give up all of this, inevitably to experience sadness and loss. For patients who have been significantly emotionally deprived, the loss of the "holding environment" of therapy may be extremely painful.

Added to the loss of the therapist as a real object is the loss of the therapist as a transference object. The therapist of the idealizing transference is the therapist with powers and capacities derived from fantasy, who is capable of fulfilling old developmental needs and realizing wishes. In this capacity, the therapist may be seen as essential, transforming, having the power to save or change the person's life. Termination confronts the patient with reality; a transformation of this kind may not happen. Ideally, transference-related needs, and the understanding and work of mourning required to deal with them, have taken place during the middle phase. In practice, the ability to cope with mourning is variable. Some patients feel intolerably let down and become depressed, indicating that insufficient resolution has occurred and termination is unlikely to take place successfully.

Self-Analytic Capacity

Throughout the process of psychotherapy, a patient should be developing and accruing the ability to step back and observe the self ("observing ego"). With education, understanding, and practice, self-analysis gradually becomes more automatic, more effective in dealing with internal emotional distress, a property of the patient's ego. When a major life decision arises or crisis occurs, a patient has the opportunity to demonstrate self-reflection and understanding, thus offering an indication of the patient's capacity to do the psychotherapeutic task. This self-analyzing capacity gives evidence that the patient is cognizant of the constitutional givens and experiences, the personal life story that created who the patient came to be. This has been variously described as the creation of a coherent narrative (Schafer 1978), a life history (Kris 1956), or an accurate memory testing (Mahon and Battin 1981). With termination, many patients demonstrate this increased self-analytic capacity. Shane and Shane noted that self-analytic experience is not simply an intellectual exercise, it is "a heightened, self-reflective, analytically informed psychological-mindedness, a new mode of ego functioning that allows both conscious and preconscious analytic insightfulness when necessary" (Shane and Shane, 1984).

Adolescent Process

Similar themes and similar requirements mark the end of adolescence and the termination of psychotherapy. Deidealization of the therapist (or parents), mourning, acceptance of human failings and humanity, development of a unique identity and sense of self, and the ability to separate without destruction of the object are all tasks of normal adolescence and a psychodynamic psychotherapy. Psychotherapy revives this adolescent process, but with the opportunity for greater resolution and consolidation of the "rites of passage" that allow for the "leaving of home." Both the ending of a therapy and the ending of adolescence signal the arrival of the capacity to think existentially, and therefore to appreciate that each person has an ordinary and yet unique life story, which can be influenced by the personal choices that are made.

LIFE GOALS AND TREATMENT GOALS

Ernst Ticho (1972) usefully and clearly described the difference between "life goals" and "treatment goals." He viewed mental illness as an interruption and distortion of a developmental process. Psychodynamic therapy as a treatment method aims to remove the causes of the interruption so that development can resume and proceed. Once this "treatment goal" is achieved, the patient can move on to reach "life goals." Life goals are defined as those goals that the patient has and would try to fulfill if full potential were available. Life goals are then the goals of the patient's "true self" (Winnicott 1960). Life goals might be professional, personal, inter-personal, athletic, creative, etc.

Treatment goals involve the removal of obstacles that stand in the way of the patient being able to discover potentialities, i.e., removal of neurotic impediments resulting in the "conflict-free" pursuit of life goals. Treatment goals might be, for example, increasing the capacity for mature personal relationships with a concomitant decrease in (narcissistic) self-centeredness, increasing frustration tolerance, improving the capacity to endure anxiety, suffering, and depression, and facilitating the maturation of the superego (for example, improving the capacity of the superego to be more tolerant and loving, or more ethical and moral). Distinguishing treatment goals from life goals is important. Difficulty relating to another human being is not the same thing as being unable to find a suitable life partner. Psychological receptivity does not insure opportunity. Psy-chotherapy hopes to make possible; unfortunately, opportunities in the current reality may be restricted.

A common life goal that can begin a therapy is the search for a love relationship. While it is remarkable that many people find their future part-ner "right under their nose" during the work of psychotherapy, some un-fortunately do not. Opportunities may be limited by age, lack of exposure to potential partners, health constraints, etc., and not simply limited by psy-chological readiness. These limitations, which could result in an inability to realize life goals, should not be a criterion for continuing therapy; however, the resolution of treatment goals should be a reason to continue the treat-ment. Winnicott's provocative comment comes to mind: "You may cure your patient, and not know what it is that makes them go on living. It is of first importance for us to acknowledge openly that absence of psychoneu-rotic illness may be health, but it is not life" (1967, 371).

The following example makes the distinction between life goals and treatment goals:

> The patient, Lucy, was a twenty-three-year-old woman, who came to treatment approximately six months after moving to the city in which she currently lived.
> Lucy told her new therapist that she had moved to this city in or-der to seriously pursue a career as a tennis pro. It had been her long-time dream. Lucy's mother, deceased for almost a year, had been a professional dancer. Her father was a successful college athletic coach. Lucy felt that the move to the new city was essen-

tial to the fulfillment of her dream. Nevertheless, Lucy found herself unable to work. She dieted, stayed in her house, and spent
time with a recently acquired girlfriend, who also dieted and
stayed in her house (or in Lucy's house). Lucy was anxious, blue,
and felt very alone. All of this made it almost impossible to pursue
her tennis, for which she apparently had very significant talent.
Lucy had had a "ton" of psychotherapy, ever since childhood. She
had had multiple therapists, necessitated by multiple moves. Now
she felt a need to find a therapist again.

Lucy's mother had been a highly unstable, anorexic woman who
was addicted to diet pills. Lucy's parents had divorced when she
was five years old. Throughout her childhood and young adulthood, Lucy's mother had been severely underweight, and at times
the mother was frighteningly underweight. This later situation had
necessitated numerous hospitalizations. Periodically, Lucy's
mother threatened to sue the father for custody of Lucy and her
brother (the father had custody); nevertheless, the father continued
to be concerned about the mother and to help her financially. On
one occasion the father moved Lucy and her brother to another
city because he feared that the mother would try to kidnap the
children.

Lucy's mother eventually died of heart failure (a consequence of
her anorexia) when Lucy was twenty years old. Lucy's mother died
slowly and horribly, wasting away and refusing to help herself.
Lucy was in a position to observe this tragedy close at hand.

Lucy's father was the only stable figure in her life, and she was
excessively attached to him. A large part of Lucy's depression had
to do with the separation from this only reliable object, partially
substituted for by the friendship with the new girlfriend.

Lucy had had a checkered school career. Because of her tennis
involvement, much of Lucy's school life was spent on the road,
during which time she was home schooled. Lucy's brother also had
significant difficulties. He became a cocaine addict, worked at
lower-level jobs, and was alienated from the rest of the family.

Despite all, Lucy was an attractive, bright, insightful, warm
young woman, who sought out an attachment to a stable (therapeutic) object, and was curious about herself and desirous of moving forward. All of this was in favor of her being able to benefit
from more treatment, but Lucy was exhausted at the thought of
putting herself in one more therapeutic situation.

Lucy knew that she had to pursue treatment because she found
herself having great difficulty managing her anxiety and depression. She was haunted by memories of her mother's death and life.

Lucy felt guilty for every advantage she had, or success she might wish for or achieve, because her mother had no more chances ("survivor guilt"). Additionally, Lucy wanted to be "famous," a "household name," this was an attempt to restitute her crumbling self-image and to reverse history. As an adolescent Lucy had felt shamed and shunned by her peers and their families in the suburb in which she had lived. Unfortunately Lucy's mother's condition had been well known to those around her. Thus despite her financial status and athletic success, Lucy felt like "trash." Struggling to maintain her self-esteem, Lucy's "ego ideal" was grandiose and unrealistic (not from an absolute lack of talent, but lack of opportunity, connections, and fortitude), and she felt despairing about herself whenever she thought that she might not be able to realize her dream (ego ideal).

Lucy's great strengths lay in her intelligence, curiosity, and strong and intact moral guide (superego). She knew what was right and what was wrong. Lucy also had an ability to choose a therapist who could be helpful to her, and then commit herself to an attachment to the therapist and the treatment. Gradually Lucy learned about herself and her themes, as the following summary shows.

1. Lucy had "survivor guilt." She felt that it was wrong to enjoy life and be successful when her mother was dead. She felt responsible for her failure to save or give her mother a reason to live, and blamed herself for her mother's death. Lucy learned to understand that her mother had been drowning of her own accord, and that no intervention, whether it was at Lucy's behest or someone else's, could have saved her.

2. She understood the theme of "trash" vs. the "household name." Lucy saw that she had alternated from one view of herself to the opposite view of herself, unable to find a happy medium.

3. Lucy analyzed her separation anxiety and its relationship to her attachment to her father. She worked through the "romantic" relationship with her father, causing her to become bored with him and desirous of an independent life.

4. Lucy saw, but only in the context of the therapist's interpretation, the transference function that the therapist served for her, of supporting and increasing the functioning of her ego strengths, allowing her in the therapist's presence to operate as though she had a more flexible and loving superego and ego ideal.

Lucy got a job as a saleswoman, selling tennis rackets at a tennis club. Within a remarkably short period of time, she was promoted to the assistant manager position at the pro shop of the club. Shortly after this, she was serendipitously spotted by a recruiter from another company, who offered her an opportunity to be a regional manager for a women's tennis wear line. The job required a move to another city. Lucy wanted to make this move, because she had started a relationship with a visiting tennis pro who happened to live in that city.

Only after accepting the job did Lucy realize that she had attached herself to the tennis pro, not so much because of the love of the man but in an attempt to find a "good mother." In so doing, she had put herself in the position of losing the "real" good mother, in the person of the therapist.

How do we understand Lucy and her situation from the standpoint of distinguishing between life goals and treatment goals? Lucy now had an opportunity for a "true" career with a plausible future. While she had found her "sea legs" in the city in which the therapist lived, she had no close friends to hold her back, and no place to go except for the job at the pro shop. Recall that Lucy's original reason for the move was to relocate and become "famous"; she now recognized that "fame" was not a viable career path. Ultimately, Lucy would only be staying for her therapist. Was this enough reason to give up a chance to pursue a career with significant potential?

On the one hand, Lucy's therapist thought that the continuity of the treatment might be enough of a reason for Lucy to stay. The therapist felt that Lucy's improved functioning, and indeed her ability to function so well, was directly related to the transference function that the therapist provided. Lucy was able to "borrow" the therapist's guiding ethics (superego function), ego strengths, and belief in Lucy's ability, in order to see herself differently and perform at a greater capacity. Additionally, her therapist didn't want Lucy to go. The therapist was fond of Lucy and felt maternal toward her; she wanted Lucy to remain a little bit longer in her protective sphere. The therapist wrestled with herself, in order to be able to support her patient to move on. The therapist mourned only within herself, in order to help and allow Lucy to mourn aloud for the loss of the real relationship with the therapist. Lucy moved on with her life.

Termination requires acceptance, by both the patient and the therapist. The patient has sometimes to accept a less-than-perfect solution, and the therapist, like the parent, must sometimes accept that what can be done is only what can be done; sometimes, this doesn't feel like enough.

PREMATURE TERMINATION

In thinking about termination, a therapist looks back and reviews where the therapy began. What was the initial formulation; what were the goals of the treatment; and were the goals delineated and understood, worked through, or revised over time? If new goals appeared or were established, how completely were these new goals resolved? In approaching the end, a therapist asks, When looking at the overall functioning of the patient in question, where are we now?

With each patient, certain choices are made about what is really possible. What is reasonable within the framework of each person's life? Reality constraints include age, situation, capabilities, and psychological capacity. How psychologically minded is the person, and how much intrapsychic flexibility is present and/or possible to mobilize? Added to this is the question of time. How much time is available? Is this a short-term treatment, for which one has to delineate goals sharply, or is time relatively unlimited? To this is also added the question of intensity. How intensively can the treatment be pursued: once a week, twice a week, or more often? As a broad generality, the more intense the treatment, the greater the possibility for change. Should treatment be interrupted prematurely, secondary to the patient's situation or the therapist's situation, having a solid sense about the formulation, including both "treatment" and "life" goals, will better allow the therapist to summarize for the patient: What has been accomplished, what needs further work, what issues have not been addressed that would have been useful to work through, what may resolve by itself after the therapy has ended?

When a patient raises the possibility of termination, particularly if the therapist has not considered this as well, a question must be asked. Does the wish to stop find origin in realistic life demands, such as financial hardship, a new and unavoidable job demand, an illness? If the answer is no, sometimes even if the answer is yes, a therapist is left to wonder if the desire to terminate has other important psychological motivations. The desire to terminate may reflect a resistance; for example, the avoidance of shame, anxiety, guilt, conflict, or depression. The desire to stop may reflect the expression of a negative transference toward the therapist. The desire to terminate may hide a concern about the therapist's character. Is the therapist trustworthy? The patient may not be aware of the reason for the wish to stop; even if a conscious reason for stopping exists, underlying motivations may still not be conscious. It is the therapist's job to investigate the matter.

Unfortunately, a patient's motivation for termination is often unclear. Even in the case in which a therapist intuitively knows that a significant process is silently unfolding, it may not be possible to sufficiently grasp or describe it to the patient in time to change the patient's mind. The therapist's own countertransference, lack of data regarding the patient's story, or lack of sufficient time to make sense of that story, can sometimes make an understanding of the patient's motives impossible. At times, a therapist can only acknowledge concern. When a negative transference or resistance is obvious, even with the most skilled, correct, and empathic exploration, a therapist may not be able keep the patient in the psychotherapeutic process.

AFTER THERAPY

What happens after the psychotherapy ends? Gradually the experience of therapy is further internalized; insights gained and capacities achieved become more completely the patient's own. The therapist's voice recedes. Confidence is gained as the patient negotiates stresses and strains. The patient's view of therapy evolves, particularly during the first year following termination. The mental awareness of the therapy experience itself may lessen; with time, a group of memories may consolidate, revolving around certain nodal moments. These "moments" recall the concept of the "screen memory": emotionally significant understandings from before, during, and after the therapy are woven together into a "picture" or "series of pictures." The therapist becomes a less important and vivid figure as repression occurs, and memory proves itself to be uniquely human.

With a successful psychotherapy, psychological functioning is expanded. Transference repetitions still transpire, but the intensity of transference-based wishes has diminished, and therefore the rapidity with which the graduated patient can step back and reflect increases. Old desires, sensitivities, and defensive postures still appear and occur in the living of life, but most are better understood and more likely to be adaptively addressed. Appropriate concern and help from others can be accepted, but the ability to soothe oneself is also available when times are hard and no one is immediately available to help. Finally, the inevitable limitations and disappointments of life can, at least some portion of the time, be viewed with humor.

There are always limits to change; this should not make for despair on the part of the therapist. After all, Freud once observed,

> Our aim will be not to rub off every peculiarity of human character for the sake of a schematic "normality," nor yet to demand that the person who has been 'thoroughly analyzed' shall feel no passions and develop no internal conflict. (1937a, 250)

That makes sense, doesn't it?

REFERENCES AND READINGS

Blum, H. P. (1989). The concept of termination and the evolution of psychoanalytic thought. *Journal of the American Psychoanalytic Association* 37: 275–95.

Freud, S. (1912). Recommendations to physicians practicing psychoanalysis. *Standard Edition* 12: 109–20. London: Hogarth Press, 1958.

———. (1937a). Analysis terminable and interminable. *Standard Edition* 23: 209–53. London: Hogarth Press, 1964.

———. (1937b). On beginning the treatment. *Standard Edition* 12: 123–44. London: Hogarth Press, 1958.

Hurn, H. T. (1971). Adolescent transference: a problem of the terminal phase of analysis. *Journal of the American Psychoanalytic Association* 18: 42–57.

Kris, E. (1956). The recovery of childhood memories in psychoanalysis. *Psychoanalytic Study of the Child* 11: 54–88.

Loewald, H. W. (1988). Termination analyzable and unanalyzable. *Psychoanalytic Study of the Child* 43: 155–66.

Mahon, E., and D. Battin. (1981). Screen memories and termination of a psychoanalysis: a preliminary communication. *Journal of the American Psychoanalytic Association* 29: 939–42.

Norman, H. F., K. H. Blacker, J. D. Oremland, and W. G. Barrett. (1976). The fate of the transference neurosis after the termination of a satisfying analysis. *Journal of the American Psychoanalytic Association* 24: 471–98.

Novick, J. (1982). The timing of termination. *International Journal of Psycho-Analysis* 15: 307–18.

———. (1990). Comments on termination in child, adolescent, and adult analysis. *Psychoanalytic Study of the Child* 45: 419–36.

Ornstein, P. H., and A. Ornstein. (1985). Clinical understanding and explaining: the empathic vantage point. In *Progress in Self Psychology*, vol. 1, ed. A. Goldberg. New York: Guilford Press.

———. (1994). On the conceptualization of clinical facts in psychoanalysis. *Journal of the American Psychoanalytic Association* 75: 977–94.

Pfeffer, A. Z. (1961). Follow-up study of a satisfactory analysis. *Journal of the American Psychoanalytic Association* 9: 698–718.

———. (1963). The meaning of the analyst after analysis. *Journal of the American Psychoanalytic Association* 11: 229–44.

Rangell, L. (1982). Some thoughts on termination. *Psychoanalytic Inquiry* 2: 367–92.

Schafer, R. (1978). *Language and Insight*. New Haven, CT: Yale University Press.

———. (1979). Character, ego-syntonicity, and character change. *Journal of the American Psychoanalytic Association* 27: 867–91.

Shane, M., and F. Shane. (1984). The end phase of analysis: indications, functions, and tasks of termination. *Journal of the American Psychoanalytic Association* 32: 739–77.

Sterba, R. (1934). The fate of the ego in analytic therapy. *International Journal of Psycho-Analysis* 15: 117–26.

Ticho, E. A. (1972). Termination of psychoanalysis: treatment goals, life goals. *Psychoanalytic Quarterly* 41: 315–33.

Winnicott, D. W. (1960). Ego distortion in terms of true and false self. In *The Maturational Processes and the Facilitating Environment*. New York: International Universities Press, 1965.

———. (1967). The location of cultural experience. *International Journal of Psycho-Analysis* 48: 368–72.

ABOUT THE AUTHORS

Dr. J. Mark Thompson is a training and supervising psychoanalyst and the Director of Education at the Los Angeles Psychoanalytic Institute. He is assistant clinical professor of psychiatry at the UCLA School of Medicine. He has taught at both UCLA and the Los Angeles Psychoanalytic Institute for many years, and has been recognized as an outstanding teacher. He has lectured widely on psychodynamic psychotherapy, obsessive-compulsive phenomena, and affect regulation. He is in the private practice of psychiatry and psychoanalysis.

Dr. Candace Cotlove is a training and supervising psychoanalyst at the Los Angeles Psychoanalytic Institute and an assistant clinical professor of psychiatry at the UCLA School of Medicine. She has taught at both UCLA and the Los Angeles Psychoanalytic Institute for many years. Dr. Cotlove is in the private practice of psychiatry and psychoanalysis. She has special interests in the areas of child development and the analysis of character and character pathology. She also has had many years of experience with the treatment of couples, the treatment of early and late adolescent children, and the problems of young adulthood.